lonely planet

Hawai'i Island (The Big Island)

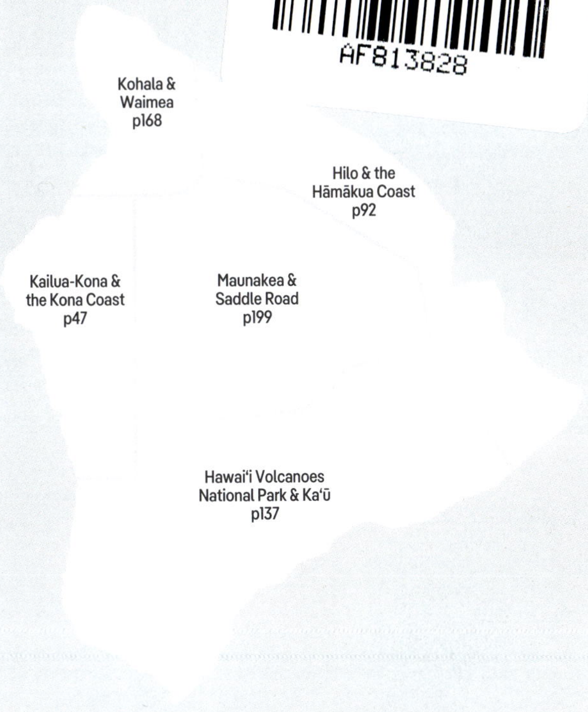

Jade Bremner, Catherine Toth Fox, Ashley Harrell, Regis St Louis

BILLY MCDONALD/SHUTTERSTOCK

Punalu'u Black Sand Beach Park (p162)

CONTENTS

Land Acknowledgement

Lonely Planet acknowledges that the state of Hawai'i rests on the unceded lands of the Kanaka Maoli (Native Hawaiians). We honor their sovereignty and connection to their lands and waters, as well as their enduring commitment to a sustainable future for Hawai'i. Lonely Planet encourages you to learn more about the history of the Kānaka Maoli, and support their continued efforts to preserve the state's fragile ecosystems for future generations by being a mindful visitor. We also encourage you to consider volunteering and connecting with a local organization during your stay. For more information, see gohawaii.com/malama.

TONY WALTHAM/ROBERTHARDING/ALAMY

Kīlauea Caverns of Fire (p114), Kazumura Cave

HAWAI'I ISLAND (THE BIG ISLAND)

THE JOURNEY BEGINS HERE

It's a rare thing to be able to regularly view an erupting volcano. Hawai'i Island's highly active, mighty Kīlauea (a non-explosive shield volcano) is its biggest draw. Red-hot spewing lava can be watched in real time from viewing platforms, even from a restaurant. Thanks to constant eruptions from Hawai'i Island's four active volcanoes, the land is regularly created and destroyed on Hawai'i's largest isle, often dramatically altering the landscape.

Come to Hawai'i Island for community life, waterfall-filled valleys fit for ancient kings, and Mother Nature at her most powerful.

Jade Bremner

@jadeob

Jade is a journalist and editor specializing in adventure travel. She has authored more than 60 books.

My favorite experience is exploring the eerie underworld of **Kīlauea Caverns of Fire** (p114), where ancient lava tubes twist beneath the ground in the 41-mile-long Kazumura Cave.

WHO GOES WHERE

Our writers and experts choose the places that, for them, define Hawai'i Island.

AXEL KOEHLER/SHUTTERSTOCK

I was lucky enough to witness a dramatic fountaining episode in which **Kīlauea volcano** (p140; pictured) shot lava nearly 1600ft in the air, and a rock storm rained down over Hawai'i Volcanoes National Park and surrounding areas. It was hands down the most astonishing natural event I have ever experienced. In the days that followed, I was continually finding small pieces of volcanic material in my hair. Worth it!

Ashley Harrell

@where_smashley_went

Ashley is a California-based journalist and national parks bureau chief for SFGATE. She's co-authored more than 50 Lonely Planet guides across the Americas, Southeast Asia and Africa, and researched the Hawai'i Volcanoes National Park & Ka'ū chapter for this book.

DOUGLAS PEEBLES PHOTOGRAPHY/ALAMY

Kealakekua Bay (p86; pictured) is both an important historical site and a place of unrivaled beauty. The crystal-clear waters are teeming with marine life, which you can explore on your own by hiking down a rugged trail and snorkeling amid vibrant coral reefs. It's a slow, thigh-burning return journey – the better to make you slow down and appreciate the sweeping views over the coastline.

Regis St Louis

@regisstlouis

A frequent contributor to Lonely Planet, Regis has written dozens of guidebooks covering travel in the tropics. He wrote the Kailua-Kona & the Kona Coast chapter.

JOHN DE MELLO/ALAMY

When I first stopped by **Rising Tide Poke** (p193) in Hāwī after hiking down to Pololū Valley, there wasn't any *poke*. Odd, I thought, until I talked with the owner, who explained her husband was on his way from fishing and would come back in an hour or so. That's how fresh the fish is – straight from the boat. I did come back, and the *poke* didn't disappoint. Neither did the smoked *pipi kaula*, cucumber kimchi, and pickled onions.

Catherine Toth Fox

@catherinetothfox

Born and raised on O'ahu, Catherine is a travel and food writer, children's book author and frequent contributor to Lonely Planet. She wrote the Kohala & Waimea chapter.

Pololū Valley Trail
Descend into a verdant valley with a beautiful windswept beach (p194)

Maunakea
Stargaze on Earth's 'tallest' mountain (p210)

Keauhou Harbor
Watch graceful giant creatures on a manta ray snorkel tour (p54)

Greenwell Farms
Taste some of the world's best coffee in the legendary Kona region (p80)

Kealakekua Bay
Explore coral forests below the Captain Cook monument (p87)

Ka Lae
Drive to the southernmost point in the US (p160)

Hāmākua Coast
Road trip to the Waipi'o Valley past plantation towns and pounding surf (p92)

'Akaka Falls
Take a hike to rainforest-shrouded Pe'epe'e cascade (p118)

Hilo Farmers Market
Soak up local life, sample fresh island fruits and buy handcrafted goods (p96)

Kīlauea Caverns of Fire
Explore an underground lava tube and weird formations created by ancient eruptions (p114)

Hawai'i Volcanoes National Park
Peer into the crater of the mighty steaming Kīlauea (p140)

0 — 50 km
0 — 25 miles

LAVA LAND

Hawai'i Island is made up of six volcanos, four of which are active. From verdant farms growing crops with volcanic soil, to barren rocky moon-like lava fields, rare fauna, and forest-clasped lava tubes – the natural power of Hawai'i's youngest island lies all around. Lucky visitors will get to see mighty Kīlauea – home to the Hawaiian god of fire Pele – as it's erupting. Don't forget your camera for a once-in-a-lifetime photo of belching smoke and molten lava pouring out.

Volcano Warnings

Exploring active volcanoes should be done responsibly. Before hiking, check for updates on recent activity at the Kīlauea Visitor Center or on the US Geological Survey *(USGS; usgs.gov)* website.

Check the Cams

Find out if Kīlauea is erupting by visiting the live USGS cameras on YouTube. At the time of writing, eruptions were lasting between six and 10 hours, but can continue for weeks.

Permits

These are required for overnight backcountry volcano exploring. Get a permit up to seven days in advance from the Backcountry Office (p144).

Maunakea volcano (p210)

BEST VOLCANO EXPERIENCES

Drive to the summit of ❶ **Maunakea** (p210) for sunset above the clouds and some of the best stargazing on Earth come nightfall.

Peer into smoking craters surrounded by lava flow at the mind-blowing ❷ **Hawaiʻi Volcanoes National Park** (p140).

Descend into the crevices of the Earth and the longest lava tube ever measured, Kazumura Cave, at ❸ **Kīlauea Caverns of Fire** (p114).

Tour ❹ **Chain of Craters Road** (p145) on the edge of cranky Kīlauea for fuming steam vents and southern slopes where hardened lava meets the sea.

Walk the family-friendly ❺ **Kaulana Manu Nature Trail** (p202) to see rare plant life, which thrives in high-altitude volcanic landscapes.

OCEAN ENCOUNTERS

Hawai'i Island's diving and snorkeling opportunities are simply phenomenal. Visibility can reach a staggering 80ft to 100ft in its pristine lava coves and turquoise waters. Marine-life-spotting possibilities are endless – clouds of colorful tropical reef fish and endangered *honu* (green sea turtles), plus manta rays and pods of spinner dolphins are daily sights, while November to April is migrating humpback season. Snorkeling sites are easily accessible, though a boat is required for the more remote dive sites.

Protect Coral

Reef-safe mineral sunscreen is required (by law) when diving and snorkeling Hawai'i Island. Don't handle or break coral with fins or feet; these valuable habitats take years to grow.

Responsible Encounters

Numerous endangered, threatened and indigenous species can be found in Hawai'i Island's waters. Help ensure their survival by avoiding feeding, interacting or swimming with aquatic creatures (p244).

Highs & Lows

Remember not to ascend to the lofty heights of Maunakea or Maunaloa within 24 hours of a dive, to avoid getting the bends.

Diver near lava tubes, Kona (p56)

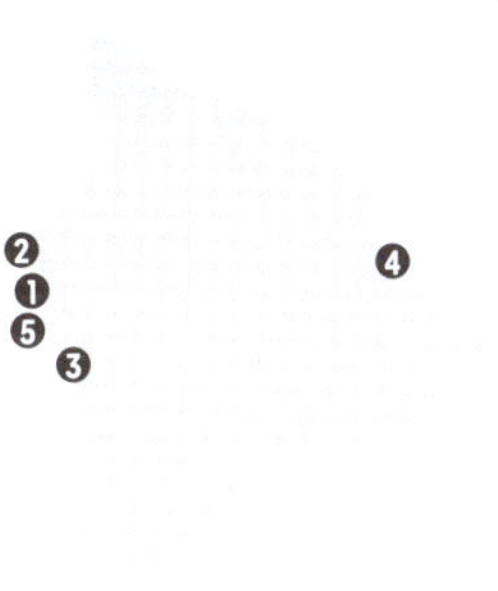

BEST MARINE-LIFE SPOTTING

Swim through the lava tube at dive site ❶ **Suck 'Em Up** (p57) near Kaiwi Point, which got its name by literally sucking then depositing divers at the surface.

Divers can see green turtles use a 'turtle cleaning site' north of Kona, dubbed ❷ **Turtle Pinnacle** (p57), where small fish feed on the algae on their shells.

Snorkel at beautiful and historic ❸ **Kealakekua Bay State Historical Park** (p86) for an aquarium of coral forests and colored tropical fish.

Join a whale-watching tour with ❹ **Hilo Ocean Adventures** (p102) to see North Pacific Humpback whales as they migrate between Alaska and Hawai'i.

Embark on a surreal and beautiful ❺ **blackwater dive** (p58) off the west coast to see pelagics drift out of the darkness, and bioluminescent marine life glow in the dark.

DOUG PERRINE/ALAMY

Manta rays, Keauhou Bay (p58)

ISLAND THRILLS

The varied terrain on Hawaiʻi Island is a paradise place for adrenaline junkies. Within a short drive, there are jungles to zipline through, wild, steep valley hikes, and truly unique marine experiences. Operators save you time thinking about logistics and gear and offer peace of mind. But solo adventurers with the right preparation can go it alone.

Be Prepared

Extreme adventures take planning. Make sure you have the right gear, including sturdy footwear for hikes, plus a hat, sunscreen and lots of water. Always check the weather forecast before you set off.

Cell Signal

Be aware that many valleys and remote areas of Hawaiʻi Island do not have phone signal. Tell someone before you set off on an adventure and let them know when you are expected back.

BEST HEART-PUMPING EXPERIENCES

Join ❶ **Blue Hawaiian Helicopters** for an aerial tour of Hawaiʻi Island's most active volcano Kīlauea (p144) and a bird's-eye view of the eruption zone.

Join a ❷ **Sea Quest** (p59) snorkel tour off Keauhou Bay for manta rays up to 14ft long gliding out of the darkness and feeding in the plankton-rich waters south of Kona.

Rappel 120ft down the side of ❸ **Kulaniapia Falls** (p104) in a high-altitude, thrilling adventure, then bring the heart rate back down with a swim in the pool below.

Soar over a 250ft waterfall with ❹ **Hawaii Zipline Tours** (p120) through a 450ft ravine on Hawaiʻi Island's east coast.

Hike the eight-hour ❺ **Maunakea Summit Trail** (p213) starting at 9200ft, then climbing almost 4600ft. Expert hikers only.

CHASING WATERFALLS

Hawai'i Island has an estimated 500 waterfalls, most of them in the east – particularly the northeast – of the isle. They range from skinny cascades of 1400ft plus, to voluminous, fast-rushing drops. Some you can swim in, others are better for photographs. Some are hidden, others sit right off the roadside and most are surrounded by lush, verdant valleys.

FROM LEFT: NICHOLAS ROMANAKIS/SHUTTERSTOCK, TROY TRAN/SHUTTERSTOCK

Tours

Some of Hawai'i Island's secret waterfalls are surrounded by private land and are best explored by tour. These offer uncrowded hikes to cascades and swimming in waterfall pools.

Waterfall Safety

Avoid swimming in waterfalls during the rain. Flash floods can make usually calm swimming areas turn to rapids and can create deadly flooding.

Health

Never enter water with open wounds. Freshwater streams and pools often contain bacteria, which can enter through open skin.

BEST CASCADES

Witness the magnificent ❶ **Rainbow Falls** (Waiānuenue, p100; pictured far left) from a scenic overlook – visit in the morning for kaleidoscopic colors in the mist of the cascade.

Cool down with a refreshing swim in the inviting pool surrounding the 80ft-high ❷ **Wai'ale Falls** (p100), after a short trek through tropical rainforests near Hilo.

Take a stroll to the 442ft ❸ **'Akaka Falls** (p118; pictured left) surrounded by lush rainforests and tropical plants.

See the triple cascade at ❹ **Umauma River** (p121), where you can swim, kayak and paddleboard in the pools.

Visit the off-the-beaten-track ❺ **Kamae'e Falls** at Botanical World Adventure (p123) for an awesome cascade in a lush valley – you'll likely have the view to yourself.

ISLAND BEACHES

Lava flows have historically destroyed many of Hawai'i Island's beaches, but the rugged Hawaiian island shouldn't be written off as a beach destination. Numerous postcard-perfect white sandy beaches can be found in the northwest, and striking ebony-sand beaches hide between soaring emerald valleys carved by pounding waves. Getting to them is part of the adventure; the best ones are secluded, and usually only accessible by 4WD tracks or hiking trails.

FROM LEFT: CRIS D/SHUTTERSTOCK, MOHANNAD KHATIB/SHUTTERSTOCK, MEANDERING TRAIL MEDIA/SHUTTERSTOCK

Lifeguards

Lifeguards are often on patrol at bay beaches. Check ocean conditions before wading out in remote spots. Strong undertows and currents can be fatal. For a list of patrolled beaches, see oceansafety.hawaii.gov/list-of-lifeguarded-beaches.

Gear & Refreshments

Many Hawai'i Island beaches are remote and undeveloped – it's advisable to bring water, sunscreen and a picnic, plus all the beach equipment you might need (snorkels, umbrellas, chairs etc).

Turtles & Seals

Stay at least 50ft from endangered Hawaiian monk seals and 150ft from a mom with pups, and do not disturb or touch endangered green sea turtles.

Maunakea Beach (p175), Kohala

BEST BEACH VISITS

Uncrowded, crescent-shaped ❶ **Maunakea Beach** (Kauna'oa Beach; p175) is the one you'll see in brochures, with powdery sand, gentle turquoise waters and wonderful snorkeling.

Uncrowded ❷ **Kīholo State Park Reserve** (p65) is a black-sand beauty with regular sea turtle sightings and a swimmable lava tube.

Family-friendly ❸ **Richardson Ocean Park** (p102) in Hilo makes up for very little sand with calm pools of tropical fish for snorkeling and green-sea-turtle-spotting.

For a remote and rugged black-sand beach in a valley clasped by pleated hillsides, follow the steep switchbacks for 0.75 miles along the ❹ **Pololū Valley Trail** (p194).

Hike 2.5 miles along the rugged boulder-filled trail to ❺ **Makalawena Beach** (p63) to be rewarded with pillow-soft sand and piercing blue-green waters.

LOCAL LIFE & CULTURE

Community is at the heart of Hawaiian culture; *'ohana* means family and so much more – it's more of a philosophy about the mutual care for relatives, friends and neighbors. Visitors who want to meet locals and learn about traditions and heritage can do so through vibrant community events, exhibitions and happenings around the island.

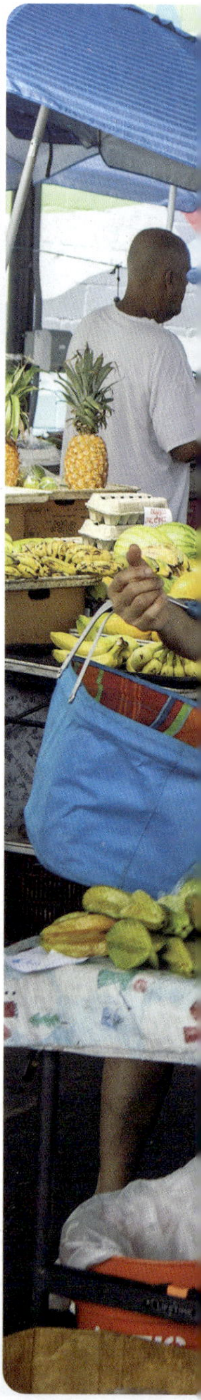

FROM LEFT: TIMBRE/SHUTTERSTOCK, EMANUELE STANO/ALAMY, DOUGLAS ZIMMERMAN/SHUTTERSTOCK

'Ohana

The *'ohā*, the shoot of the *kalo* plant (taro; pictured), a staple crop, can be seen around the island. People in an *'ohana* – a term derived from the same word – are seen as branches of a single living system.

Shared Meals

Traditional meals are typically communal. You can see this in action at beach parks all over the island. Beach gatherings include potlucks, sunset picnics, and barbecues that welcome neighbors and friends.

Talk Story

The local tradition of relaxed, meaningful conversation can happen anywhere, from riding on the local free bus to camping in one of the county parks. Starting a conversation is very much part of local life.

Hilo Farmers Market (p96)

BEST COMMUNITY HAPPENINGS

Join a local farmers market, such as ❶ **Kamuela Farmers Market** (p186), ❷ **Hilo Farmers Market** (p96) and ❸ **Hāmākua Harvest Farmers Market** (p127), brimming with community life, inexpensive eats and live music.

Attend ❹ **Hilo's Merrie Monarch Festival** (p104) for a celebration of Hawaiian hula dance, accompanied by traditional music and food.

Meet creatives, musicians, and friends for food and conversation at ❺ **Hōlualoa First Friday** (p68), a monthly community event.

Visit the magnificent ❻ **Lyman Museum** (p112) in Hilo to learn about Hawaiian culture and community.

Celebrate Hawai'i's local music, food and community at ❼ **Laupāhoehoe Music Festival** (p33) on the northeastern coast every April, to celebrate the spirit of aloha.

REGIONS & CITIES

Find the places that tick all your boxes.

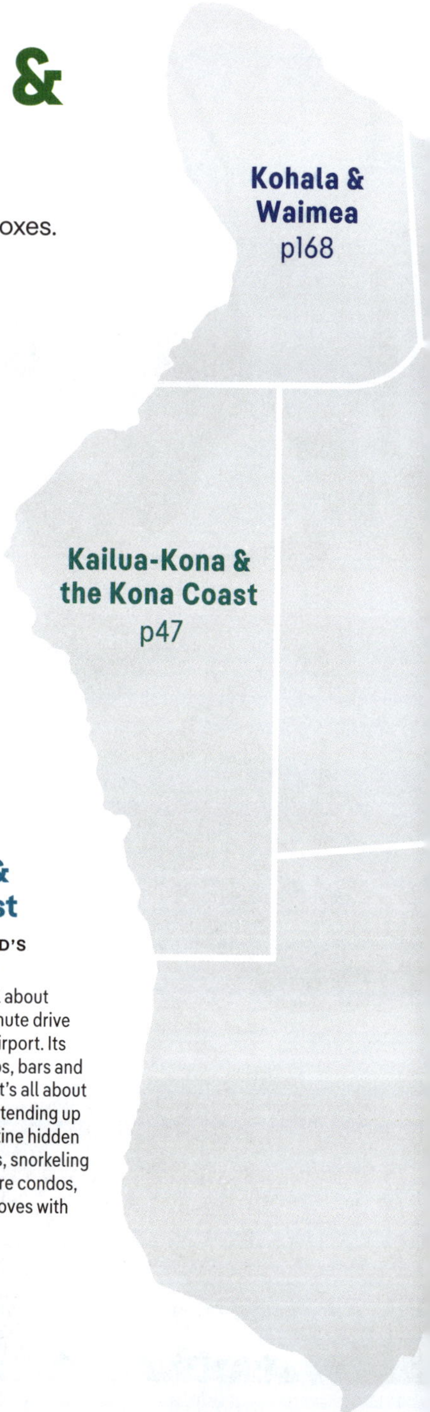

Kohala & Waimea

ANCIENT HAWAIIAN CULTURE, RESORTS AND WINDSWEPT VISTAS

South Kohala is dotted with giant hotel complexes and their adjacent golf courses. Inland barren lava fields give way to brochure-ready soft white-sand beaches. Geography dramatically changes to grassy hills and dense forests on the northwest peninsula. In Waimea, sweeping grassland, scattered with cattle ranches, combines with a sleepy town and vibrant arts scene, plus outstanding dining options, independent shopping, and a terrific farmers market.

Kailua-Kona & the Kona Coast

GATEWAY TO THE ISLAND'S WESTERN WONDERS

There's a 'built for tourists' feel about Kailua-Kona, which is just a 10-minute drive south of the Kona International Airport. Its main seafront drag has hotels, shops, bars and restaurants. Along the Kona Coast, it's all about beach life. North of Kailua-Kona, extending up to Kohala, lava deserts lead to pristine hidden beaches with white sand, surf breaks, snorkeling spots and dive sites. To the south are condos, guesthouses, and smaller rocky coves with dreamy sunset views.

Hilo & Hāmākua Coast

THUNDEROUS WATERFALLS, HISTORIC TOWNS AND RAINFORESTS

Hawai'i Island's capital is a look at a Hawai'i that has disappeared on other islands. This is a real working town with a diverse population, wonderful museums, tropical gardens and a vibrant farm-to-table foodie scene. High annual rainfall ensures its hillsides are always glistening and nearby waterfalls are always thundering. Fertile emerald landscape extends from Hilo to Waipi'o Valley. An unforgettable drive winds along the rugged coastline, with stops at quaint towns filled with cute cafes and boutique shops. To the south, the community of Puna is built in an active rift zone, and has long lava tubes to explore.

Hilo & the Hāmākua Coast p92

Maunakea & Saddle Road p199

Maunakea & Saddle Road

LOFTIEST PLACE AND STARGAZING EPICENTER

Crossing the belly of Hawai'i Island by car, the main thoroughfare between Kona in the west and Hilo in the east (Saddle Road/State Rte 200) is a beautiful drive. Drive past soaring pastures, view giant volcanoes and stretch legs on high-altitude hikes. Saddle Road is the gateway to Maunaloa and mighty Maunakea, whose lofty slopes offer the best view of the night sky you can get. Classic sea resort land turns to *paniolo* (cowboy) country in and around Hāwī.

Hawai'i Volcanoes National Park & Ka'ū p137

Hawai'i Volcanoes National Park & Ka'ū

EXPLOSIVE VOLCANOES, MULTICOLORED BEACHES AND UNDEVELOPED COUNTRYSIDE

Containing both the largest volcano in the world and one of the most active, this is where you can peer into an erupting smoky crater and hike around a lava wonderland. The jaw-dropping drive along Chain of Craters Road zigzags down hardened lava fields to the piercing blue ocean. Kids will go giddy exploring subterranean lava tubes. Meanwhile, Ka'ū, the land of large ranches, has forested highlands with grazing hoofed animals, windswept empty coastlines, high cliffs and the southernmost point in the US. The latter is about as far from 'tourist town' as you can get.

STEVEN GREAVES/GETTY IMAGES

'Akaka Falls (p118), near Honomū

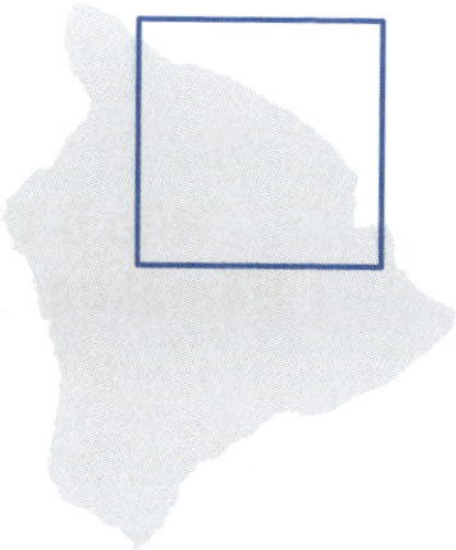

ITINERARIES

Hawai'i Lost In Time

Allow: 5–6 days **Distance:** 49.4 miles

Hawai'i Island's largest city, Hilo, is a former plantation town with historic storefronts and a thriving food scene, thanks to nearby produce and a diverse Indigenous and immigrant population. History gives way to botanical gardens, waterfalls and rainforests along the Hāmākua Coast.

1

HILO 2 DAYS

Fuel up in Hawai'i Island's capital with a healthy breakfast and island-grown coffee at a bohemian or mom-and-pop cafe such as **Paul's Place** (p100), before wandering town and visiting the **Lyman Museum** (p112; pictured) and learning about Hawaiian culture. Hit downtown's **Hilo Farmers Market** (p96) to peruse locally made gifts and stop for a street-food *poke* lunch. Pay a visit to the **Pacific Tsunami Museum** (p109) to see how the area survived two tsunamis, before wandering the **Hawai'i Tropical Bioreserve & Garden** (p123) on the outskirts of town.

2

HONOMŪ 1 DAY

Start early to view **Rainbow Falls** (p100; pictured) and take a refreshing dip in nearby **Wai'ale Falls** (p100), before grabbing freshly baked pastries in one of Honomū's cute wooden-fronted buildings, such as **The Hive** or **Mr Ed's Bakery** (p122). Head into the hills for the next waterfall of the day – the mighty rainforest-shrouded **'Akaka Falls** (p118), thought to be the highest free-flowing waterfall in Hawai'i. Finish your day with **Hawaii Zipline Tours** (p120), soaring over tropical farmlands.

FROM LEFT: JOHN ELK III/ALAMY, LOUIELEA/SHUTTERSTOCK, ANGUS MCCOMISKEY/ALAMY, DAMIEN VERRIER/SHUTTERSTOCK

3

HONOKA'A ⏱1 DAY

Join a *paniolo*-style horseback ride with **Wailea Horseback Adventures** (p121) in the rural Hakalau countryside, before stopping for a picnic and swim at **Umauma Falls** (p121). Spend the afternoon exploring the laid-back town of **Honoka'a** (p126), with its terrific museum, vintage theater (pictured), and pastel-colored buildings dating to the late 1800s. While here, try Hawai'i-made chocolate at **Honoka'a Chocolates** (p128) before settling in for the evening at **Honoka'a Public House** (p128) in town, an atmospheric watering hole inside the original wooden Historic First Bank of Hilo building.

4

WAIPI'O VALLEY ⏱1 TO 2 DAYS

Grab a cup of locally grown coffee at **Lean-To Farm Hawai'i** (p130) before joining a **Waipi'o Valley Shuttle Tour** (p133) to take in the verdant cliffs (pictured), soaring views, and wild, empty beaches of the sacred 'Valley of the Kings.' Afterwards, peruse handmade Hawaiian timber pieces at **Waipi'o Valley Artworks** (p134). Experienced hikers with their own kit can embark on the epic and strenuous **Muliwai Trail** (p133), zigzagging up the side of Waipi'o's western wall and crossing several gulches before camping overnight at the remote Waimanu Valley Campground.

ITINERARIES

Ocean Encounters

Allow: 7 days **Distance:** 118.6 miles

Beach lovers can do no better than Hawai'i Island's west coast. It has coves of all personalities – hidden windswept coves, postcard-perfect white sandy crescents, fierce rocky shores, deserted bays below soaring cliffs, and even one with green sand.

Below: Kamakahonu Beach (p50), Kona; Right: Ka Lae (p160)

1

NORTH KOHALA 1 DAY

Hike into Hāwī's **Pololū Valley** (p194) in the northwest, where pleated emerald valleys stretch into the horizon; a short, steep mile-long trail leads to an untamed black-sand beach, ideal for a picnic. Take the scenic route through North Kohala via Waimea on **Kohala Mountain Road** (p190) for jaw-dropping green pastoral views, and see three of the island's powerful volcanoes in the distance: Maunakea, Maunaloa and Hualālai. Stop in **Waimea** (p182) for excellent farm-to-table restaurants.

2

SOUTH KOHALA 1 DAY

Beach-hop southern Kohala's coastline, where idyllic bays of soft white sand, such as **Hāpuna Beach** (p176), are offset by sparkling electric-teal waters. Beyond the beaches, culture and history can be found in the form of several ancient heiau (temples), petroglyphs and fishponds in the area, where morsels were raised for *ali'i* (chiefs and royalty); many are still stocked with *awa* (Hawaiian milk fish).

3

KAILUA-KONA 2 DAYS

Wander the tourist shops for gifts and fill bellies with local *grinds*, before renting a board at **Boss Frog's** (p39). Surf if there are waves, paddleboard if there are none, at surf spots – **Pine Trees** (p57) to the north of town, or **Banyans** (p57) and **Kahalu'u Beach Park** (p53) to the south. The latter has decent snorkeling in the bay. Families flock to tiny peaceful **Kamakahonu Beach** (p50), while **Magic Sands Beach** (p50) draws crowds at sunset.

4

KONA COAST ⏱ 2 DAYS

Take a boat along the coastline or snorkel with one of the many operators leaving from **Keauhou Harbor** (p54), bound for the mesmerizing **Kealakekua Bay State Historical Park** (p86), where Captain James Cook landed. This wonderful snorkeling site is a natural aquarium of aquatic life, including shoals of kaleidoscopic fish, green sea turtles and spinner dolphins. Cook was killed at this bay – an obelisk on shore marks his death. By night, book a manta ray night snorkel by torchlight with **Sea Paradise Hawaii** (p61) in the plankton-rich waters of Keauhou Bay to watch majestic 14ft manta rays glide past.

5

KA LAE ⏱ 1 DAY

Drive through Ka'ū to **Ka Lae** (South Point; p160) by 4WD for an utterly different perspective – rural ranches lead to windswept beaches, below high cliffs with soaring views of nothing but deep blue ocean. Have a healthy home-cooked Filipino meal at **Pele's Eye** (p166), located at the home of the couple that owns it. They mostly use local ingredients grown on-site.

***Detour:** Mahana Bay, or **Green Sand Beach** (p156), is a rare thing – the greeny tint here is caused by crystals of olivine (known as Hawaiian diamonds) created in high-heat environments. Find it via a dusty, windy coastal hike 2.5 miles east of South Point.*

WIRESTOCK CREATORS/SHUTTERSTOCK

Maunaloa volcano (p208)

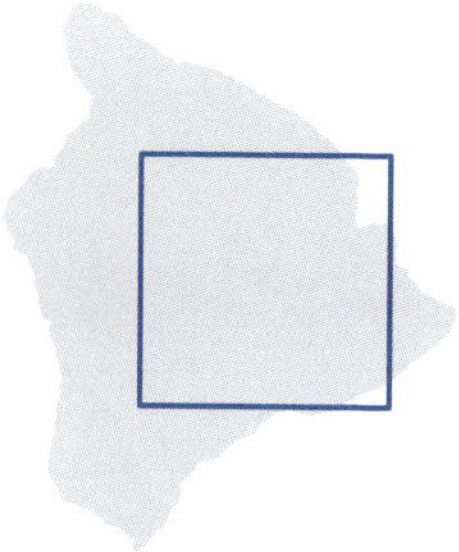

ITINERARIES

Volcanic Adventures

Allow: 5 days **Distance:** 90 miles

Six volcanoes make up Hawai'i's youngest island. Two, Māhukona and Kohala, are dormant. Hualālai, Maunakea, Maunaloa and Kīlauea, however, are very much active – the latter pair last erupted in 2022 and 2026 (correct at the time of writing). Maunakea and Maunaloa, the world's tallest and largest volcanoes, can both be summited.

1

HAWAI'I VOLCANOES NATIONAL PARK ⏱ 2 DAYS

The enormous **Hawai'i Volcanoes National Park** (p140; pictured) has six of Earth's climate zones. Climbing from sea level to 13,000ft, drives cover rugged lava fields, hikes traverse ash desert and rainforest flora, and paths descend into calderas, showcasing the power of Hawai'i Island's two most active volcanoes: Maunaloa and Kīlauea. The **Halema'uma'u** (p141) crater regularly billows smoke and spews lava.

2

SADDLE ROAD ⏱ 1 DAY

The main cross-island route from east to west climbs the hump of Hawai'i Island, bisecting its two biggest volcanoes – the loftiest, Maunakea (13,803ft/4207m), and the largest, Maunaloa (13,681ft/4170m). Road-tripping here offers different worlds, moon-like lava fields, lush tropical rainforests and rolling green pastures – all in one hit. Stretch your legs on hikes such as the easy half-mile **Kaulana Manu Nature Trail** (p202) to view high-altitude flora.

FROM LEFT: DOUGLAS ZIMMERMAN/SHUTTERSTOCK, FAINA GUREVICH/SHUTTERSTOCK

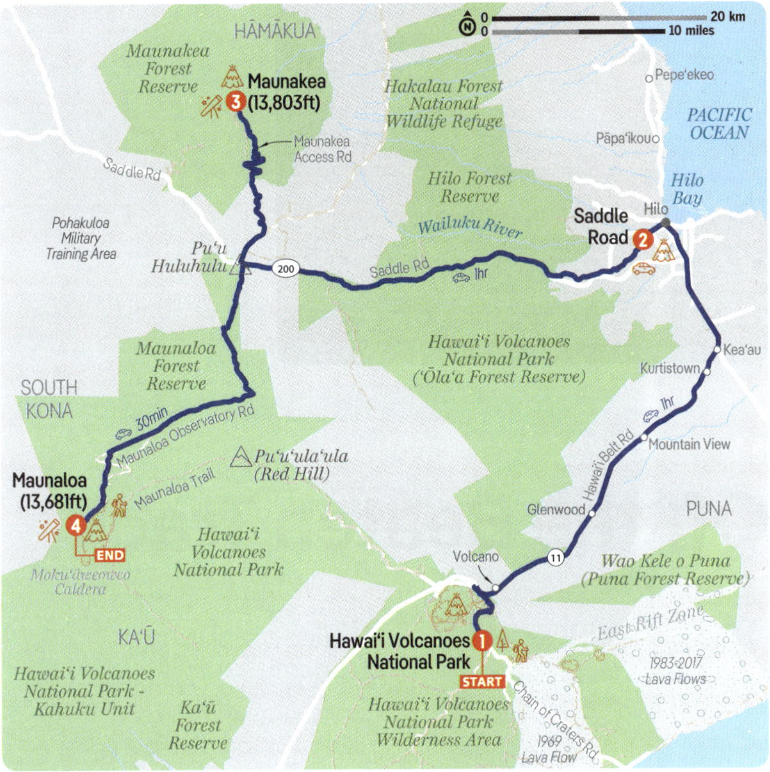

3

MAUNAKEA 1 DAY

Mighty **Maunakea** (p210; pictured), measured from its underwater base to its summit, soars over 30,000ft (higher than Everest, although some of it sits underwater). The half-paved, half-gravel 4WD **Maunakea Observatories Access Road** (p212) winds to the volcano summit for epic sunsets and some of the best stargazing on Earth (thanks to unparalleled clarity). Join a star tour at **Maunakea Visitor Information Station** (p210) after dark.

4

MAUNALOA 1 DAY

Maunakea gets all the attention, but **Maunaloa** (p208; pictured) is only 122ft shorter and is just as thrilling to explore. The **Maunaloa Observatory Road** (p209) is a lesser-traveled single-lane road winding through otherworldly volcanic terrain to the volcano's only observatory. Next to the entrance to the road is the terrific 2.5 mile **Pu'u Huluhulu** hike (p204), around a forested volcanic cinder cone with soaring views of Maunakea and Maunaloa.

CHRIS FINCH PHOTOGRAPHY/SHUTTERSTOCK, MNSTUDIO/SHUTTERSTOCK

Kīlauea volcano (p140)

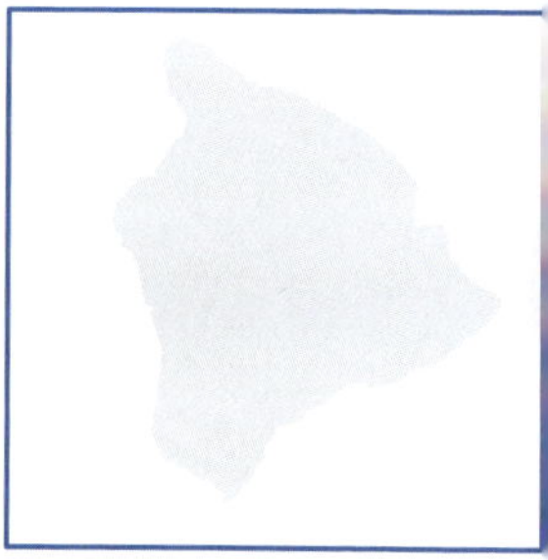

ITINERARIES

Off the Beaten Track

Allow: 4 days **Distance:** 178 miles

For those who have a good chunk of time on Hawai'i Island, have ticked off the major sights and want to get far, far away from the crowds, this driving route offers scenic views galore and something refreshing – the chance to indulge in laid-back local life on farms, explore empty trails and indulge in lesser-known island wonders.

1

KA'Ū 1 DAY

This area below the Kona Coast couldn't be more different from its neighbor. Hotels, restaurants and tour operators give way to open pastures, ranch living and wind-ravaged coastline. **Manadina Farm** (p166) is a delightful stop along Ka'alaiki Rd, offering guided tours through a permaculture food forest with the chance to take lots of freshly picked produce home with you. Meanwhile, descend into the centuries-old lava tubes of **Kula Kai Caverns** (p158; pictured), for a chance to roam labyrinthine passageways used by ancient Hawaiians for shelter.

2

KEA'AU 1 DAY

Hidden in the sleepy residential area of Kea'au is a terrific muddy, jungly hike to the remote, picturesque, black-and-white-sand Hā'ena Beach, known for its *honu* (green sea turtles). Ten miles inland, the **Kīlauea Caverns of Fire** (p114) – reportedly the longest and deepest lava tube in the world – join one of the tours into the dark cavities of Hawai'i Island.

3

WAIMEA (KAMUELA) ⏱1 DAY

Hawai'i Island's cowboy capital (p182) is where passions run high for rodeo and horseback riding through rolling green hills. **Paniolo Heritage Center** (p185) is the place to learn about Hawai'i's cattle ranching industry and lifestyle, while various ranches and stables will get visitors living it, trotting or cantering through breathtaking countryside.

4

HĀWĪ ⏱1 DAY

The tiny Western-style town of **Hāwī** (p192) in the north has a big appetite. It's barely two blocks – but punches above its weight when it comes to bohemian cafes and locavore dining, galleries and artisan gifts; try **Mi Ranchito** (p193; pictured). Sample interesting takes on Hawai'i regional dishes and flavorsome fare using locally sourced produce.

WHEN TO GO

The climate can be completely different within a short drive on Hawai'i Island. But at ground level it's always warm and tropical year-round.

One of Hawai'i Island's most intriguing qualities is its diverse weather. It has 10 climate zones in a relatively small area (the longest part of the island is only 93 miles wide). In a short drive you can find yourself in tropical monsoon, dry arid desert or snowy winter conditions on the high peaks. Visitors to Hawai'i Island can have multiple types of vacations, from lying on the beach in the west's dry climate to exploring lush green tropical rainforests and tumbling waterfalls in the east, thanks to an abundance of rainfall. Warm weather can be found year-round with the warmest months being August and September and the coolest February and March.

Accommodations Lowdown

High seasons are less about weather and more about worldwide public holidays, with increased demand for accommodations in August during school holidays and in December, around the festivities.

I LIVE HERE

CHASING RAINBOWS

Breeani Kobayashi is the hotel general manager at SCP Hilo *@scphilo*

As a native of Hilo, I love the rainy season – November through April. As Hawaiians, we believe that rain is a sign of a blessing and a symbol of growth and abundance. When the rain comes, it takes the old and replenishes us with new growth. In Hilo it rains on average 130in a year, so we have lots of blessings. After a hard downpour, I enjoy going to Rainbow Falls, where there's a high chance of seeing rainbows in the morning.

FROM LEFT: SCSTOCK/SHUTTERSTOCK, HAWAII PRODUCTION/SHUTTERSTOCK

Rainbow Falls, Hilo (p100)

HIGHS & LOWS

At sea level the weather remains a consistent 75–85°F, but there's always the option to cool right down atop Hawai'i's highest mountain, Maunakea, which mainly hovers around 32°F and dips to -19°F in the cooler months.

Weather Through the Year: Kailua-Kona

JANUARY	FEBRUARY	MARCH	APRIL	MAY	JUNE
Ave. daytime max: **82°F**	Ave. daytime max: **82°F**	Ave. daytime max: **82°F**	Ave. daytime max: **84°F**	Ave. daytime max: **84°F**	Ave. daytime max: **85°F**
Ave. rainfall: **2.4in**	Ave. rainfall: **1.5in**	Ave. rainfall: **2.2in**	Ave. rainfall: **2.2in**	Ave. rainfall: **2.5in**	Ave. rainfall: **2.4in**

WEST SIDE

Locals call the leeward side of the island the 'sunny side.' This is the ultimate beach weather destination, remaining dry most of the year thanks to the high mountains in the middle of the island, which stop most of the rain coming from the east.

Cultural Festivals

Merrie Monarch Festival Named after King David Kalākaua, the 'merrie monarch' who restored Hawaiian traditions during his reign, the Merrie Monarch Festival in Hilo (p104) is a big sell-out three-day celebration of the Hawaiian hula dance. Book accommodations a year in advance. **March or April**

Lei Day Hawai'i celebrates Lei Day (p104) in spring. Hilo's Kalākaua Park has lei-making demonstrations and music, plus hula and floral arrangements. **May**

King Kamehameha Day A public holiday (p104) across Hawai'i Island and Hawai'i state, honoring the monarch. The biggest celebrations occur in the small northern town of Kohala where he was born, with a *pā'ū* parade with horses, flowers and hula. **June**

Laupāhoehoe Music Festival For a taste of Hawaiian music, this festival (p33) at Laupāhoehoe Point Beach Park on the Hāmākua Coast draws a crowd with Hawaiian crafts and cultural demonstrations such as *poi* pounding. **April**

Food & Drink Festivals

Kona Coffee Cultural Festival With artisan markets, lantern parades and farmer talks, this festival (p68) celebrates local caffeinated brews and more. **November**

Farm Fest The place to meet local growers and try in-season produce fresh from the fields. It's part of **Honoka'a Western Week** (p127) in Hāmākua. **May**

Kona Brewers Festival Craft-beer fans can try the most inventive new local brews paired with local *grinds* (food) at this beer festival, which donates proceeds to local charities. **March**

Ka'ū Coffee Festival For live cultural performance plus all things coffee, from learning how to make a proper cup of Joe to discovering how coffee is produced, head to this coffee festival (p158) in the small southeast town of Pāhala. **April or May**

I LIVE HERE

BOATING

Dante Leuenberger is a boat captain at Fair Wind Cruises *@fairwindcruises*

Kona has beautiful weather year-round. June to August offers warmer water temperatures and the vibrant atmosphere of summer vacation. November through April is humpback whale season, a delightful annual spectacle that always inspires awe. During fall and late spring, Kealakekua Bay is quieter and more peaceful – marine life feels it as well and is often more active. But you can't go wrong visiting Kona any time of year.

Lei making

EAST SIDE

Humid ocean air is pushed into Hawai'i Island via the east or windward side, which receives abundant rainfall year-round. Hilo gets more than 270 days of rain a year on average; these are not continuous downpours, but come in short and long bursts (in summer and winter respectively), feeding the lush green rainforests in the area.

JULY	AUGUST	SEPTEMBER	OCTOBER	NOVEMBER	DECEMBER
Ave. daytime max: **86°F**	Ave. daytime max: **87°F**	Ave. daytime max: **87°F**	Ave. daytime max: **86°F**	Ave. daytime max: **85°F**	Ave. daytime max: **82°F**
Ave. rainfall: **2.8in**	Ave. rainfall: **2in**	Ave. rainfall: **2.8in**	Ave. rainfall: **2in**	Ave. rainfall: **1.6in**	Ave. rainfall: **1.7in**

FROM LEFT: MARIDAV/SHUTTERSTOCK, YOULI ZHAO/SHUTTERSTOCK

GET PREPARED FOR HAWAI'I ISLAND

Useful things to load in your bag, your ears and your brain.

Clothes

Dining out With warm weather all year round, shorts and flip-flops are typical attire. Hawai'i Island is a casual place: restaurants will not turn away those in the latter, but most wear jeans, trousers or casual dresses for an evening out. Only certain high-end resorts require visitors to wear a smart dress or blazer.

Outdoor activities Pack casual sportswear for active pursuits such as horseback riding and ziplining, and bring hiking boots with ankle support for exploring rugged volcanic terrain. A raincoat or umbrella is useful for exploring Hilo and the Hāmākua Coast, where sudden downpours are common. Take rash vests and reef-safe sunscreen to protect from the sun when surfing and snorkeling.

Etiquette

Be polite, courteous and patient – island time is slower than in big cities.

Learn the pronunciations of Hawaiian words where possible – an attempt is appreciated.

Don't enter private property or walk on sacred sites.

Don't take away lava or shells, and ask before picking fruit or flowers on private property.

Don't take off a lei garland in front of the person who gave it to you – it's rude.

Volcano summits A warm padded coat (or skiwear) is necessary for summiting Maunakea or Maunaloa, which can drop to 32°F at night.

READ

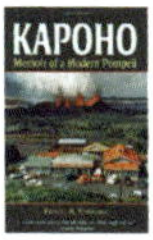

Kapoho: Memoir of a Modern Pompeii (Frances Kakugawa; 2011) Memories of the town of Kapoho, which no longer exists after being eradicated by lava flow.

The Sound of Hilo Rain (Roy Kodani; 2014) Tales of the old plantation days in Hilo, and the lessons learned from those times.

Volcano: A Memoir of Hawai'i (Garrett Hongo; 1996) Part memoir, part natural history by an elegant poet, who spent long periods in the town of Volcano.

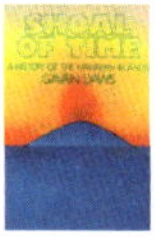

Shoal of Time (Gavan Daws; 1968) Engrossing and accessible narrative on the history of the Hawaiian Islands.

Words

Aloha (uh loh huh) Used as a greeting instead of hello and goodbye, to signal love, peace and compassion.

Mahalo (mu haa low) Thank you.

'A'ole pilikia (ah oh lay pee lee kee ah) You're welcome/No problem.

Howzit? (how zit) How are you?

Kapu (ka poo) Taboo. On signs it means no trespassing or keep out.

Wahine (wah hee neh) Woman.

Kāne (kah neh) Man.

Keiki (keh ee kee) Children. Look for the *keiki* menu in restaurants.

Kūpuna (koo poo nah) Elders, who deserve the utmost respect in Hawai'i.

Kama'āina (kah mah ie nah) People of the land – Native Hawaiians or locals.

'Ohana (oh hah nah) Family or community.

Shaka (shah kah) Hand gesture also known as the 'hang loose sign'. It's used as a greeting and to say thanks.

'Ono grinds (oh no grinds) Good local food.

Poke (poh kay) Raw fish rice bowl.

Spam musubi (mu su bee) Snack made of crispy spam and rice and wrapped in seaweed, served at service stations and hole-in-the-wall joints.

'Ahi (ahh he) Yellowfin and bigeye tuna.

Loco moco (loh koh moh koh) Hamburger patty with a fried egg, gravy and rice, served for breakfast at fast-food joints and diners.

Poi (poy) Local food made steamed, of pounded taro.

Kālua pua'a (kah loo ah poo ahh) Pork slow-roasted in an underground oven.

WATCH

Lava flow, Kīlauea 2018 eruption

Kīlauea: Hawai'i on Fire (Peter Chinn; 2020) NOVA documentary on the carnage that ensued as a result of the 2018 eruption.

Hometown Legends (Kolby Akamu Moser and Nainoa Lange; 2022) Beautiful documentary highlighting the Hawai'i Island *kūpuna* (older people) and the value they bring to society.

Seeds of Hope (Danny Miller; 2012) Interviews with Hawai'i Island farmers about the everyday challenges they face competing with development and its effect on the population, thousands of whom are malnourished.

Black Widow (Cate Shortland; 1987) Crime drama with scenes filmed at Mauna Lani Resort, and in Hilo's Kaikodo Building.

LISTEN

Kona Town (Pepper; 2002) Three-piece reggae rock band from Kona, influenced by Sublime.

Tell U What (Brittni Paiva; 2012) Groovy American award-winning *'ukulele* player, bassist, guitarist and keyboardist.

Lei Lehua (Mark Yamanaka; 2018) Hilo falsetto vocalist with Japanese heritage and Hawaiian soul.

E Walea (Kalani Pe'a; 2016) First Hawaiian music recording artist to win a Grammy (for Best Regional Roots Music Album), born in Hilo.

REALINA/SHUTTERSTOCK

Hula dancers

TRIP PLANNER

THE HAWAIIAN ARTS

Spanning dance, music and textiles, Native Hawaiian arts remain a powerful cultural force. Media include *kapa* (geometric designs on textiles), wood and stone carvings, tattoos and hula. These disciplines are a way for visitors to further understand local Indigenous Hawaiian genealogy, spirituality and symbolism.

Types of Cultural Arts

Cultural arts on Hawai'i Island are embodiments of the Hawaiian spirit and history. They include labor-intensive methods *kaula* (braiding), *hīpu* (knot making), and *ulana* (plaiting) – all typically done with trees and plants, and used to make pots, clothing and bedding. Designs are often decorated with geometric patterns, especially on *kapa* fabric (made of paper-thin tree bark). Hawaiian *kakau* (tattoos) also use similar designs, repeating certain symbols and depicting the wearer's social standing.

Hula dance dates back hundreds of years and tells stories through rhythmic foot movements and choreography against music performed with traditional instruments, including the *pahu* drum, *ukeke* bow, and *'ohe hano ihu* (bamboo nose flute). Dancers usually wear lei adornments – garlands or wreaths made with flowers or other items. Hula movements convey various things, including *pua* (flower), *pali* (cliff), *makani* (wind), *aloha* (love), *kai* (ocean), and *hale* (house).

Wood carvings, meanwhile, are embedded in wider Polynesian culture; tiki statues often represent Hawaiian gods and are used to ward off evil spirits.

Spiritual & Wider Significance

'When people hear the word "craft," they think it's something done just during our free time, like a hobby,' explains Kaaiohelo McAfee-Torco, cultural advisor at Four Seasons Resort Hualālai, 'but these disciplines are a way of life. This is how our ancestors survived.' This relates to creating pots and clothing, but also hula, which was a form of communication. 'Hula is actually like our Hawaiian database; we didn't have a written language. It's a lot more than just entertainment.'

BUY HAWAIIAN

Authentic Hawaiian crafts are harder to come by than cheap imitation imports. Shop carefully when seeking out original works and expect to pay fairly for them (read: a lot). Markets are a good place to get lower-cost items directly made by the trader – enquire about their practices before you make a purchase. Reliable shops include the following:

Waipi'o Valley Artworks Featuring 100 of the island's artists and a huge collection of woodwork.

Volcano Art Center (p141) A terrific collection of wood, art and jewelry, inside Hawai'i Volcanoes National Park.

Kimura Lauhala Shop (p71) A large selection of woven goods in Hōlualoa.

Llosh Winne Art and Design (p192) The place for hand-carved *koa*, tamarind and pine wood bowls in Kapa'au.

Hilo Farmers Market (p96) Good place to find local crafts sold directly by sellers. These change and vary month to month.

All Hawaiian-made items are created with a sense of purpose. 'Almost everything has some kind of deeper and spiritual connection,' says McAfee-Torco. When considering the growth of the material, a plant may have a physical representation of a Hawaiian god or goddess or embody the living. Taro, the main food staple in Hawai'i, for example, is considered to be part of the *'ohana* (family). 'It's considered the oldest of the human race – if we care for our older sibling, then our older sibling [the plant] will take care of us,' says McAfee-Torco.

In *kapa* making, it takes a year for the plant to actually grow. 'We spend time with that plant, and know when it's the correct time to pick the leaves and harvest. There's a very deep relationship with the environment and the material we're working with, to produce the best product possible.' The materials used in this medium are as important to Hawaiians as the end product: 'We ask permission from the forest to remove an item from a forest that we intend to use.'

Genealogy of Hawaiian Crafts

Most authentic Hawaiian 'crafts' can be attributed to a maker. 'There's kind of like a genealogy of who you learn from,' explains McAfee-Torco. 'I know who my *kapa* teacher is, and I know who that person learned from and her teacher's teacher and so on. It's kind of how you can determine their credibility.' Knowing how to do these cultural practices is both a burden and a privilege, she explains, since there is a responsibility to pass on the craft to the next generation. 'That knowledge cannot end with you.' However, these are not things people can ask to become a master at, 'but the knowledge will be shared if they're ready and open to learn.'

HULA EVENTS ON HAWAI'I ISLAND

More than half a century old, Hilo's **Merrie Monarch Festival** *(merriemonarch.com)* takes place around Easter, with competitive hula dancing. Keauhou's **'Iolani Luahine Hula Festival** *(nawaiiwiola.org)* is a more intimate event taking place in January with hula presentations and workshops. Atmospheric hula performances take place outdoors in Hawai'i Volcanoes National Park run by the Volcano Arts Center *(volcanoartcenter.org)*. **Laupāhoehoe Music Festival** *(laupahoehoemusicfestival.org)* is an opportunity to listen to traditional music and watch hula dance overlooking the Hāmākua Coast in March or April.

The rest of the year, various commercial hotel *lū'au* offer an easily digestible snapshot of hula dancing, varying in degree of authenticity. Among the most popular are performances at the **Legends of Hawai'i Lū'au** at Hilton Waikoloa Village and the **Voyagers of the Pacific Luau** at the Royal Kona Resort. These include communal buffet meals with traditional Hawaiian dishes such as *kālua* pig, fresh island fish, *lomi lomi* salmon and *poi*, plus music, entertainment and other Polynesian rituals. Hula events are often an opportunity to buy local Hawaiian artisan products too.

DOUGLAS ZIMMERMAN/SHUTTERSTOCK

Hilo Farmers Market (p96)

THE FOOD SCENE

Lush hillsides where anything will grow, a diverse population, and an ocean full of fresh seafood ensure an extraordinary eating scene on Hawai'i Island

Food is a huge part of life on Hawai'i Island and eating here is a unique culinary experience. It is over food that the *'ohana* (family) gathers, at a beach barbecue or picnic that friends meet up, and at the fruit and farmers markets that communities come together. The Hawaiian custom of caring for the land and a local emphasis on sustainability mean it's easy to find organic food, from the flavorful veggies that go from farm to plate to the fruit hanging on trees on the roadside. Combine this with a multicultural population – Hawaiians brought chicken and pigs, plus taro and coconut, while the Japanese immigrants of the 19th and 20th centuries added rice, soy sauce and chilies to the local diet, and Portuguese ranchers sweetened things up with sugared bread and fried *malasadas* (donuts). Eating establishments are typically casual, ranging from hole-in-the-wall outlets and diners, to laid-back cafes and restaurants. Meals are done early on Hawai'i Island: 6am for breakfast and 6pm for dinner. Restaurants are often closed by 9pm.

Food Markets & Fruit Stands

These are places to try in-season food and dive into Hawai'i Island community life. Local farmers markets are typically a weekly event, even in small towns, and offer a chance to meet growers, find out about local practices and sample everything from cheese and chocolate to local veggies. They often have food trucks and live performers to entertain folks tucking into their food.

Best Hawaiian Dishes

POKE
Raw fish cubes, commonly salmon or tuna, in a bowl of rice with sides such as kimchi.

HAWAIIAN PLATE
Affordable dish with chicken, beef, or pork, rice and a side of mac and cheese.

SAIMIN
Noodle soup dish served with *kamaboko* or Spam and diced green onions.

CHOCOLATE HAUPIA CREAM PIE
Thickened coconut milk and chocolate in a pie crust.

Fruit stalls and shacks, meanwhile, can be found all over the island, literally on the side of the road. Some are more permanent than others (and take card payments), but all are terrific places to pick up exotic, often completely organic, seasonal produce at a great price.

Japanese Food

The first Japanese immigrants arrived in Hawai'i at the end of the 19th century, after the Native Hawaiian population was decimated by Western diseases. Workers were required on the sugar plantations, which were crucial for Hawai'i's economy. Immigrants brought classic Japanese recipes and cooking techniques, which have evolved in Hawai'i over the decades to create dishes like *poke*. Hawai'i's abundance of fresh fish means sushi in Hawai'i can be phenomenal, while ramen and other staple dishes are arguably better in Hawai'i than anywhere else outside Japan. Hawai'i Island's Hilo and Kona areas have an abundance of excellent Japanese restaurants.

Shave Ice

Hawai'i's most famous dessert came about thanks to Japanese plantation workers, who used their machetes to cut blocks of ice in the field and covered the shavings with fruit juice and sugar to help them cool down in the hot sun. Over the decades, shave ice creations have evolved to include fillings such as ice cream and toppings – including a classic condensed milk 'snow cap' to exotic fruits from *liliko'i* (passion fruit) and banana, and ultra-processed sweet varieties with cola- or bubble-gum-flavored syrup. Cups of shave ice can be bought all over Hawai'i Island, but the craft bowls at Kula Shave Ice stand out, with organically grown and locally sourced fruit, organic cane sugar, and even filtered water for the ice.

BLUESTORK/SHUTTERSTOCK

Shave ice

DRONG/SHUTTERSTOCK

DARE TO TRY LOCO MOCO

While the name might be unappetizing, translating to 'crazy snot' in Spanish, the hearty *loco moco* dish (pictured; consisting of a hamburger patty on rice, with a fried egg and slathered with gravy) is anything but. Born in Hawai'i Island's biggest town, Hilo, it can now be found all over Hawai'i.

Legend has it that the dish was created in 1949 by a teen baseball team member named George Okimoto (who was studying Spanish at Hilo High School) when he requested a new dish from the no-longer-open Lincoln Grill diner. The owners offered him a big bowl of rice smothered with a hamburger steak and brown gravy; he nicknamed it *loco*, the Spanish for 'crazy', and *moco*, because it rhymed. It went down so well that it eventually became a staple in Hawai'i. In the decades following, an egg was added, and it's also possible to find it served with oysters, bacon, ham, Spam, tofu, *kālua* pork, Portuguese sausage, teriyaki beef and teriyaki chicken.

LAULAU
Large taro plant leaves wrapped around pork or fish and slow-baked in an underground oven.

LOMI LOMI SALMON
Salted raw salmon served with onions, tomatoes and hot peppers.

KĀLUA PORK
Also called *kālua pua'a*. Slow-roasted pork that falls off the bone, traditionally made in an underground oven.

POI
Taro root paste with a flavor similar to sweet potato; low in fat, high in vitamins.

Local Specialties

Poke & Sushi

Suisan Fish Market (p105) Take-out poke bowls in Hilo Bay served with uber-fresh fish brought in from the adjacent ocean that morning.

Poke N Sides (p96) Solid *poke* bowls with delicious dressings and melt-in-the-mouth fish, in a laid-back outdoor setting at Hilo Farmers Market.

Umekes Fish Market Bar & Grill (p61) Take-out *poke* counter in Kona with dozens of fish varieties and superb *poke* nachos, made with crispy wonton chips.

Hilo Bay Cafe (p105) Delicious rolls prepared with super-fresh ingredients in an open kitchen in a Kona cafe setting.

Da Poke Shack (p60) Reliable Kona counter-serve joint, steps from the ocean, for top express *poke* at a fair price.

Hard Drinks

Ola Brew (p99) Creative crafts with local flavors like *liliko'i* lime milkshake IPA, plus hard juice and cider.

Kona Brewing Company (p53) Probably Hawai'i's most famous beer, serving 'liquid aloha' and refreshing lagers.

Volcano Winery (p155) Grapes grown on Maunaloa's slope and creative fruit fusions.

Big Island Brewhaus (p185) Home-brewed beers served in goblets and 12 beers on tap.

Sweet Treats

Big Island Candies (p99) Enormous showroom factory and shop in Hilo, with a huge gift shop selling its standout chocolate.

Mauna Loa Macadamia Nut Visitor Center (p105) Chocolate-covered nuts galore at this factory and visitor center.

Honoka'a Chocolate (p128) Home-grown Hawaiian chocolate, with free tastings at the Mamane St store – try the smooth coconut dark milk and rum-infused chocolate bar.

Two Ladies Kitchen (p99) Handmade rainbow-colored *mochi* with island-inspired flavors. Expect a long line.

Puna Chocolate Company & Cafe (p101) Serves up chocolate made from 100% Hawai'i-grown cacao, which comes in liquid hot chocolate or as bars and candy varieties.

Sugar Coast Candy (p101) Old-fashioned Hilo sweet shop with taffy and nostalgic sweets.

MEALS OF A LIFETIME

Manta (p176) Upmarket open-air sunset dining in Kauna'oa Bay with farm-to-table dishes, infused with Hawai'i Island culture.

Hilo Bay Cafe (p105) Exceptional 'ahi *poke* bowls and sashimi in a sleek contemporary Japanese space with Hilo Bay views.

The Fish & the Hog (p185) For salivatingly good southern barbecue plates, with perfectly smoked meat and Hawaiian-style *grinds*.

Lava Lava Beach Club (p174) Gorgeous laid-back palm-fronted ocean setting and mind-blowing seafood mains, bursting with flavor and color.

'Ulu Ocean Grill & Sushi Exceptional sushi served at the raw fish bar; or against the west coast oceanfront views.

Harmoni Foods (p128) Top Korean lunch spot serving bibimbap rice bowls and tacos made with local ingredients.

THE YEAR IN FOOD

SPRING

Lychees (pictured) are best from May to September, when their floral aroma and crisp sweetness peak. Water-rich melons and strawberries are also best during the same months.

SUMMER

Sweet and delicious apple bananas are available all year round but are best from June to October, as are mangoes, dragon fruit (pictured) and *liliko'i*, plus cucumbers, which can taste bitter in winter.

FALL

Kabocha squash (pictured; Japanese pumpkin) is halfway between a squash and a pumpkin with sweet, earthy flesh – it is best bought between June and March for maximum flavor.

WINTER

Avocados (pictured) are generally a winter fruit. Look out for Hawai'i Island's giant ones – they can grow as large as footballs. Rambutans (spiky orb-shaped sweet fruit) are best from October through March.

FROM LEFT: LEXEY KAMENSKIY/SHUTTERSTOCK, CHUANPIT POOLSAWAT/SHUTTERSTOCK, NUNGNING20/SHUTTERSTOCK, LAURAGVG/SHUTTERSTOCK

GERALD PEPLOW/SHUTTERSTOCK

Surfing, Kona (p60)

TRIP PLANNER

SURFING HAWAI'I ISLAND

Riding waves has been part of Hawaiian culture for centuries, and was popularised in the US following Duke Kahanamoku's visit to Huntington Beach in the early 1900s, where he demonstrated surfing to a crowd of spectators. Hawai'i Island's surf scene mainly revolves around Kailua-Kona.

Board Riding Geography

Hawai'i Island is not as well known as O'ahu for its surf scene, but many cite it as the birthplace of surfing, and the activity is hugely culturally significant here. Those who do ride waves will find many lesser-known, harder-to-access, less-crowded spots on Hawai'i Island. Surfing here is not for the faint-of-heart: active volcanoes mean that lava flows are constantly shaping the landscape, and on its journey to the ocean, lava can create or destroy surf breaks. Coastlines on Hawai'i Island are typically volcanic and rugged, with shallow reefs that damage fiberglass boards (most rental shops only rent out epoxy or foamie boards). Winter swells are not as large as those on the other islands, due to Hawai'i Island's position southeast of Maui, meaning it's a good option for intermediate surfers who don't want to ride huge waves. Waves are best ridden in the morning, before the trade winds turn onshore.

The Kona Coast

This area receives offshore trade winds, resulting in cleaner waves. Beginners and intermediates will enjoy surfing at Kahalu'u Beach Park, where there's a family-friendly beach and a rock wall that protects the bay from big surf. Beginner lessons take place here. Two miles north is the local spot Banyans, a consistent intermediate spot over exposed reef. Further north are the pristine white-sand beaches of Kekaha Kai State Park, with an advanced wave to the north of Mahai'ula Beach named Kawili Point. Meanwhile, Kawaihae Harbor offers sheltered beginner right-hand waves, which work with west-northwest swells.

PREDICTING THE SURF

Surf cams It's now easy to check the surf without even leaving the house by using surf cams. These are set up at popular spots to face the ocean and are live-streamed to your device. Off-the-beaten-track or 'secret' spots don't have surf cams, but auto-generated predictions for these (based on swell and wind patterns) can appear on surf report websites (including surfline.com), although these are not 100% accurate.

Current hazards, tide times and weather Check **Hawai'i Beach Safety** *(safebeachday.com/county/big-island)* for current hazards at Hawai'i Island beaches, and **Surf News Network** *(surfnewsnetwork.com)* for tide times and incoming weather.

Local knowledge Surf shops and businesses have the inside track when it comes to local beaches; some do their own forecasts and post conditions on their websites (see livebeaches.com for beach cams).

THE SPORT OF KINGS

Surfing was created by Native Hawaiians who named it *he'e nalu* ('wave sliding'). While there are early depictions, dating to the 12th century, it's unknown when Polynesians actually first started riding boards. It's thought that wave riding began in outrigger canoes, before big heavy boards were carved from *'ulu*, koa and *wiliwili* wood. Smaller waves were more commonly ridden in ancient times, before the light fiberglass boards of today.

Hawai'i Island has a sacred connection to surfing, as King Kamehameha (born on the island) is believed to have ridden his first wave at Kamoa Point (also known as Lyman's surf break), south of Kona. The activity was reserved for *ali'i* (chiefs and royalty) and waves were ridden for cultural, religious and political reasons. Temples were built at surfing beaches so that chiefs and commoners could pray for waves. At Kamoa Point there is still a rocky grandstand of sorts where people would watch the king surf, plus a grandstand where lower-level *ali'i* would watch the highest *ali'i* surf. Beyond the grandstand, battered by several hundred years of tides, the Haleaaaama heiau (temple) was once dedicated to surfing. Ku'emanu heiau, south of Kahalu'u Beach Park, is where people would also pray for surf.

Hilo

East Hawai'i Island's Hilo area has a scattering of intermediate surf spots, including the 'Bay' opposite Hilo town, and an exposed reef break at Richardson Ocean Park, which mainly gets groundswell, but works at all times of the year and is popular with bodyboarders. It breaks left and right, but can get crowded. The surf breaks over boulders and rocks on the ocean floor, with occasional strong currents. A stream meets the sea at Honoli'i Beach, where a large pond forms a great natural swimming area when there is no surf. During swells, fast left and right peaks break into the stream.

Hāmākua Coast

Things get really wild on the dramatic black sandy Waipi'o Bay, with the lush Kohala mountains rising thousands of feet from the beach, which only has local 4WD access due to the road being prone to rockfall and erosion. It offers a consistent sandy bottom break for experienced surfers only, with incredible views from the lineup. East of the beach are Kaluahine Falls and Waiulili Falls. It's considered a locals-only spot.

MOHANNAD KHATIB/SHUTTERSTOCK

Hāpuna Beach State Recreation Park (p176)

Puna

Pohoiki was the island's premier surf area until lava damage from the Kīlauea eruption ruined 20 breaks in 1991. Pohoiki Bay in Isaac Hale Beach Park had three surfable breaks; and waves could be big. This is an example of how the island's active volcanoes can drastically change the surf scene. In theory, eruptions could create new future surf spots, as the seabed is always evolving.

South Hawai'i Island

Surf can often be blown out on the windswept south, but in the right conditions, great waves can be found, including fun lefts at the black-sand and pebbled Kāwā Bay and rocky South Point. Nearby is a famous (and potentially dangerous) cliff-jumping location, located at the island's southernmost point – prone to currents.

Off the Beaten Track

Surfers with a sense of adventure can go in search of empty, off-the-tourist-radar waves. These spots require hiking with your board through hot lava terrain or driving a super-high-clearance 4WD vehicle.

Expert spots include Makalawena on a beautiful, white, ultra-soft sandy beach, with consistent surf during northwest swells in the winter months. Pine Trees near Kona International Airport is a wave magnet at the white-sand Keāhole Point, and is another off-the-beaten-path spot to seek out via a hike or 4WD adventure. It's an exposed reef break with groundswells from west-northwest and a popular barbecue spot – it can get crowded at weekends.

HAWAI'I ISLAND SURF OPERATORS

Kona Boys In the biz for more than 25 years, with knowledgeable, friendly staff at Kamakahonu Bay, in Kona.

Hilo Ocean Adventures Friendly family-run store with a cheap selection of foamies.

Kona Surf Company Stocking a range of epoxy mini longboards, plus shortboards and foamy surfboards, at Kahalu'u Beach Park.

Miller's Surf Renting boards for 20-plus years; carries soft tops and performance boards in Kona.

Boss Frog's Some of the cheapest foamie and epoxy surfboard rentals in Kona.

Orchid Land Surfboards Selection of surfboards and rental boards on the Bayfront in downtown Hilo.

Hulakai Hawaii On Hilo Bayfront, with surfboard rental plus boards for purchase.

Surfing Etiquette

Share waves, and don't drop in (if someone is already on the wave – don't take off; priority is given to those closest to the peak). When paddling out, don't paddle into the clean face of the wave – this prevents surfers from being able to maneuver on the wave and can cause accidents. Give respect to locals and don't bring big groups of tourists to lesser-known spots. Make friends with the locals where possible, or better still go surfing with a local. As a newcomer to a lineup, don't expect to get every wave – tourists are at the bottom of the food chain.

BODYBOARDING

The first 'bodyboard' was ridden at Kona's Honl's Beach, around 2 miles from Kamoa Point where King Kamehameha learned to surf. Desperate to ride the waves near his house, but not owning a surfboard, California transplant Tom Morey fashioned a small board out of scrap foam and newspaper in 1971 and called it a 'boogie board.' In 1977, he produced almost 100,000 boards, and Honl's Beach is still the boogie-boarding capital of Kona. Multiple bodyboarding competitions have been held on the Hawaiian Islands since, with riders scoring points for drop-knee and stand-up surfing, plus spins and aerobatics – aerials, 360s, front flips and backflips. Visitors can rent a boogie board/bodyboard at most surf shops. Hāpuna Beach, Hawai'i Island's largest sandy beach, is a great place to start. Old Airport Beach, Magic Sands and Ho'okena are also bodyboarding spots.

FROM LEFT: RS SMITH PHOTOGRAPHY/SHUTTERSTOCK, JAMES R.D. SCOTT/GETTY IMAGES

Hiking near 'Akaka Falls (p118)

THE OUTDOORS

With vibrant ocean life, volcanoes and tropical rainforests, life on Hawai'i Island is an outdoor person's dream.

It's hard to find a more suitable destination for adventurous pursuits. Hawai'i Island is only 90 miles wide, meaning much of its shapeshifting terrain can be experienced in a day. Hawai'i's largest island has snorkeling with manta rays, tumbling waterfalls to chase, active volcanoes to peer into, high-altitude hiking on Hawai'i's tallest peak, road trips through moon-like settings, and dense tropical landscapes to get lost in. The youngest island in the archipelago, Hawai'i Island is alive and growing, thanks to eruptions, meaning adventures are always changing with the terrain.

Walking & Hiking

Hawai'i Island is great for hiking, offering something utterly different from other hiking destinations – wide-ranging ecosystems, from starkly beautiful volcanic terrain to lush tropical rainforests. However, much land is private, and off-the-beaten-path places require pre-planning. The well-traversed hikes are usually easy to tackle and accessible. Family-friendly ambles include the short Kaulana Manu Nature Trail, for high-altitude flowers in bloom and views of soaring volcanoes, while the magnificent Hawai'i Tropical Bioreserve & Garden is a living museum with eye-poppingly colorful flowers and 2500 plant species. Walkers of all abilities can discover pounding waterfalls in the east of the island, while experts (with a lot of pre-planning) can attempt a calf-pounding climb along the Maunakea Summit Trail, ascending 4500ft to the summit (13,803ft). Hawai'i Island's north is all about the staggeringly verdant valleys of Waipi'o and Pololū, with their lush pleated hillsides (the former requires shuttle access). In the southeast, kids will giggle with excitement wandering the long dark underground lava tubes dotted around the island, including in Hawai'i Volcanoes National Park.

Nail-Biting Thrills

ATV DRIVING
Rev around Hawai'i Island's rugged terrain by ATV with the **Umauma Experience** (p121) on the east coast.

SURFING
Ride waves at the beautiful palm-tree-fronted (experienced-only) surf spot at **Honoli'i Beach Park** (p102).

HIGH-ALTITUDE HIKING
Ascend the island's tallest mountain by foot on the experts-only **Maunakea Summit Trail** (p208).

FAMILY ADVENTURES

Join a zipline tour and white-knuckle it over the 250ft **Kolekole Waterfall** (p120).

Snorkel with Fair Wind at the dreamy **Kealakekua Bay State Historical Park** (p86).

Hike the short but steep **Pololū Valley Trail** (p194) for soaring lush views and an empty beach.

Chase waterfalls along the Hāmākua Coast, starting at **Rainbow Falls** (p100), swimming under **Wai'ale Falls** (p100), and hiking to the mighty **'Akaka Falls** (p118).

Paddleboard at Hilo Ocean Adventures then head to the calm waters of **Reeds Bay Beach Park** (p102).

Horseback ride Hawaiian *paniolo* style through farmlands with Pacific Ocean views with **Wailea Horseback Adventures** (p121).

Rappel down the 120ft drop of **Kulaniapia Falls** (p104) into a gorgeous valley, suitable for older kids.

Snorkeling & Diving

Hawai'i Island has phenomenal snorkeling and diving opportunities. Marine life thrives on the vivid coral sculptures and volcanic reefs in the island's crystal-clear waters, where visibility can be as much as 80ft to 100ft. Divers can have a unique underwater experience exploring sunken lava tubes or night snorkeling or diving with graceful giant manta rays (p58), which flock to the plankton-rich waters off the west coast. Take a boat or kayak to Kealakekua Bay State Historical Park (p86) for an underwater paradise with a natural aquarium of tropical fish, plus *honu* (Hawaiian green sea turtles) and frequent sightings of spinner dolphin pods. On the east coast are a string of beach parks, including Richardson Ocean Park, with several natural break walls (created by lava), forming still, child-friendly snorkeling pools abundant with marine life, including giant sea turtles, some 4ft long.

ACTION AREAS

For the best outdoor locations, see p42

Snorkeling, Kealakekua Bay State Historical Park (p86)

Stargazing

Once the sun goes down, the stars come out, and so do the telescopes on Hawai'i's highest mountain, Maunakea. Hawai'i Island is considered one of the best astronomical sites on planet Earth, particularly the high-altitude slopes of Maunakea and Maunaloa, which have low moisture and almost zero light pollution. Maunakea Visitor Information Station is a superb spot for amateur stargazing, with or without fancy kit, thanks to its clear, dark and dry skies free from light pollution. After dark, clusters of stargazers crane their necks to see twinkling galaxies, shooting stars (it's possible to see more than a dozen an hour here) and planets lighting up the sky. Want the skies all to yourself? Stay overnight at the lofty and rustic Maunaloa Cabin just off the Maunaloa Observatory Trail, during a challenging backcountry hike across one of the largest active volcanoes in the world.

HELICOPTER RIDES

Fly above waterfalls, valleys and coastline, plus peer into an active volcano with **Blue Hawaiian Helicopters** (p144).

SHARK DIVING

Embark on a heart-pounding encounter with tiger sharks at Crescent Beach with **Kona Honu Divers** (p57).

CAVING

Descend into the dark underworld of the Kazumura Cave in Puna on a caving tour with **Kīlauea Caverns of Fire** (p114).

LAVA SPOTTING

Kīlauea regularly erupts. Its spewing magma, viewable at **Hawai'i Volcanoes National Park** (p140), is a sight to behold.

ACTION AREAS

Where to find Hawai'i Island's best outdoor activities.

Beaches

1. Green Sand Beach (Papakōlea; p156)
2. Punalu'u Black Sand Beach Park (p162)
3. Kua Bay (Manini'ōwali Beach; p64)
4. Hāpuna Beach (p176)
5. Honokōhau Beach (p67)
6. Makalawena Beach (p63)
7. Ho'okena Beach Park (p79)

Snorkeling/Diving

1. Kealakekua Bay (p86)
2. Kahalu'u Beach Park (p53)
3. Two-Step (p89)
4. Blackwater dive (p59)
5. Manta Ray diving/snorkeling at Keauhou Bay (p54)
6. Māhukona Beach Park (p196)
7. Richardson Ocean Park (p102)

Surfing

1. Pine Trees (p57)
2. Banyans (p57)
3. Honoli'i Beach Park (p102)
4. Kahalu'u Beach Park (p53)

Walking/Hiking

1. Pololū Valley Trail (p194)
2. Nāpau Crater Trail (p144)
3. Kīlauea Iki Trail (p141)
4. Nāhuku (Thurston Lava Tube Trail; p141)
5. Kahuku Unit (p149)

Scenic Drives

1. Kohala Mountain Road (p190)
2. Maunakea Observatories Access Road (p212)
3. Chain of Craters Road (p145)
4. Māmalahoa Highway
5. Maunaloa Observatory Road (p209)

HAWAI'I ISLAND

THE GUIDE

Chapters in this section are organized by hubs and their surrounding areas. We see the hub as your base in the destination, where you'll find unique experiences, local insights, insider tips and expert recommendations. It's also your gateway to the surrounding area, where you'll see what and how much you can do from there.

Honu **(green sea turtle)**
MARTY WAKAT/SHUTTERSTOCK

For places to stay in Kailua-Kona & the Kona Coast, see p91

LOUIELEA/SHUTTERSTOCK

Above: Kailua-Kona (p50); Right: Coffee cherries

Researched by
Regis St Louis

Kailua-Kona & the Kona Coast

GATEWAY TO THE ISLAND'S WESTERN WONDERS

Golden beaches, aquamarine waters and arts-loving towns set the stage for exploring Kona's enchanting attractions on both land and sea.

The west side of Hawai'i Island (the Big Island) has long captivated visitors with its relaxed settlements, easy-to-reach beaches and near perfect weather, thanks to over 300 days of annual sunshine. The laid-back town of Kailua-Kona is a fine gateway to the island, with a handful of key historic sites that date back to the days of King Kamehameha, who made Kona the capital of his newly united kingdom. Nearby, you can explore lava deserts and sandy shorelines or plan a one-of-kind adventure, like snorkeling amid manta rays or paddling an outrigger canoe while learning about ancestral Hawaiian traditions.

LELIZ/SHUTTERSTOCK

Head from the coast into the interior, and the winding roads lead up into an entirely different backdrop amid the forested slopes of Hualālai. Here morning sunshine and afternoon shade (and periodic showers) create ideal conditions for growing coffee, with small independently owned farms producing some of the world's best java. You can tour coffee farms, some of which date back to the mid-19th century, and sample rich roasts, or perhaps catch one of the area's big events – like the Kona coffee festival in autumn.

The tiny settlements in the area provide a window into culture, and you can explore galleries and arts centers, vintage dining rooms and innovative chocolate-makers (with the farm out back), before heading higher up the mountain for hikes amid cloud forest. Keep heading further south to reach more stunning coastline, including ancient Hawaiian sites and a magnificent bay of crystal-clear waters teeming with marine life.

THE MAIN AREAS

KAILUA-KONA
Wide-ranging west-coast adventures. **p50**

HŌLUALOA
Art and Kona coffee. **p68**

KEALAKEKUA & SOUTH KONA
Ancient history overlooking marine-rich waters. **p77**

Find Your Way

Kona stretches along over 40 miles of rugged coastline – with upland forests and coffee farms overlooking the ocean – on the island's western shore. Attractions spotlighting the region's history, culture and natural places are just a short drive away.

Kailua-Kona, p50

Dine and sip cocktails by the waterfront, stroll past historic sites and enjoy seaside adventures, including beach-hopping and snorkeling amid manta rays.

Hōlualoa, p68

Tucked among fruit trees, coffee plantations and cloud forest, this breezy artists enclave brims with shops and galleries, with memorable hikes nearby.

Kealakekua & South Kona, p77

Southern hub for ocean activities and jaunts through history, whose curvy roads are flanked with charming settlements, gardens and snack stands.

CAR

By far the easiest way to get around is with your own set of wheels, which allows you to hit the beach, coffee farms and other far-flung attractions at your leisure. Rideshares and taxis are available but pricey.

BUS

The free Hele-On Bus runs Monday through Saturday, and has generally reliable service (more punctual in the mornings). It's mostly used by commuters and resort employees, and may not leave at times convenient for travelers.

EXETER_ACRES/SHUTTERSTOCK

Makalawena Beach (p63), North Kona Coast

Plan Your Time

Wherever you go, bring snorkel gear. Try to balance beach time with Kona coffee-sipping, scenic drives, hikes in the forest and visiting the island's best historical parks.

Pressed for Time

- Start the day with beach-hopping: don't miss the lounging sea turtles in **Kaloko-Honokōhau National Historical Park** (p66) or the spectacular sands at **Makalawena Beach** (p63). Stroll the **downtown** (p52) in the afternoon, have a seaside dinner at **Magics Beach Grill** (p53) and take a **nighttime dive** (p58) with manta rays.

Three Days to Travel Around

- Join a morning paddling trip in **Kealakekua Bay** (p86) or hike the **Ka'awaloa Trail** (p86). Discover the past at **Kona Coffee Living History Farm** (p82) and take a coffee tour at **Greenwell Farms** (p80). Leave time for shopping and snacks in **Hōlualoa** (p72) and **Kainaliu** (p84).

SEASONAL HIGHLIGHTS

SPRING

Expect low-season prices and perfectly sunny weather. You can still spot humpback whales in March, while May marks the start of mango season.

SUMMER

It's peak season. The seas are calmer for snorkeling and swimming. Catch big events like **Queen Lili'uokalani Canoe Race** (p62).

AUTUMN

Prices drop in late fall. In October there's the **Ironman** (p92); in November, you can sip stellar java at the **Kona Coffee Cultural Festival** (p68).

WINTER

Besides the holidays, winter rates are relatively reasonable. Surf's up, weather's lovely and it's peak season for humpback whale-watching.

Kailua-Kona

AQUATIC ACTIVITIES | PHOTOGENIC BEACHES | HISTORIC SITES

GETTING AROUND

It's easiest to get around with your own set of wheels, but be prepared for heavy congestion in downtown Kailua-Kona. You'll also have to factor in limited and sometimes pricey parking. You can get around by the free bus service, **Hele-On** *(heleonbus.hawaiicounty.gov)*, which runs hourly. There's also **HiBike** *(hawaiislandbike.com)*, the local bike-share program. For a higher-quality ride, you can rent rent from **Bike Works** *(bikeworkskona.com)*.

TOP TIP

You don't have to spend a lot to eat *'ono kine grinds* (good food), but you'll usually have to venture further afield than Ali'i Dr, where many of the waterfront restaurants are disappointing and overpriced.

The waterfront settlement of the Kona Coast gets called a half-dozen different names: Kailua-Kona, Kailua, Kailua Village, Kona Town, Downtown or even just Town. The truth is, this 1-mile stretch along Ali'i Dr is less an urban hub and more an economic center and tourist enclave, with restaurants, shops and curiosities designed to serve both cruise-ship passengers and independent travelers who base themselves at the area's hotels and B&Bs.

The settlement makes a handy base for booking boat tours and manta ray night experiences, and you can pack your day by visiting beaches, snorkeling spots and ancient Hawaiian sites. Most Big Island visitors will pass through here at some point, walking the waterfront, munching a shaved ice treat and watching the sunset while lingering over a meal or a mai tai. Dig beneath the surface by visiting historic buildings and landmarks that help tell the story of Hawai'i.

Kona's Closest Beach

MAP P51

Family-friendly favorite

Most of Kailua-Kona's shoreline is rocky and somewhat rough, but there are a few notable exceptions, and a short drive north or south you'll find additional options.

Tucked between Kailua Pier and Ahu'ena Heiau, **Kamakahonu Beach** is the town's premier swimming area, where ocean waters are calm and usually safe for kids. Concession stands rent all kinds of beach gear, and this is a perfect spot for learning stand-up paddleboarding (SUP), since it has both gear vendors and calm water. This is also a good spot to teach kids snorkeling basics.

Bask on a Beach Near an Ancient Site

MAP P55

Scenic sands and ruins

About five minutes south of Kona you'll find **La'aloa Bay Beach Park** (also called Magic Sands Beach, White Sands or

SIGHTS
1 Kamakahonu Beach

ACTIVITIES
2 Atlantis Submarines
3 Body Glove Hawaii
4 Kona Boys Beach Shack
5 Kona Honu Divers

SLEEPING
6 Courtyard by Marriott King Kamehameha's Kona Beach Hotel
7 Pacific 19
8 Royal Kona Resort

EATING
9 808 Grindz Cafe
10 Huggo's on the Rocks
11 Izakaya Shiono
12 Poi Dog Deli
13 Umekes Fish Market Bar & Grill
14 Willie's Hot Chicken

DRINKING & NIGHTLIFE
see 8 Don's Mai Tai Bar
15 Kona Brewing Company
16 Oceans
17 Ola Brew Co

SHOPPING
18 ABC Stores
19 Kona Inn Shopping Village
20 Puna Chocolate Company
21 Tasty Kona

WANDER THE PAST IN KAILUA TOWN

On a seaside stroll, you'll enjoy lovely views while visiting major Kona landmarks from the 19th and 20th centuries.

START	END	LENGTH
King Kamehameha's Kona Beach Hotel	Kona Inn	0.7 miles; 1 hr

Inside ❶ **King Kamehameha's Kona Beach Hotel** (p91), you'll find dozens of historical paintings by legendary artist and Hawaiian historian Herb Kawainui Kāne. Hawaiian war weapons, featured garments and more are also on display. Head through the hotel to ❷ **Kamakahonu Beach** (p50), a lovely patch of sand. To your right, you can admire (from a distance) ❸ **Ahu'ena Heiau**, a replica of a temple favored by King Kamehameha; in fact he died at this sacred spot in 1819. Stroll out to ❹ **Kailua Pier**. This was once a cattle-shipping area where animals were forced to swim to steamers waiting to transport them to Honolulu slaughterhouses. Follow Ali'i Dr past restaurants and bars overlooking the water to ❺ **Moku'aikaua Church**, an 1836 landmark made of lava rock and crushed coral. To peer inside you'll have to time your visit for 10am Sunday services (when all are welcome). Across the street, the ❻ **Hulihe'e Palace** is a two-story, lava-rock house built in 1838 by Hawai'i's second governor, 'John Adams' Kuakini. Get a look inside by pre-booking a guided tour with Daughters of Hawaii *(daughtersofhawaii.org)*. Continue another few minutes to the ❼ **Kona Inn** (p62). Once a high-end hotel, today the 1928 building houses shops and restaurants. Head out back for pretty bay views from the grassy lawn.

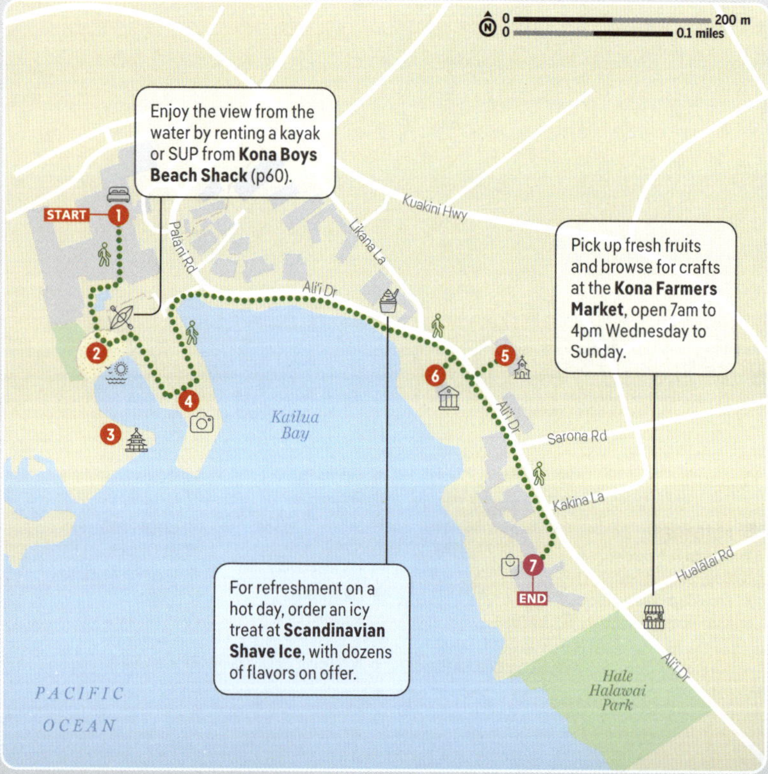

La'aloa Beach). This small beach lacks shade but is a prime spot for enjoying the view over turquoise water, relaxing on the shore or catching a magnificent sunset. Note that the waves here are usually powerful. You'll see bodysurfing and bodyboarding, but this is not a place for the inexperienced (visitors have gotten seriously injured here from the undertow and strong shore breaks, earning the beach the nickname 'Tragic Slams'). La'aloa is always packed. Go early to score one of the free parking spots in the lot across the road.

Just south of the sands, you can follow a walkway past remnants of the **La'aloa Ahupua'a** (a historic land division) that ran from the shore to the mountain. Interpretive signs point out important sites, including an ancient boundary wall, the remains of an 800-year-old former heiau (temple) and a platform where a *ku'ula* (a stone imbued with the spirit of a fisherman's god) was placed.

Grab a Bite Beside the Beach

MAP P55

Seafood and views

Right beside La'aloa Bay Beach Park, **Magics Beach Grill** *(magicsbeachgrill.com)* has a fabulous setting for a bite or a drink throughout the day (open 11am to 8:30pm). Reserve a table overlooking the sea, and tuck into fish and chips, fresh catch of the day or braised short ribs while sipping creative cocktails like the black lava mezcalita. Outside the restaurant is **Magics Beach Shack** (open 8am to 4pm), with breakfast (burritos, acai bowls) and lunch fare (tacos, chips and salsa), plus coffees, cold drinks and cocktails.

Snorkel off Kahalu'u

MAP P55

Fish-viewing off a rocky beach

Some 1.3 miles south of La'aloa Bay Beach Park, **Kahalu'u Beach Park** is another popular destination for some seaside activity. When the conditions are calm this rocky shore offers some excellent snorkeling, and the bay is usually tranquil owing to an ancient breakwater built to create better fishing conditions. The shallow, protected cove teems with marine life, and snorkelers regularly spot butterflyfish, parrotfish, surgeonfish and triggerfish, among others, and the occasional sea turtle shows up to feed on algae. The lifeguard-staffed park has outdoor showers, restrooms, drinking water and picnic tables. If you're driving, arrive early to maximize your chances at a parking spot.

SNORKELING ESSENTIALS

Safety The water is often calmest, and the crowds thinnest, in the morning. Check conditions and avoid going when there's high wind/high surf. Don't snorkel alone.

Reef conservation Do your part to protect the coral by wearing reef-safe sunscreen or, better yet, skip the sunscreen (some reputedly reef-safe brands aren't very good for marine life) and wear a rash shirt instead. And of course, try not to touch anything.

Lava rocks It's wise to wear water shoes to avoid cutting up your feet on the sometimes jagged or slippery stones along the water line.

Gear rental Many places rent high-quality snorkeling gear, including **Snorkel Bob's** *(snorkelbob.com)*, which even has corrective lenses for near-sighted folks, and **Kahulu'u Bay Surf & Sea** (p54).

DRINKING IN KAILUA-KONA: OUR PICKS

MAP P51

Oceans: This buzzing bar and grill with outdoor seating has a decent draft beer selection, daily food specials and live music most weekends. *3pm-2am*

Kona Brewing Company: The anchor of Hawai'i's microbrewery scene. Its lush backyard makes a fine backdrop for cold beers, pizza and fish tacos. *11am-9pm*

Don's Mai Tai Bar: Inside the Royal Kona Resort. Soak up the views of crashing surf while sipping up the tropics in the form of a legendary cocktail. *6:30am-9:30pm*

Ola Brew Co: The inviting taproom showcases Ola's fine satisfying brews, hard seltzers and pub fare, and it draws a fun local crowd. *11:30am-10pm Mon-Sat, to 8pm Sun*

KONA'S MAGNIFICENT COASTLINE

Manu Powers, owner of Sea Quest Hawaii (p59) *@seaquesthawaii*

This coastline is so incredibly beautiful, rugged and untouched, and the water is crystal clear. There are all of these sea caves – technically they're giant lava tubes and they're all along this coast. If you get out on a boat, you can see them so clearly, and skilled boat captains can pull the vessels into the sea caves; each one is different with its own unique ecosystem. You'll also see bottlenose and spinner dolphins, turtles, monk seals and resident whales like the false killer whales, which essentially look like large dolphins. And if you visit from December to March, you can see the incredible humpback whales. You'll likely see them on every trip you take during whale season.

Just up from the beach and across the street, **Kahulu'u Bay Surf & Sea** *(learntosurfkona.com)* rents out snorkel gear (snorkel set per day/week $18/40) as well as stand-up paddleboards (two/four hours $35/55) and surfboards (two/four hours $25/35). You can also book a surf or a SUP lesson.

Airport Turned Nature Site

MAP P51

Tide pools and succulents

For more of a local experience, head a mile northwest of Kailua-Kona to **Old Kona Airport State Recreation Area**, a grand spot for picnicking, jogging and fishing. The beach area is studded with lava rock, which means the swimming isn't great, but the tide pools teem with life, including the occasional napping sea turtle. Just in from the shore, you can follow the Maka'eo Walking Path, a 1-mile loop that takes you past a community-maintained garden with a diverse array of plants, including some unique succulents.

Combing the Shores

MAP P56

Sunsets and lava rocks

Another tide-pooling destination is **Wawaloli Beach**, lying some 7 miles north of Kailua-Kona. At the *makai* (seaward) end of the access road to the Natural Energy Laboratory of Hawaii Authority, this quiet locals' beach is perfectly positioned for sunsets – never mind the jets flying overhead. At high tide, the protected tide pools along the lava-rock coastline overflow; at other times, the same pools (especially the more southerly one) are a perfect spot for teaching kids to swim. Water shoes recommended for maneuvering amid slippery and sharp rocks. Facilities include restrooms and outdoor showers.

Secluded Alula Beach

MAP P56

Peaceful shore for spotting marine life

Head north to Honokōhau Small Boat Harbor and drive to the very end, where you can park atop hardened lava on the left side. You'll need to walk carefully over lava rocks down to **Alula Beach**, a small, sandy cove where there are no facilities, trash cans or lifeguards (locals call this Dog Beach). Fish are abundant over a sloping reef here, and turtles, rays and sharks are sometimes spotted. Stay out of the nearby channel, as there's frequent boat traffic, and don't be surprised to see shore divers around.

Take a Snorkeling Boat Trip

MAP P55 & P56

Half-day sea adventures

To snorkel further afield, take a cruise from **Honokōhau Small Boat Harbor** or **Keauhou Harbor**, with various outfitters offering trips (see p53). Opt to depart in the morning, when conditions are calmer and clearer. Tour prices range from around $140 to $230 depending on the number of stops, and typically include snorkel gear, beverages and snacks; book ahead online for discounts. Tours aboard Zodiac rafts are zippy

HIGHLIGHTS
1 La'aloa Bay Beach Park (Magic Sands Beach)

SIGHTS
2 Kahalu'u Beach Park
3 Keauhou Harbor
4 La'aloa Ahupua'a

ACTIVITIES
5 Anelakai Adventures
6 Banyans
7 Eka Canoe Adventures
see 5 Fair Wind
see 2 FBI Surf School
8 Four Mile
9 Kahalu'u Bay Surf & Sea
see 2 Kona Mike's Surf Adventures
10 Lyman's
see 5 Sea Paradise
see 5 Sea Quest

SLEEPING
11 My Hawai'i Hostel
12 Outrigger Kona Resort & Spa

EATING
13 Da Poke Shack
14 Kenichi Pacific
15 Magics Beach Grill
16 Magics Beach Shack

SHOPPING
17 Ali'i Gardens Marketplace

SIGHTS
1 Alula Beach
2 Honokōhau Small Boat Harbor
3 Wawaloli Beach

ACTIVITIES
4 Ala Kahakai National Historic Trail
5 Aquatic Life Divers
6 Big Island Divers
7 Garden Eel Cove
8 Golden Arches
9 Hawaii Forest & Trail
see 5 Jack's Diving Locker
10 Kaiwi Point
11 Keāhole Point
12 Ocean Eco Tours
13 Pine Trees
14 Suck 'Em Up
15 Turtle Pinnacle

SLEEPING
16 Honu Kai B&B
17 Mango Sunset B&B

and thrilling, and often explore sea caves, lava tubes and blowholes. Expect a bumpy ride, though, and no toilets. Catamarans are much larger, smoother and comfier but can't get as far into coves. Many dive boats also let snorkelers ride along at a decent price.

SNORKELING DOWN SOUTH

If you're on a boat tour, chances are you're making a stop at the famous Kealakekua Bay and its protected northern end, **Ka'awaloa Cove** (p86). This is a premier snorkeling spot, a sacred site for Native Hawaiians and where Captain Cook first set foot on the archipelago.

Diving Adventures

MAP P51, P55 & P56

Explore top sites below the surface

The Kona Coast makes an excellent launchpad for undersea adventures. Near shore, divers can see steep drop-offs with lava tubes, caves and diverse marine life. Top sites include **Four Mile**, a rocky bay filled with reef fish, eels, sea stars and the occasional shark, and **Alula Beach** (p54), where divers may encounter resident tiger sharks.

In deeper waters there are dozens of popular dive sites: **Garden Eel Cove** has a healthy reef, a manta ray cleaning station and quite a few garden eels, while **Turtle Pinnacle** features (you guessed it) abundant turtles. **Suck 'Em Up** offers a long lave tube where white-tip reef sharks hang out, and right beside it, divers can swim into a collapsed lava structure appropriately named **Skull Cave** to spot crustaceans and more white-tips. At **Golden Arches**, divers swim through a lava rock arch with white sand beneath it, and a nearby drop-off sometimes features mantas and sharks.

Advanced-only sites include **Keāhole Point** (aka Pipe Dreams), an abandoned OTEC pipe now teeming with coral and other marine life (including frog fish!), and **Kaiwi Point**, where turtles, large fish and eagle rays congregate near hulking mounds of coral.

Most dive boats launch from Honokōhau Small Boat Harbor, and the average cost of a standard two-tank dive (including all gear) is between $190 and $230. Multiday PADI Open Water certification programs range from $600 to $1000. Recommended operators include **Aquatic Life Divers**, **Big Island Divers**, **Kona Honu Divers** and **Jack's Diving Locker**.

Take a Submarine Trip

MAP P51

Stay dry spotting marine life

For visitors who would love to experience the undersea environs but without getting wet, book an excursion with **Atlantis Submarines** *(atlantisadventures.com; adult/child $160/72)*. This real-deal sub descends up to 100ft into a coral-reef crevice and explores nearby shipwrecks. The battery-powered sub has 26 portholes, carries 48 passengers and explores down below for around 45 minutes. Children must be 36in tall to ride. You can sometimes find discounted rates online.

Ride Kona's Top Waves

MAP P55 & P56

Surfing reliable breaks

Hawai'i Island is the youngest of all the Hawaiian Islands, which means it has fewer beaches and surf spots than its neighbors. But there are some good options, regardless of your experience level. Keep in mind the best waves are in the winter months of November to March.

Local experts surf at **Banyans**, north of Magic Sands, which is known for its northeast winds, shallow reef and urchins – but also excellent hollow waves. Another good ride is out at Kohanaiki Beach (aka **Pine Trees**), an exposed reef break south of the airport. At **Lyman's** (also known as Kamoa Point), south of Banyans, you'll find a reliable left-hand break.

Novices should focus on the consistent and beginner-friendly waves of **Kahalu'u Bay** (p53). Further out, you'll find more advanced-level surf.

LEARN MORE ABOUT LYMAN'S

For more information about the rich history of surfing and bodyboarding on the Big Island, such as King Kamehameha's famous wave-riding at Lyman's, see p37.

ROBJ808/SHUTTERSTOCK

TOP EXPERIENCE

Manta Ray Night Experiences

A night snorkel or dive with Pacific manta rays is one of Hawai'i Island's great highlights. The ocean at night is spooky enough, but to see these graceful, gentle creatures with 8ft to 14ft wingspans glide out of the darkness and perform backflips as they feed is unforgettable. You'll also get a deeper understanding of the rays thanks to knowledgeable guides who lead the experience.

DID YOU KNOW?

Manta-watching is enormously popular, and boat overcrowding has led to poor practices – some boats anchor on reefs, destroying coral, and mantas can sometimes swim dangerously close to boat propellors. Do some research before you book.

Manta Ray Night Snorkeling

There are two locations where night manta experiences take place: the original site in Keauhou Bay (in front of the Outrigger Kona Resort) is referred to as **Manta Village**, while a more northerly site up by the airport is called **Manta Heaven**. The chance of seeing mantas is slightly higher at Manta Village, but at Manta Heaven, divers who do see mantas tend to see more of them (as many as 40 have been spotted at once). If you're snorkeling, Manta Village is preferable, as there often fewer boats there, and rarely any divers.

PRACTICALITIES

- mantapacific.org
- per person $130-200
- 75min tours nightly

If you go with **Sea Quest** *(seaquesthawaii.com)* you'll only have a five-minute ride on a rigid-hull inflatable raft to the snorkel spot, and staff members have deep knowledge of the mantas. You'll be given a wetsuit and snorkel gear, and put in the water with a floating metal ladder-rig that you'll hang onto as mantas coast beneath you. A powerful light is attached to the ladder rigs, which attracts a buffet of plankton and, subsequently, mantas. While clutching the rig you may feel a bit restricted, but it is illegal in the state of Hawai'i to touch manta rays, and the floating ladders are a preventative tool that guards against accidental contact. The tours last just over an hour and typically cost $130 to $140. Other reputable companies that run snorkel trips to Manta Village include **Fair Wind** (p61; *fair-wind.com)* and **Sea Paradise** (p61; *seaparadise.com)*.

For a slightly different way of experiencing the mantas at night, **Anelakai Adventures** (p61; *anelakaiadventures.com; per person $200)* and **Eka Canoe Adventures** *(ekacanoeadventures.com; per person $120)* send small groups out in traditional outrigger canoes. Guests may remain in the canoes to view the mantas from the surface, but they can also hop into the water and snorkel.

Manta Ray Night Diving

Manta night diving can involve either one tank or two. The latter option includes a preliminary reef dive around sunset, and the second dive takes place at Manta Heaven after dark. To witness the manta spectacle, divers descend to what's referred to as 'the campfire,' where bright lights positioned on the bottom attract plankton (which in turn attracts manta rays). The magnificent creatures perform a sort of ballet, swooping in, rising face-to-face through the water column and, at times, gliding just above the heads of the divers. Kona is the only place in the world where this happens, and it's truly awe-inspiring.

The cost ranges from around $155 to $240, depending on the number of dives, and includes basic dive gear. A number of reputable companies offer manta night dives, but our top pick is **Aquatic Life Divers** *(aquaticlifedivers.com)*, with top-notch gear and personable, knowledgeable dive masters. Also recommended are **Big Island Divers** *(bigislanddivers.com)*, **Jack's Diving Locker** *(jacksdivinglocker.com)* and **Kona Honu Divers** *(konahonudivers.com)*.

LOOK, DON'T TOUCH

Manta rays have no stingers and are harmless to humans. Humans, however, are a massive threat to manta rays, due to overfishing and entanglements in fishing nets. Touching them is also harmful; manta rays are covered in a mucous film and when it's removed, they become more susceptible to bacterial infections.

TOP TIPS

- If you are prone to motion sickness, take medication. The rocking motion as you float on the water can cause seasickness.
- Show up a few minutes early to give yourself time to find a parking spot.
- A wetsuit, snacks, juice, water and hot drinks (post-trip) are usually provided.
- The later in the evening your tour takes place, the fewer boats you'll see in the water.
- Bring an underwater camera, towels and something warm to wear afterwards.
- If you don't see any mantas, many companies will allow you to join another tour at no charge (space permitting).

HISTORICAL SNAPSHOT OF KAILUA-KONA

Despite the touristy vibe in certain areas, Kailua-Kona holds a significant place in Hawaiian history. Kamehameha the Great lived his last years here, worshipping at Ahu'ena Heiau, his own temple. Soon after his death in 1819, his son Liholiho broke an important *kapu* (taboo) by dining with women. The old ways suffered another blow when the first missionaries sailed into Kailua Bay in 1820 and converted the Hawaiians to Christianity. In the 19th century, the town was a leisure retreat for Hawaiian royalty. Hulihe'e Palace was a favorite getaway for King David Kalakaua, a talented patron of the arts, including hula, music and literature. Since the 1970s Kailua-Kona has been the Big Island's economic powerhouse, fueled by tourism, retail and real estate.

Take a Surf Lesson

MAP P51 & P55

Top schools

If you've never tried surfing but want to give it a go, book a two-hour class with **Hawaii Lifeguard Surf Instructors** *(surflessonshawaii.com)*. Skilled, personable instructors here have a minimum of 15 years' surfing experience and are all certified lifeguards. It's also a Native Hawaiian family-owned and -operated outfit. The private group lessons start at $115 per person for a group of three or more, while a two-person lesson costs $295 and a one-on-one lesson costs $195.

Other recommended schools include **Kona Mike's Surf Adventures** *(konamikes.com; 2hr group/private lesson $124/210)* in Kona town, and **FBI Surf School** *(fbisurf.com; 2hr group/private lesson $150/199)*, a friendly outfit run by beloved local surf dude Ossian. If you just need to rent a board, **Kahalu'u Bay Surf & Sea** *(learntosurfkona.com)* is your spot: surfboards start at $20 for two hours, SUP boards are $35 for two hours, and the shop also does group lessons starting at $139 per person.

Hop on a SUP or Boogie Board

MAP P51

Get active on the sea

For those who have never tried SUP, the **Kona Boys Beach Shack** *(konaboys.com)* organizes lessons (group/private $129/179) as well as more ambitious coastal paddling tours, and rents SUP sets (per hour/day $29/99) and kayaks (per hour/day from $19/64) right on Kamakahonu Beach – which, sheltered as it is, is perfect for learning SUP basics. If body-boarding is your jam, drive five minutes south to **Honl's Beach**. It was here, in 1971, that Tom Morey tested the Boogie Board (the brand-name version of the most popular type of bodyboard). The sandy beach here is small, and sharp rocks make the water unfriendly to casual swimmers, but as you may guess, the area is quite popular with local bodyboarders.

Paddle an Outrigger Canoe

MAP P51

The iconic Hawaiian adventure

Sure, you could easily rent a kayak. But when in Hawai'i, why not try out the traditional watercraft of the ancient Polynesians: the double-hulled outrigger canoe. After all, this is how the island's first inhabitants arrived here, and immersing in the local culture is both a soul-satisfying and sustainable way to explore Hawai'i Island's marine environs.

EATING IN KAILUA-KONA: OUR PICKS

MAP P51 & P55

Da Poke Shack: A bustling spot with some of the freshest and tastiest *poke* on the Big Island. The line is always long, so plan accordingly. *10am-4pm* **$$**

Kenichi Pacific: Ignore the mall setting and savor the Pacific Rim fusion cuisine, including miso black cod and Hawaiian *ono* (white-fleshed wahoo). *4:30-9pm Tue-Sun* **$$$**

Willie's Hot Chicken: Order at the counter then grab a picnic table and enjoy the laid-back setting, live music (Thu-Sun) and cold beers. *11am-9pm Mon-Sat, to 8pm Sun* **$$**

Huggo's on the Rocks: Perched over the water, with sunset views, tropical cocktails and casual fare (ceviche, *kālua* pork sandwiches, fish and chips). *noon-9pm* **$$**

RITU MANOJ JETHANI/SHUTTERSTOCK

Kona Boys Beach Shack

If you're only in town for a few days, you can learn the basics from **Kona Boys** at Kamakahonu Beach. On a one-hour excursion (per person $69), you'll get a workout while learning about the area's long history and with luck see spinner dolphins or other marine life. **Anelakai Adventures** *(anelakaiadventures.com)* offers a two-hour morning excursion (per person $150) paddling a double-hull canoe and departing from Keauhou Bay.

Another option is to join the recreational canoe paddling excursions of **Kai 'Opua Canoe Club** *(kaiopua.org)*, one of the oldest outrigger canoe clubs in the state of Hawai'i. Note that you need to be invited as a guest by a current member or register online as a member (adult/youth annual fee $200/100), which helps support this vital organization. Once enrolled as a member you can join a paddling session that departs from Kamakahonu Beach most mornings.

See a Spectacular Canoe Race

Powerhouse paddling competitions

To see how outrigger-canoeing pros do it, catch a race while you're on the island. Check out the January-to-May race schedule of the **Hawaii Island Paddlesports Association** *(hipa.clubexpress.com)* for the latest events, which happen in Kona and Hilo. If you're around over the Labor Day weekend

BEST BOAT TOURS

Sea Quest (p59) Well-run company with rigid-hull inflatable rafts that take passengers on one-, two- and three-stop snorkel adventures that cover much of the South Kona Coast.

Body Glove Hawaii Popular three-hour catamaran dinner cruises along the Kona Coast, as well as four-hour super-raft snorkel trips with stops in two places.

Fair Wind The *Fair Wind II*, a two-story catamaran with two 15ft-long waterslides, sails to Kealakekua Bay from Keauhou Bay every morning.

Sea Paradise Highly recommended outfitter offering morning and afternoon snorkel cruises on a 50ft-long catamaran with a friendly, professional crew.

Ocean Eco Tours Head off in search of large marine animals on a four-hour small group 'offshore safari,' with snorkeling and an underwater video included.

EATING IN KAILUA-KONA: OUR PICKS

MAP P51

808 Grindz Cafe: Hole-in-the-wall eatery serves classic *loco moco* (rice topped with eggs, gravy and the meat of your choice). *7am-1pm* $

Poi Dog Deli: A veritable sandwich heaven, this shop is decked out in funky island art and the owners are all about social justice. *10:30am-6pm Mon-Sat* $

Izakaya Shiono: Linger outdoors over perfect morsels of sushi and sashimi, plus steaming ramen and unagi bowls. *11am-1:30pm Mon-Fri & 5-9pm Mon-Sat* $$

Umekes Fish Market Bar & Grill: Come here for several variations on delicious *poke pūpū*, and chase them with fish tacos, or a grilled catch of the day. *11am-9pm Mon-Sat* $$

BEST STORES IN KAILUA-KONA

Puna Chocolate Company Breathe in the heady scent of dark chocolate while browsing handcrafted bars or perhaps sipping a cacao Manhattan from the bar in back.

Kona Inn Shopping Village Browse for craft items, jewelry, surf wear and artwork amid the stores of this small waterfront complex.

Tasty Kona Friendly spot for coffees, candles, beach blankets, shell necklaces, skincare products and eye-catching Star Wars–esque posters featuring Hawaiian backdrops.

Ali'i Gardens Marketplace Around 2 miles south of the center, this open-air shopping center has stalls of arts, crafts and produce.

ABC Stores One of several ABCs on Ali'i Dr, this one has all the Hawaiian essentials, including T-shirts, jewelry, snack food, gift ideas and alcohol, all at fair prices.

MIKE BRAKE/SHUTTERSTOCK

Canoes, Queen Lili'uokalani Canoe Race

(late August or early September), don't miss the world's largest outrigger canoe competition: **Queen Lili'uokalani Canoe Race** *(qlcanoerace.com)* features four days of racing, bringing over 2500 paddlers from all across the globe. Saturday is the main event, with the challenging single-hull 18-mile race from Kailua Bay to Hōnaunau. There's also a torchlight parade Saturday night and an awards *lū'au* on Sunday.

Plan Your Land Adventure

MAP P56

Guided hikes and birdwatching

If you're keen on a guided, far-flung day outing in Hawai'i Island's greenest depths, contact Kona-based **Hawaii Forest & Trail** *(hawaii-forest.com)*. From the always-popular Mauna Kea Summit & Stars Adventure ($315) to hikes that take you through volcanic landscapes (adult/child $259/234) and guided birdwatching excursions ($275) in Hakalau Forest National Wildlife Refuge, these expert naturalists and eco-sustainability stewards have you covered. You can also book a three-hour Kohala Canopy Adventure (adult/child $245/220) with ziplining and rappelling in Kohala.

Beyond Kailua-Kona

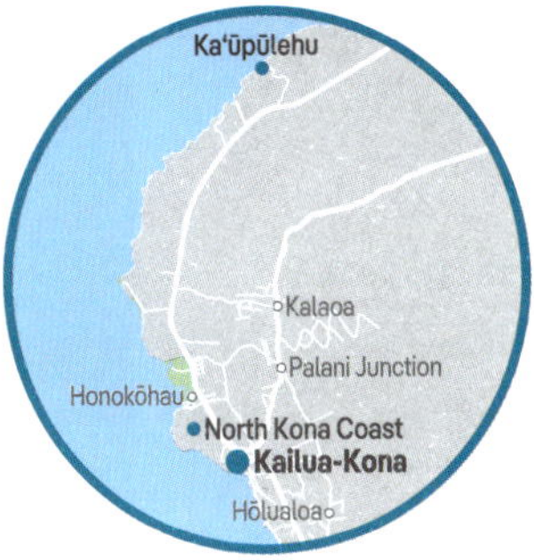

Untamed and arid, the North Kona Coast is where the bright blue Pacific meets surreal lava fields.

North Kona runs 33 miles from Kailua-Kona up the coast along Queen Ka'ahumanu Hwy (Hwy 19), encompassing busy Honokōhau Harbor, the sacred Kaloko-Honokōhau National Historical Park, an international airport and a vast desertscape of jet-black and rust-colored lava, extending for miles before a crashing sea. Walking across the *'a'ā* (rough, jagged lava) under the beating sun is like stumbling across a foreboding, otherworldly landscape. But once you plunge into the turquoise depths of North Kona's remote beaches, snorkel among its foraging green sea turtles and take in a magical sunset from the wave-lapped sands, you'll realize all that ankle-wrenching was worth it. The sun is intense because of the reflection off the lava and sea – bring a wide-brimmed hat, sunglasses and ample (reef-safe) sunscreen.

Places

GETTING AROUND

Hele-On runs at least one daily bus out to the resorts north of Kailua-Kona. Otherwise, North Kona is an easy drive; just be aware of heavy traffic conditions around the airport during peak hours (7am to 9am and 3pm to 6:30pm). Keep in mind parking is easiest early in the day, and lots can fill by 10am. Note that mile markers decrease as you head north.

North Kona Coast

TIME FROM KAILUA-KONA: **20MIN**

Explore the beaches of Kekaha Kai

Some of the prettiest beaches on the island are found at **Kekaha Kai State Park** *(free)*, located some 11 miles north of Kailua-Kona, and backed by a vast desert of unforgiving black lava. To reach the 1600-acre park, take the chunky lava road between Miles 90 and 91 on Hwy 19 (4WD recommended, not required). The easiest access point is the parking lot for **Mahai'ula Beach**, where you'll have a short walk to the salt-and-pepper sand, rocky tide pools, shaded picnic tables and toilets (bring your own drinking water). The gate to access the road to the shore is open from 8am to 6:30pm.

If what you're after is an almost-deserted scoop of soft, white-sand beach cupping brilliant blue-green waters, it's worth the extra effort to reach **Makalawena Beach** ('Maks') instead. You'll need to take the same access road, but at the

BEST AIRBORNE EXPERIENCES

UFO Parasail Enjoy up to 10 minutes of airtime with UFO, which operates two- and three-person 'flights' out of the King Kamehameha hotel (from $116 per person).

Paradise Helicopters Kona-based helicopter tours (one hour from $500 per person) take in volcanoes, waterfalls, beaches and rainforests.

Mauna Loa Helicopter Tours This reputable company does shorter, more affordable tours (20- to 30-minute flight from $229) that take in the spectacular Kona coast.

Flight of Aloha Experience the thrill of flying without leaving terra firma through an immersive theater experience (adult/child from $35/30) in the King Kamehameha hotel.

Tropicbird Flight Service If a scenic flight feels too tame, why not learn to fly a training aircraft with an FAA Certified Flight Instructor?

CHRIS FINCH PHOTOGRAPHY/SHUTTERSTOCK

Kua Bay, North Kona Coast

junction before the parking lot, turn right. Park on the shoulder, then walk north for 30 minutes across the lava and sand dunes. This string of idyllic coves absorbs crowds so well you'll still feel like you've found paradise. The northernmost cove is sandier and gentler, while the southernmost cove is (unofficially) a nude sunbathing spot. Swimming, snorkeling and bodyboarding are popular, but beware of rough surf and rocks in the water.

Enjoy a day at Kua Bay

If you're ready to brave the crowds, continue just a bit further north to **Kua Bay** (also known as Manini'ōwali Beach). The sublime crescent-shaped white-sand beach is fronted by sparkling waters in alternating bands of pale cyan, deeper turquoise and rich blue. Expect first-rate swimming and excellent bodyboarding, along with good snorkeling by the rock outcroppings on the bay's north side. There's also a lifeguard station where beachgoers can inquire about conditions, which can get choppy. A paved road leads right up to the parking area, which has bathrooms and showers. If you arrive late in the day, parking is tough.

Family-friendly shores

Those with children in tow should set their sights on **Kikaua Point Park**. Access to the protected white-sand, palm-fringed cove is via a private country club. There are just 28 parking spots (plus two spots for people with disabilities); you're best off arriving before 8:30am or sometime around 1:30pm, after the initial wave of visitors leaves for lunch. Facilities include restrooms, outdoor showers and drinking water. If you like the vibe at Kikaua, you'll love the scalloped, palm-fringed coves of **Kukio Beach**, which is part of the **Four Seasons Resort Hualālai**. The sand is soft, the swimming is good and there's a paved trail leading north along the rocky coastline to another beach. Enter through the Four Seasons security guardhouse and request a parking pass (the lot rarely fills up). Facilities include restrooms, outdoor showers and drinking water.

Beachcombing at Kīholo State Park

A bit further up the coast is the relatively unvisited **Kīholo State Park Reserve**. With its pristine turquoise waters and shoreline fringed with coconut trees, this is a series of beaches rather one continuous stretch. The main beach (near the parking lot) is pebbly and swimming is fine when seas are calm, while other parts of the bay are popular sunning areas for sea turtles. A walk north at low tide takes you past the Queen's Bath, a lava tube filled with clear freshwater. Continuing north, you'll pass a gargantuan private estate with a yellow mansion and tennis courts (keep a respectful distance). Eventually, you'll cross a bridge and come to Wainanali'i Pond, a sea turtle haven. Remember to stay 10ft away.

Ka'ūpūlehu

TIME FROM KAILUA-KONA: **20MIN**

Relax and dine at Kona Village Resort

Once a thriving fishing village on the North Kona Coast, Ka'ūpūlehu was wiped out by the 1946 tsunami and abandoned until the Kona Village Resort opened here in 1965. The celebrity haven and favorite vacation spot of Steve Jobs closed in 2011 after more tsunami damage, but reopened with a fabulous facelift in 2023 as **Kona Village** *(rosewoodhotels.com/en/kona-village)*, a Rosewood Resort. Spread over 81 acres, the sustainably run resort makes a fabled base on the island, but nonguests can book a spa treatment at **Asaya** or reserve a table at **Moana**, which has a sterling reputation for its Pacific Rim cuisine (don't skip the tableside pineapple upside down cake). For something more casual, try the **Kahuwai Cookhouse & Market**, an airy spot for ceviche, fish tacos and wood-grilled short ribs. For sunset drinks, head to the beachside **Shipwreck Bar**, where you can sip a prize-winning mai tai while munching on sushi around a former schooner-turned-outdoor bar.

Dine at the Four Seasons

Apart from its luxurious accommodation, the **Four Seasons Resort Hualālai** *(fourseasons.com/hualalai)* has several outstanding dining spots for a special occasion. At **'Ulu** you can book an alfresco table overlooking the lapping waves, while enjoying imaginatively prepared pan-Asian cuisine – with 75% of ingredients sourced from the island. **Noio** is another seaside standout for sushi and high-end Japanese cooking. For something different, you can tuck into grilled steaks and black truffle risotto at **Miller & Lux Hualalai**, or explore coastal Italian-inspired recipes at the **Beach Tree**.

DON'T SWIM WITH DOLPHINS

It's not a good idea to seek out dolphins – known locally as *nai'a* – in the wild. In fact, as of 2021, it's actually illegal to swim within 50yds of them. Dolphins, including the local spinner dolphin (the most commonly encountered species on Hawai'i Island) are social creatures with complex behavioral patterns and schedules. Part of that schedule is rest, which generally takes place from 10am to 2pm in shallow sandy-bottom coves and protected bays. Swimming with dolphins during this time disrupts their crucial rest phase. Young spinner dolphins are curious creatures, and they will often swim to interact with nearby humans. Their investigation in turn awakens their parents, thus robbing entire pods of much-needed rest. Read more about the protection of Hawai'i's dolphins on p244.

ERIC BRODER VAN DYKE/SHUTTERSTOCK

'Aimakapā fishpond

TOP EXPERIENCE

Kaloko-Honokōhau National Historical Park

This 1160-acre national park may be the Kona Coast's most underappreciated ancient Hawaiian site. Hidden among lava fields lies evidence of the innovations that allowed Hawaiians to thrive in this hostile landscape: fishtraps, lava planters used to grow taro and other staples, plus the *ahupua'a* (land division) between Kaloko and Honokōhau that gives the park its name. There are also heiau (temples), burial caves and petroglyphs.

DON'T MISS

- Honokōhau Beach
- 'Ai'ōpio Fishtrap
- Pu'uoina Heiau
- Ala Kahakai National Historic Trail
- Kaloko Fishpond
- 'Aimakapā Fishpond

Visitor Center

The park's main entrance is off Hwy 19 between Miles 96 and 97, where there's a parking lot and a small but informative ranger-staffed visitor center. This is a great place to get your bearings and some advice about how to spend your time in the park, which was established in 1978 to celebrate and preserve the ancient Hawaiians' way of life.

PRACTICALITIES

● nps.gov/kaho ● free ● 8:30am-4pm daily

There's a short interpretative trail with signage about why they settled among these seemingly inhospitable lava fields and managed to achieve a balance with their natural surroundings. The trail extends to the Ala Mauka Makai Trail, which passes some petroglyphs on its way to Honokōhau Beach (about 0.75 miles one way).

Honokōhau Beach

This postcard-pretty, hook-shaped **beach** is a mix of black lava, white coral and wave-tossed shells, and just standing on the shore you'll often see *honu* (green sea turtles). Look for them munching on *limu* (seaweed) around the ancient **'Ai'ōpio Fishtrap** at the beach's southern end, where early inhabitants raised the lava wall and placed nets across the openings to catch fish. Beside it you'll find **Pu'uoina Heiau**, an ancient temple signifying the importance of the fishtrap and nearby fishponds. Strict rules were in place to ensure that fish were only harvested from the pools in times of abundance, which kept the fishery from depleting. Inland, you'll also notice anchialine ponds - pools of brackish water that make unique habitats for marine and plant life.

'Aimakapā Fishpond

If you walk up Honokōhau Beach along the Ala Kahakai National Historic Trail for a few minutes, you'll soon reach 'Aimakapā - the largest fishpond on the Kona Coast. Ancient Hawaiians constructed it behind the dunes to hold fish they planned on eating, and they also dug channels from the pond to the ocean, allowing water to flow in and out with the tides. Rare native waterbirds such as *ae'o* (Hawaiian black-necked stilt) and *'alae kea* (Hawaiian coot) use the aquatic plants lining the fishpond for nests, and nearby, you'll find the ancient remains of a *hōlua* (lava-sledding course). Other birds to seek out are black-crowned night herons, often seen carefully watching for fish by the water's edge, and great frigatebirds, easily recognizable by their forked tails and and pterodactyl-like shape when soaring overhead.

Kaloko Fishpond

Continue another 1.5 miles north along the Ala Kahakai National Historic Trail and you'll reach Kaloko Fishpond. It's especially fascinating because its massive rock retaining wall has been rebuilt in the traditional way - dry stacking, with no mortar or shaping of the rocks - so it can once again be fished as it was in ages past. Some speculate that the bones of Kamehameha the Great were secretly buried in a cave nearby.

Alternatively, you can reach this site by driving north from the park's visitor center on Hwy 19 until you reach a separate entrance at Ala Nui Kaloko Rd. Note that the wall is closed to foot traffic, so you'll need to walk about a mile around the fishpond to reach the other side. Sometimes sections of this trail may be closed due to stinging ants.

ALA KAHAKAI NATIONAL HISTORIC TRAIL

The park's 2.5-mile stretch of this historic trail is a small piece of the 175-mile ancient footpath, restored in 2000 to preserve Hawaiian culture. The path linked travel routes up along the coastline, and it extends from Puna on the eastern shoreline down to the island's southernmost point (Ka Lae) and up the west side, terminating at the northern tip ('Upolu Point).

TOP TIPS

- Go in the early morning, late afternoon or when skies are overcast, to avoid the intense midday heat.
- Don't climb on, move, alter or deface any rock structures.
- Don't disturb or come within 10ft of the threatened *honu* (green sea turtles) that haul out here to rest and bask in the sun.
- Avoid stinging ants by staying on trails and refraining from sitting on the ground or touching trees or bushes.
- The water is usually too cloudy for snorkeling, and signage asks that visitors respect the sacred site by refraining from sunbathing, playing games or picnicking.

Hōlualoa

BOHEMIAN VILLAGE | SHOPS & GALLERIES | FESTIVALS

GETTING AROUND

Hōlualoa village lines Hwy 180 (Māmalahoa Hwy), north of the Hualālai Rd intersection. You'll find parking along the side of the road – just be careful pulling off, and make sure you're fully off the roadway. Once here, you can stroll the length of the village within a few minutes. Take care when crossing the road (use the crosswalks) as some drivers blaze through the town. There are no public transportation options in the area.

TOP TIP

On the first Friday of each month (5:30pm to 8:30pm), the galleries and boutiques of Hōlualoa host a block party, with art openings, live music and food vendors. Find other happenings on holualoavillage.com.

The further up the mountain you get from Kailua-Kona, the more artsy, residential and rural it gets (not to mention cooler and damper), until all of these qualities mush into one misty bohemian village: Hōlualoa. Perched at 1400ft on the lush slopes of Hualālai, this tiny settlement has come a long way from its days as a remote, one-donkey coffee crossroads. Today Hōlualoa's ramshackle buildings hold a small but diverse collection of galleries and shops, some of which are owned by renowned artists. During special events and holidays, the little village of Hōlualoa becomes a veritable mountainside art gallery. Regardless of when you visit, there's never a bad time to explore this fascinating corner of Hawai'i.

Although the census-designated area called 'Hōlualoa' extends to the sea and includes much of Ali'i Dr, when locals speak of Hōlualoa they are referring to the upcountry enclave described here, plus the surrounding mountainside and agricultural areas.

Get Caffeinated at an Arts Fest

World-class coffee and crafts

The rich cultural heritage of Hōlualoa is something worth planning an entire trip around experiencing. Consider visiting during one of the big events here, when the streets come alive and the arts are put front and center. In early November, during the **Kona Coffee Cultural Festival** *(konacoffeefest.com)*, you can take part in coffee and tea harvesting, catch live performances and hone your skills during coffee barista training. The main event is the Hōlualoa Coffee and Art Stroll, where you can taste free samples from over two dozen coffee producers and then vote for your favorite. There are also food trucks and loads of makers selling everything from handmade soaps and jewelry to vintage clothing and ceramics. It typically happens on Sunday (9am to 2pm) on the main drag, roughly between Ipu Arts and Antioch Church Hōlualoa.

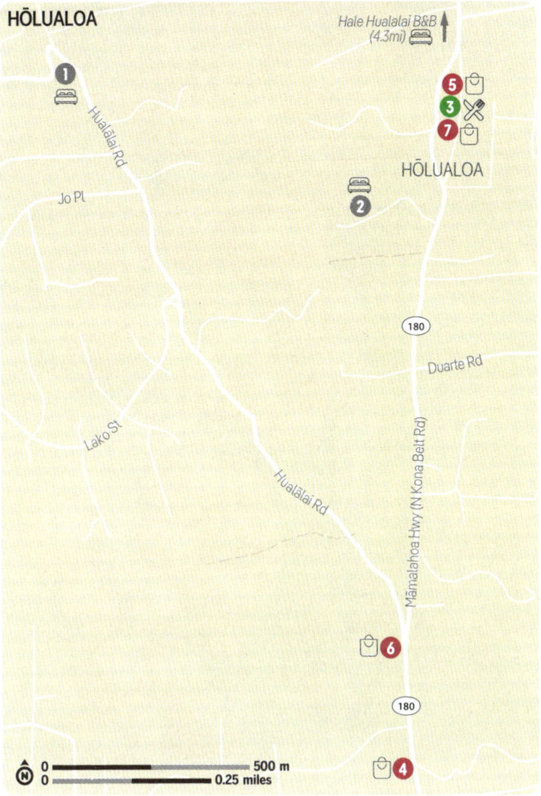

SLEEPING
1 Hale Maluhia Country Inn
2 Holualoa Inn

EATING
3 Hōlualoa Garden & Kitchen
see 3 Uncle Kimo's Coffee Shop

SHOPPING
4 Doris' Place
5 Ipu Arts
6 Kimura Lauhala Shop
7 Petals & Provisions

Dine in a Lush Garden

Meals and Kona coffee

At aptly named **Hōlualoa Garden & Kitchen** *(visitholualoa.com)*, you can dine in a verdant setting of ferns, palms and tropical blooms. The wide-ranging menu includes breakfast, bistro fare and Hawaiian classics. Hours vary, but it's closed Monday and Tuesday. Reserve ahead.

If you're just after a coffee, you can stop in the adjoining **Uncle Kimo's Coffee Shop** in front (open 7am to 11am Wednesday to Sunday). Here you can sip fine coffees made from 100% Kona beans grown exclusively on a family-run 157-acre estate.

TRACING HŌLUALOA'S HISTORY

Named after the ancient Hawaiian sport of sledding down steep slopes, Hōlualoa (from *hōlua* for wooden sleds and *loa* for long) was the heart of a rich agricultural region that stretched from the mountains to the sea. The arrival of Europeans brought dramatic changes to the land and the island's ethnic mix. Coffee was first introduced in the region in the 19th century, and by the early 20th century, Japanese families played a key role as independent coffees farmers and store owners. Hōlualoa entered a new phase in 1967 when Bob and Carol Rogers founded the Kona Arts Center. In the decades that followed, more artists were drawn to the area, opening galleries and helping to cement the town's reputation as an epicenter of creativity.

PRAWEENA STYLE/SHUTTERSTOCK

Join the Holiday Celebration

Tree lighting, art and music

If you're around in early December, don't miss the **Music & Light Festival** *(holualoavillage.com/festival)*. Typically held on the first Saturday (5:30pm to 8:30pm), the Christmas celebration features a tree-lighting ceremony, as well as live music, an appearance by Santa and special events held in Hōlualoa's galleries and shops.

Shop for Local Treats

Gourmet items and crafts

Inside a retrofitted 1920s-era service station, **Petals & Provisions** *(petalsprovisions.com)* is well known for its lovely floral arrangements. But there's much more on offer inside this small but well-stocked shop selling mostly island-made products. You'll find local spices, honey, chocolates, macadamia spread, salami and gourmet spreads, as well as clothing and housewares. On Tuesdays and Thursdays, you'll also find fresh bread here.

Coffee cherries

Browse Lauhala Crafts

Hats, baskets and crafts

Four generations of Kimuras have sold *lauhala* (*hala* plant) products in **Kimura Lauhala Shop**, making it as much a landmark as a business. The *lauhala* hats, placemats, baskets and tote bags showcase the fine craftsmanship and quality materials. You'll also find handmade jewelry, aloha shirts and more.

Sample Crack Seed at Doris' Place

A one-of-a-kind local favorite

Opened in 1948, **Doris' Place** is a small convenience store on the highway that's a much-loved local institution for its cold drinks and kind staff. Stop in for sodas, beer, chips, candy, popsicles and most importantly 'crack seed.' These are dried fruits sold by weight and displayed in several dozen big glass jars near the freezer. They come in varieties like sour apple, spicy pineapple chili, cherry plum and lemon blossom hibiscus.

WALKING TOUR

A Stroll Through Hōlualoa

Saunter down Māmalahoa Hwy through the quaint enclave of Hōlualoa, checking out the art, picking up souvenirs and grabbing tasty roadside coffee and snacks. The galleries feature unique works and make for excellent shopping, and oftentimes the artists themselves are present to answer questions and 'talk story.' A Japanese cemetery offers further insight into the local culture. Just be mindful of the traffic, and take extra care when crossing the road.

1 Ipu Arts

Begin at this magnificent shop full of *ipu* (gourds) decoratively carved with Hawaiian imagery and dyed using an ancient method unique to Ni'ihau island. The art form had been lost for over a century until a scholar rediscovered it in 1980, and today the shop owner and a small community of gourd carvers continue to create new works.

The Walk: Head south along Māmalahoa Hwy, passing a restaurant with outdoor tables (Hōlualoa Garden & Kitchen, p69), then look for the coffee truck on your left.

2 White Nene Coffee Roasters

The sleek white coffee trailer of White Nene parked on the east side of the road roasts up some of the best coffee for miles around. The small locally owned operation has perfectly brewed espresso, lattes and matcha, and there's shaded outdoor seating on the adjoining patio.

The Walk: Cross the street and walk south to the low-slung green building on your right.

3 Studio 7

The oldest contemporary fine-art gallery in Hawai'i is housed in a serene, museum-like space. On prominent display are the

REGIS ST LOUIS

Hōlualoa Japanese Cemetery

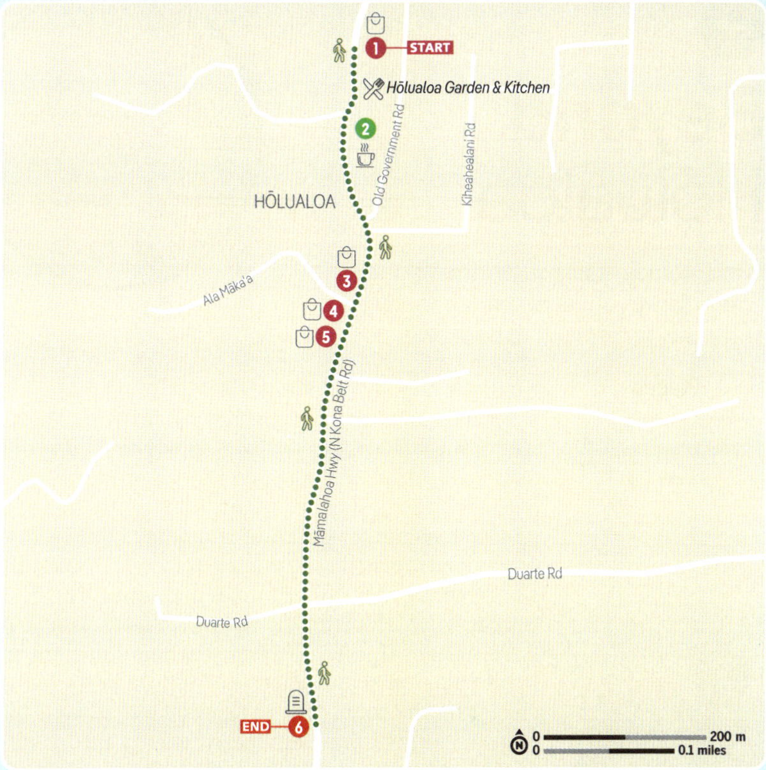

works of artist-owner Hiroki Morinoue, who is exceptional with watercolor, oil, woodblock and sculpture; and the pottery of his accomplished wife, Setsuko. Pieces draw on Japanese influences and history but are also excellent executions of contemporary art.

The Walk: It's a short hop to your next stop, which will be on the same side of the street (right).

4 Kona Treehouse

The imaginatively dubbed botanical boutique Kona Treehouse is a Kona-born indie shop that sells tiny terrariums, miniature air plants, moss bowls, water plant starter kits and beautifully illustrated books on foraging.

The Walk: Head just a few paces down the road to your next stop. It's just past the white picket fence.

5 Kona Art Collective

An excellent one-stop shop for unique gift ideas, the Kona Art Collective features the work of some 20 different Big Island artists. Ceramics, wood carvings, delicate feather work, watercolor paintings, landscape photography and handmade jewelry are among the rotating works on display. Don't miss the view over the water from the lānai in back.

The Walk: Take care when walking this stretch as the road is narrow. It's about a seven-minute walk to your final stop, which will be on the right side.

6 Hōlualoa Japanese Cemetery

The upland coffee country of the Kona coast has historically been settled and worked by Japanese immigrants and their descendants, and this cemetery, clinging to the mountain slopes and full of coral and lava-rock headstones inscribed with kanji, speaks to that heritage. The cemetery is actively visited by locals so be respectful.

Beyond Hōlualoa

Winding mountain roads lead to quaint coffee farms, unusual outdoor activities and misty forests full of birdsong.

Places

North Hōlualoa p74
South Hōlualoa p75
Kaloko p75

GETTING AROUND

Having your own wheels is ideal in this region, particularly since the Hele-On Bus doesn't run to this upland area. Uber and Lyft is an option, but you may have a long wait to find a driver, and prices can be high.

Up in the hills surrounding Hōlualoa you'll find some of Hawai'i Island's most enchanting environs: this is where high elevation, frequent cloud coverage and fertile volcanic soil come together to produce some of the island's best coffee beans. Kona coffee has had gourmet cachet for decades, and today many coffee farms have opened roadside visitor centers and gift shops, where they offer samples and tours. The best time to visit is during the harvest season, running from August through February, when 'Kona snow' (white blossoms) and 'cherries' (mature berry fruit) cluster on the coffee trees. Once you've had your fill of java, channel that caffeinated energy into a wilderness adventure: hiking through the cloud forest or taking a culturally themed ATV tour.

North Hōlualoa

TIME FROM HŌLUALOA: **10MIN**

Visiting Japan's top coffee estate

A little under 2 miles north of Hōlualoa on Māmalahoa Hwy, the 35-acre farm of **UCC Hawaii** *(ucc-hawaii.com)* belongs to one of Japan's premier coffee producers – UCC stands for Ueshima Coffee Company, which was founded in Kobe in 1935. The ocean-view farm is divine and you can take your self-guided tour during normal opening hours (9am to 4:30pm Monday to Friday). You'll get more insight into the estate by taking one of three daily guided tours ($20 per person), available Monday through Friday. For something different, take a Roastmaster Tour (also offered three times daily on weekdays). Under the guidance of a pro, you'll roast your own coffee, creating your own signature coffee under a label that you create ($50 per person, which includes two quarter-pound bags of beans).

Small-Farm coffee tour

If you'd like a side of jaw-dropping ocean views with your award-winning coffee, we suggest **Hula Daddy Kona Coffee** *(huladaddy.com)*, less than 5 miles north of Hōlualoa. Its epicurean tasting room and eco-conscious 33-acre farm is also a great place to learn about cupping and the unusual coffee-production techniques used to create the signature Kona Oli and Kona Sweet beans. The $35 tour lasts about an hour and takes place three times daily (Monday through Friday) at 9:45am, 11:15am and 12:30pm. Reserve in advance.

South Hōlualoa

TIME FROM HŌLUALOA: **10MIN**

Tap into Hawai'i's creative side

For a deeper dive into the Big Island's art community, look no further than the **Donkey Mill Art Center** *(donkeymill artcenter.org)*. The Hōlualoa Foundation for Arts & Culture created this nonprofit in 1994, and eight years later secured its community center, a 1953 coffee mill with a donkey painted on its roof. Inside there are free exhibits and a plethora of locally made art, plus lectures and workshops taught by recognized national and international artists – all open to visitors. Whether it's ceramics, printmaking, metal or fiber that interests you, there are likely to be artists you can learn from and collaborate with here; the center also puts on lots of family-friendly arts education programs. Recent workshops included paper- and kite-making, block printing and botanical painting. The center opens Wednesday to Saturday from 10am to 7pm. Go online for class schedules, prices (some activities are free) and booking information.

Ride an ATV or try woodcarving

At **Aloha Adventure Farms** *(alohaadventurefarms.com)* you can head off on a guided two-hour ATV excursion (adult/child $199/169) with a cultural component touching on Fiji, Tonga, Samoa and of course Hawai'i. At stops along the way, you'll be able to try your hand at spear throwing, drumming and coconut cracking – and will also get to taste *poi* – while learning about different aspects of Polynesian heritage. For something more arts-focused, you can carve your own tiki while learning alongside a fourth-generation master carver. There's also a fruit-tasting tour, where you might sample mangosteen, jabuticaba, cherimoya and many other exotic delicacies depending on what's in season.

Kaloko

TIME FROM HŌLUALOA: **20MIN**

Book a guided cloud forest experience

A steep, winding drive up the lower slopes of Hualālai volcano takes you to the spectacular **Kona Cloud Forest Sanctuary** *(konacloudforest.com)*. A cloud forest is a moist woodland where mist and fog are constants. Founded in 1982 by a local horticulture professor and carried on by his descendants, the sanctuary holds 70 acres of restored ranch lands, which now

EXPLORING THE KONA COFFEE BELT

Home to some of the world's best coffee, the **Kona Coffee Belt** extends for some 35 miles from north of Hōlualoa to south of Captain Cook. A trip to Hawai'i Island is simply incomplete without sampling its premier product. Exploring a coffee farm or two is also a great way to learn about the island's agricultural heritage and history. Just be sure to make reservations for tours and other activities – you won't want to have braved these steep, narrow roads for nothing. For an overview of Kona Coffee, start off with a free tour at **Greenwell Farms** (p80), and don't miss a visit to the **Kona Coffee Living History Farm** (p82) to learn more about the region's deep cultural roots.

KONA'S FAMOUS COFFEE

Karen Paterson, co-owner of Hula Daddy Kona Coffee (p75), gives insight into Kona's most famous crop. *@huladaddycoffee*

The best way to learn about Kona coffee is by taking a tour. You'll learn that coffee is a plant that requires shade, and the conditions here are simply among the best in the world. You typically get morning sun and afternoon shade, so we don't have to put up canopies as you do in many other places. You'll see how it's grown on trees, and in season you'll get to taste the somewhat bitter red cherry-sized fruit, which of course tastes nothing like coffee. You'll also go into the roasting room, and can buy the coffee right out of the roaster – which is as fresh as it's going to get.

REGIS ST LOUIS

Makāula O'oma Trails

serve as a haven for native plants and birds. It also contains demonstration gardens of non-native species, including more than 100 varieties of bamboo. Visits are guided, with 1½-hour tours along the pantropical trail (adult/child $80/40) and 2½-hour tours on the montane jungle trail (adult/child $120/60). Other activities include a one-hour soundbath meditation journey ($40) and various mindfulness forest walks. On Wednesday and Thursday, plan your day around a one-hour slow-flow yoga in the clouds class ($25). Be sure to reserve all activities ahead.

Take a hike in the forest

Less formal but nonetheless rewarding wanderings include a hike along the **Makāula O'oma Trails** *(free)*. Located within a lush forest reserve, several different trails, totaling 4.5 miles, take you through a verdant landscape dotted with *'ōhi'a* (the iconic blossoming evergreen) and *hāpu'u* (tree fern). Find the trailhead at the end of Makahi St, off Kaloko Dr, and park on the side of the road. The most popular route takes you along the Jurassic Trail, an appropriate moniker considering the prehistoric-looking foliage. Signboards show the different trails and distances to the next trail intersection. Make a 3.8-mile circuit by turning right on the Upper Jurassic Trail, which eventually takes you onto the Crosstown Trail, the Pig Skull Trail and the Pipeline Trail before completing your loop by ascending the Lower Jurassic Trail. You'll ascend about 800ft throughout the hike; allow around two to 2½ hours to complete it. There aren't many views here – hiking here is all about immersing yourself in the sights and sounds of the forest.

Kealakekua & South Kona

NATIVE HAWAIIAN HISTORY | AQUATIC ADVENTURES | COFFEE FARM TOURS

Less than a half-hour drive from Kailua-Kona, a swath of South Kona encompasses sleepy settlements, hillside coffee farms and spectacular shoreline. Kealakekua Bay is the region's standout attraction, which you can reach by kayak excursion, motorboat tour or on your own two feet, by hiking down a steep path to reach the marine-rich waters of this pristine coastline. Kealakekua, which means 'pathway of the gods,' is more than just a marine reserve. Until the late 18th century, the area was home to a thriving population center that contained residences for Hawaiian royalty, the priestly class and commoners, along with burial grounds for rulers and their families. This area is still very much a sacred site, providing a link to ancient Hawaiian culture, and it's home to one of Hawai'i's most important historical parks. Small towns like Captain Cook and Kainaliu offer fascinating gateways to the area, amid gardens, century-old restaurants and iconic landmarks – including a brilliantly painted church and a revitalized community theater.

GETTING AROUND

The Hele-On Bus runs several lines from Kailua-Kona down to Kealakekua and South Kona. Though you can reach towns like Captain Cook and Kainaliu by bus, it's not practical for reaching Pu'uhonua o Hōnaunau National Historical Park or the Ka'awaloa Trail to Kealakekua Bay. If you're driving, take care when traveling these narrow, winding roads. In the towns, parking is generally at designated (free) spots along the roadway.

TOP TIP

Plan your visit to the area carefully. Mornings are best to go snorkeling or make a boat trip to Kealakekua Bay. Some shops and restaurants in the area close one or two days a week.

Dine at a South Kona Landmark

Hawai'i's oldest restaurant

One of Kona's best-loved eateries is the **Manago Hotel** *(managohotel.com)*, a 1917 institution that began as a restaurant catering to salespeople on the then-lengthy journey between Hilo and Kona. Today the fourth-generation owners maintain the historic structure and surrounding koi pond and garden, not to mention the unchanged bingo-parlor dining room, where you'll feel as though you're stepping into another era. The menu focuses on well-executed, no-frills comfort food, including butterfish, New York steak and a much-lauded pork chop that helped the restaurant earn a James Beard award in 2023. The restaurant opens Wednesday to Saturday for lunch (11am to 2pm) and dinner (5pm to 7:30pm).

Note that despite the name, the Manago Hotel no longer offers accommodation.

HIGHLIGHTS
1 Kona Coffee Living History Farm
2 Pu'uhonua o Hōnaunau National Historical Park
3 St Benedict's Painted Church

SIGHTS
4 Amy Greenwell Ethnobotanical Garden
5 Big Island Bees
6 Captain Cook Monument
7 Great Wall
8 Greenwell Farms
9 Hale o Keawe Heiau
10 Ke'ei Beach
11 Keone'ele Cove
12 Manini Beach
13 Paleaku Gardens Peace Sanctuary

ACTIVITIES
14 1871 Trail
15 Ka'awaloa Trail
16 Kona Boys
17 Mamalahoa Hot Tubs & Massage
18 Two-Step

EATING
19 Banana Bread Spot
20 Black Rock Pizza
21 Coffee Shack
22 Ka'aloa's Super J's
23 Manago Hotel
24 Mi Lindo Michoacán
25 Randy's Huli Chicken & Ribs
26 Rebel Kitchen
27 Reel Aloha
28 South Kona Fruit Stand
29 Teshima's Restaurant
30 Theatery

ENTERTAINMENT
31 Aloha Theatre

SHOPPING
32 Déjà Vu
33 Hale Cocoa
34 Kainaliu Fresh
35 Mauna Music
36 Pure Kona Green Market

Seek out Japanese Comfort Fare

Home cooking and vintage atmosphere

For a window into local life, grab a table at **Teshima's** *(teshima restaurant.com)*, a family-run restaurant dishing up Japanese comfort food since the 1950s. The vintage setting and country-style Japanese home cooking come together into a lovely whole, and the multi-dish specials are great value. Open 7am to 2pm and 5pm to 9pm.

Step into the Famous Painted Church

An ecclesiastical masterpiece

A pulpit with a view, gravestones cradled by tropical blooms and a little chapel with floor-to-ceiling 'outsider art' make **St Benedict's Painted Church** *(thepaintedchurchhawaii.org)* a picturesque side trip. John Velghe, a Catholic priest and self-taught artist, came to Hawai'i from Belgium in 1899 and modeled the vaulted nave on a Gothic cathedral in Burgos, Spain. His trompe l'oeil artwork merges European structure with Polynesian scenery, such as Jesus casting out the devil in front of what looks like the Pololū Valley. Admission is free, though donations are gratefully accepted and help to ensure the survival of this fascinating, living piece of culture. The church opens 7am to 5pm.

Wander a Peaceful Garden

Blooms and yoga classes

Not far from the Painted Church, **Paleaku Gardens Peace Sanctuary** *(paleaku.com; adult/child $10/3)* is a tranquil 7-acre oasis with shrines to the world's major religions. You'll also find an impressive 'Galaxy Garden,' a scale model of the Milky Way created in plants. Yoga classes are held regularly ($20). It's open 9am to 4pm Tuesday to Saturday.

Enter the World of Bees

Honey tasting and beekeeping tours

Follow winding Napo'opo'o Rd off Hwy 11 to reach **Big Island Bees** *(bigislandbees.com)*, a charming little beekeeping operation where you can learn all about the world of Hawaiian honey production. The shop doubles as a small museum, where you can learn a bit about the history of honey making

BEST BEACHES NEAR KEALAKEKUA

Ho'okena Beach Park This modest, charcoal-colored beach is backed by a steep green hillside. When calm, the bay's waters are good for swimming, kayaking and snorkeling.

Ke'ei Beach Just south of Kealakekua Bay, Ke'ei Beach is an attractive cove that's mostly too rough and rocky for swimming, but draws surfers to a long reef break.

Manini Beach On Kealakekua Bay's south side, this rocky, exposed beach is usually too rough for swimming, but makes a great spot for a scenic, shady picnic.

Pebble Beach Not quite pebbles, the smoky stones of this non-sandy beach at the bottom of the Kona Paradise subdivision range from gumdrop- to palm-size. It's a popular kayak put-in and offers a good dose of peace and quiet.

EATING IN KEALAKEKUA: ROADSIDE FAVORITES

Randy's Huli Chicken & Ribs: Though open just twice a week, Randy's has a loyal following for juicy grilled *huli-huli* chicken, ribs and brisket. *9am-4pm Thu & Fri* $

South Kona Fruit Stand: Exotic fruits, tropical smoothies, Kona coffee and piping hot paninis. The upper-level patio has fine views. *10am-4pm Wed-Mon* $

Banana Bread Spot: En route to the Painted Church, stop off at this self-serve roadside stand for a loaf of banana bread with macadamia nuts. *8am-7pm* $

Ka'aloa's Super J's: Delicious home cooking, especially *laulau* (pork or chicken wrapped in taro leaves) served with *lomi* salmon. *10am-3pm Mon & Wed-Sat* $

THE END OF CAPTAIN COOK

On January 17, 1779, Captain Cook sailed into Kealakekua Bay. His visit coincided with the makahiki festival, a period when warfare was suspended. Cook's welcome was spectacular: more than 1000 canoes surrounded his ships and 9000 people hailed him. A few weeks later, Cook departed, but he soon encountered a storm and returned to the bay. Insults and suspicion replaced politeness, and after the English took the Hawaiian chief hostage and killed a couple of Hawaiians, a melee broke out. Cook was clubbed to death and dismembered in the custom reserved for high chiefs. Surviving Brits torched homes and slaughtered Hawaiians – women and children included. Eventually the Hawaiians returned Cook's skull, hands and feet – which the English buried at sea. The Hawaiians kept his femurs.

and peek at a demonstration hive. You can also taste a free sample of its award-winning, single-varietal and certified-organic honey – the rare lehua honey and dark rich macadamia nut blossom honey are outstanding. For more insight, book a one-hour beekeeping tour (adult/youth/child $30/20/10). You'll get to see how the hive is organized and what makes bees so extraordinary. Big Island Bees opens weekdays only (10am to 3pm). Reserve tours in advance.

Relax in a Hot Tub

Rejuvenating soaks and massages

At **Mamalahoa Hot Tubs & Massage** *(mamalahoa-hottubs.com)* you can soak away your aches and pains or simply enjoy the warm, watery serenity in a lush garden mini-oasis. The teak tubs, sheltered by thatched roofs that allow for stargazing, are open-sided yet private, and there's a hot waterfall shower adjoining each tub. Prices are cheaper by day (one/two person $50/60), but evenings are magical (one/two person $60/80). Many types of massage, from Swedish to traditional Hawaiian *lomilomi* and hot stone, are available (one-hour massage from $175). Reservations are required. Open noon to 8:30pm Wednesday to Saturday.

Take a Free Coffee Farm Tour

An iconic 1850 estate

One of the best coffee tours on the island is offered by **Greenwell Farms** *(greenwellfarms.com),* a 150-acre family farm established in 1850 and run by fourth-generation Greenwells. One of Kona's oldest and best-known coffee plantations, it roasts coffee cherries from more than 200 local growers. On the free guided tour you'll learn how coffee goes from seed to cup; samples are on offer before and after. Tours run for around an hour and are available every half-hour from 9am to 3pm daily; no reservations are required. For a more in-depth experience, the 2½-hour deluxe tour and tasting visits the cupping room, roasting room, farm, wet mill, nursery and dry mill. It happens at 9:30am and 1:30pm on weekdays and costs $60 per person; reserve these ahead.

EATING IN KEALAKEKUA: OUR PICKS

Coffee Shack: Bay views from an open-sided deck; munch on eggs Benedict, pulled pork sandwiches and passion-fruit cheesecake. *7am-3:30pm Thu-Tue* **$$**

Mi Lindo Michoacán: This taco stand doles out satisfying enchiladas, burrito bowls and of course tacos, plus Mexican drinks like horchata. *hours vary* **$**

Black Rock Pizza: Creatively topped pizzas (including good vegetarian options), craft cocktails and Kona brews, best enjoyed on the patio. *11am-8pm* **$$**

Reel Aloha: In a roadside complex, Reel Aloha whips up delicious *poke* bowls prepared half a dozen ways (try the California with avocado and crab). *10:30am-6pm* **$**

RITU MANOJ JETHANI/SHUTTERSTOCK

Greenwell Farms

Stroll a Botanical Garden

Endemic plants and a Sunday market

Though small in size, the 15-acre community-run **Amy Greenwell Ethnobotanical Garden** *(amygreenwell.garden)* makes a verdant backdrop to exploring 200 different species of native and Polynesian-introduced plants that predate the arrival of Captain Cook. You can check out *kalo* (taro), one of the world's oldest cultivated crops, *'ulu* (breadfruit), *hala* (whose leaves were used in weaving) and many other plants essential for survival. Knowledgeable staff and volunteers are happy to answer questions and help you find rare species. Admission is free, but donations are kindly requested. The garden opens 9am to 4pm Tuesday to Saturday, to 2pm Sunday.

If you're around on Sunday (9am to 2pm), don't miss the **Pure Kona Green Market**, a veritable town hall and gossip center for all of South Kona. Pick up some fresh fruits, bakery items and cooked dishes (including island-inspired Korean dishes). You'll also find vendors selling locally made crafts and goods – soaps, jewelry, printed fabrics.

Plan an Aquatic Adventure

Kayaking, snorkeling and SUPs

South Kona's largest pro water-sports outfitter, laid-back **Kona Boys** *(konaboys.com)* is a fixture of the local tourism scene. Kayaking, snorkeling and outrigger-canoe sailing trips visit Kealakekua Bay (p86), and you can purchase essential gear and learn the basics of surfing and SUP from these bruhs. Snorkel gear, SUP, surfboard and kayak rentals available. Call ahead for tour and gear-rental reservations.

A STUNNING BAY

Frank Carpenter,
co-CEO at Kona Boys
@konaboys

The area in front of Captain Cook monument is the most protected deep-water bay in the Hawaiian Islands. In pre-contact times, there were more Hawaiians living in this area than anywhere else, and today it remains an important and active cultural site. The waters are fantastic for snorkeling, with an abundance of fish and marine life, and it faces into the rising sun – so perfect morning conditions. The bay starts off at about 2ft, slopes down to about 25ft, then there's an underwater cliff where it plunges to a depth of 250ft. Amazingly, there's coral growth at up to 100ft. This is literally in the top 2% of the planet when it comes to visibility in the ocean.

FRANK SCHULENBURG/WIKIMEDIA/CC BY-SA 3.0

Historic coffee mill near the Uchida Farmhouse

TOP EXPERIENCE

Kona Coffee Living History Farm

In the first few decades of the 20th century, native Japanese made up more than 80% of the coffee farming families in Kona. This beautifully preserved homestead and working 5.5-acre farm provides a fascinating glimpse into the past. You can wander through buildings, chat with historical interpreters and see how the labor-intensive work was done by all members of the family a century ago.

DON'T MISS

- Kitchen demonstration
- Coffee processing
- Bathhouse
- Tenant farmer's house ruins
- Donkeys

Enter the Uchida Farmhouse

Take off your shoes and step into another century. This pristine farmhouse was home to three generations of the Uchida family between 1910 and 1994. Start off in the the kitchen (go right). There you'll see a historical interpreter taking you through a day in the life of a housewife in the 1920s. She'll show you what meals were prepared (rice and seaweed for the kids packed in a bento box for school), demonstrate hand roasting and grinding of coffee beans the family set aside for

PRACTICALITIES

● konahistorical.org ● adult/child $20/10 ● 10am-2pm Tue & Fri

its own use, and give lots of insight into day-to-day challenges without modern conveniences – no refrigeration, no indoor toilets, and transport by foot or donkey only (until jeeps were available after the war). Be sure to walk through the rest of the house. You can see photos of the family, and see the home-made futons (sleeping mats), which were made of repurposed rice bags and worn-out kimono.

See the Water Source

Just behind the house is a catchment tank for rainwater. In the days before a well was dug, most Kona farm families relied on rain as their only water source. Gutters along the house fed into the tank, which was then fed into the kitchen (a small tobacco sack was placed over the spout as a filter). The catchment was also used for the *furo,* a traditional wooden Japanese-style bathtub set on a concrete base. The water was heated underneath by using pruned coffee branches as kindling. You'll see the big pile nearby. Typically, every household member would use the same bathwater (they would wash first before entering the water), and it was often up to one of the kids to come home early from school and fire up the bath, which was an evening ritual. Afterwards, the leftover bathwater was used for washing clothes, which was a daily chore.

Learn About Coffee Processing

A few steps from the farmhouse, you'll find the buildings used for processing coffee. A farmer is on hand to take you through the steps essential to producing coffee beans: picking the fresh ripe coffee cherry, using machinery to separate the skin from the seed, soaking the seed to remove the thin coating known as parchment, then drying the seeds on an open platform. The *hoshidan,* developed by Japanese farmers here in Kona, is a rolling roof that could be moved into place if rain threatened.

Enjoy the Gardens & Farm Critters

Afterwards, wander the gardens and see the wide variety of fruit grown here, plus macadamia trees in addition to coffee. You'll likely see (or hear) roosters strutting about and there are also a few donkeys. In the evening, donkeys would bray to each other and fill the air with their plaintive sound. And locals gave these donkeys the whimsical nickname of 'Kona nightingale.'

Study Stone Fragments from the Past

Wander uphill past fruit trees on either side of you, and follow the signs to the tenant farmer's house ruins. These belonged the Shirai family, who helped out the Uchidas in the 1930s. During WWII the now empty abode was transformed into a bomb shelter.

COFFEE TO THE RESCUE

During WWII American authorities rounded up people of Japanese heritage and relocated them to internment camps. The Japanese farmers in Kona, however, were spared since they were considered vital contributors to the local economy. In fact, the US military became the main buyer of Kona coffee and bought nearly everything the Japanese farmers produced to supply American troops.

TOP TIPS

- Plan carefully. The farm opens only twice a week. You don't need a reservation to visit. The last admission is at 1:15pm.
- Parking is limited. Go around opening time to score one of the few spots. There isn't any parking on the narrow, busy road, so you'll have to come back if there's no spot available.
- Don't miss the photos near the admission desk before you leave. You can see images of the Uchida family – both formal portraits as well as at work on the farm. There are also photos of a Japanese funeral procession, landscape views from the 1940s, and a protest against donkey replacement.

JOHN S. LANDER/LIGHTROCKET VIA GETTY IMAGES

Aloha Theatre

TOP EXPERIENCE

Exploring Kainaliu

Home to one-of-a-kind shops and a bohemian air, Kainaliu is a tightly knit upcountry settlement with a mix of old and new. Park for free right along Māmalahoa Hwy, then head off on foot to explore. Among the finds: vintage stores, a chocolate shop (and cacao farm tours), restaurants for both casual and high-end fare, and an iconic theater.

DON'T MISS

- Vintage apparel from Déjà Vu
- Rebel Kitchen sandwiches
- Tropical fruits from Kainaliu Fresh
- Hale Cocoa chocolate
- *'Ukeleles* from Mauna Music
- A show at Aloha Theater
- Happy hour at the Theatery

Browse a vintage emporium

One of several vintage shops in Kainaliu, **Déjà Vu** hides untold treasures, though you'll have to dig. This is the place to find colorful aloha shirts and dresses, records, baseball caps, artwork, plastic dinosaurs, Hawaiian-themed mugs and old TWA totes.

Pick up a Ukulele

One of the best places on the island to browse for acoustic and electric *'ukulele*, **Mauna Music** *(maunamusic.com)* stocks high-quality locally made brands like Kamaka and Little River Ukuleles. If you're sticking around a while, ask about music lessons.

Grab a Bite at Rebel Kitchen

There's a palpable sense of indie pride at **Rebel Kitchen** *(rebelkitchen.com)*, a colorful lunch and dinner spot known for its bold flavors and decadent sandwiches. Try the jerk chicken or blackened *ono* (white-fleshed wahoo) sandwich, and don't neglect the pepperoni garlic fries and hearty plates of jambalaya.

Assemble a Locally Grown Picnic

Kainaliu Fresh *(kainaliufresh.com)* is a showcase of small local producers, growers and artisans. The tiny neighborhood market stocks deliciously tempting fruits and vegetables, which might mean dragon fruit, passion fruit, guava, pineapple and mangosteen, depending on what's in season. There's also fresh bread, cold drinks, Kona coffee, locally made soaps and more.

Catch a Performance

Meet one of the liveliest little community arts spaces on the island. Set in a historic 1932 building, the **Aloha Theatre** *(apachawaii.org)* hosts a lineup of plays, musicals, improv, live music and cult-favorite films. Go online for the schedule and tickets.

Book a Table at the Theatery

One of the best new restaurants on the island, the **Theatery** *(thetheatery.com)* opened to much acclaim next to the Aloha Theater back in 2024. Under notable chef Stewart Woodman, this atmospheric dinner spot has a small menu of standouts featuring local ingredients and Asian accents – like tamarind-braised short ribs or *kanpachi* (a type of yellowtail fish) with *'ulu* (breadfruit) galette. There's a bar and lounge with happy hour (4pm to 6pm and 8pm to close) deals on cocktails, beer and appetizers. It's open Wednesday to Sunday 4pm to 9pm.

Get Your Chocolate Fix

Put a boost in your step at the **Hale Cocoa** *(halecocoa.com)*, an atmospheric shop that sells a variety of chocolaty decadence as well as Kona-grown coffee beans. Beautifully packaged bars feature a mix of dark chocolate and creative blends – horchata, macadamia nuts and toasted coconut, and even maple bacon. Signboards give insight into the growing, harvesting and production cycle of chocolate and coffee. A chocolate and cafe bar doles out refreshments, from banana chocolate smoothies to *paniolo* (spicy Mexican-style) mochas.

Take a Cacao Farm Tour

Behind the Hale Cocoa, you can take a guided two-hour tour (adult/child $40/25) through a working farm that produces pineapple trees, coffee and, most importantly, cacao. You'll learn all about the production of chocolate from bean to bar, and will get to taste half a dozen varieties that are made from cacao grown on Hawai'i Island. The more abbreviated one-hour express tour (adult/child $22/17) focuses on chocolate, coffee and tropical spices, with chocolate tasting at the end. Tours take place several times a day Wednesday through Saturday (and Sunday for the express tour); reserve ahead.

ORIGINS OF KAINALIU

Like a handful of other towns on the west side of the island, Kainaliu emerged as a market center of shops and supplies to serve the coffee farmers and ranchers who settled in the area in the early 20th century. The community of roughly 1600 people is named after a Native mariner who served under King Keawenuia'umi in the 16th century.

TOP TIPS

- Be careful when crossing the road. It's best to use one of the crosswalks. Most (but not all) drivers will stop.
- You can get here by the (free) Hele-On Bus. Bus 90 and 204 connect Kainaliu with Kailua-Kona and other towns, and there are departures roughly every two hours.
- Some places close or keep limited hours on Sunday and Monday. Friday and Saturday are the liveliest days to visit (and the best chance to catch a show at the Aloha Theater).
- If you need a morning pick-me-up, grab an espresso and breakfast burrito from So'K Coffee Station, open from 4am to 10am.

REGIS ST LOUIS

TOP EXPERIENCE

Spend the Day at Kealakekua Bay

Kealakekua Bay blends natural beauty with historic importance. It's a major religious site for Native Hawaiians and also marks the spot where Captain Cook first set foot in the archipelago. The bay is a protected marine conservation area and is famous for its rich variety of sea life. Experience the allure on a kayaking excursion, boat trip or DIY hike.

DON'T MISS

- The scenic Ka'awaloa Trail
- Snorkeling amid marine life
- Cute but mischievous mongoose
- Kayaking on the bay
- Captain Cook Monument

Hiking to the Bay

The only land access to the bay is via the **Ka'awaloa Trail** (aka Captain Cook Monument Trail), which offers nice lookouts on the way down and leads right to the snorkeling cove. To get to the trailhead, turn off the Māmalahoa Hwy onto Napo'opo'o Rd and park along the narrow road shoulder (look for where other vehicles have done the same). The 2-mile descending path takes about an hour, and brings you to a gorgeous spot for snorkeling. While the hike is rewarding, snorkeling amid vibrant sea life in usually calm conditions is the real highlight.

PRACTICALITIES

● dlnr.hawaii.gov/dsp/parks/hawaii ● free ● 7am-8pm

You can enter the sea near the **Captain Cook Monument** at the northern edge of the bay. This tall white obelisk is visible from a mile away, and marks the spot where Captain Cook was killed in an armed confrontation with Hawaiians in 1779. In 1877, as an act of diplomacy, the Kingdom of Hawai'i deeded the land that the monument stands on to Britain (so yes: this is technically British soil). Behind lie some scattered stones and foundation marks, the ruins of the ancient village of Ka'awaloa.

Bring snacks and eat them before you go swimming; otherwise, clever mongooses may find their way into your bag and snatch food items while you're gone. While in the water, keep an eye out for spiky urchins. Hiking back up, the 1300ft elevation gain feels pretty steep. Allow two hours to return, bring plenty of water and wear shoes suitable for hiking.

Kayaking & Paddling

Another way to experience Kealakekua Bay is by kayak, canoe or stand-up paddleboard, although there are tight regulations around this due to overcrowding, which has had an impact on the bay. Individuals are not allowed to launch from Napo'opo'o Wharf or land at Ka'awaloa Cove, but special recreational permits for transiting the bay are available in advance from the Division of State Parks (*dlnr.hawaii.gov/dsp/parks/hawaii*), and it's possible to launch from Ke'ei Beach. The other option is a guided kayaking tour with a state-permitted outfitter like the excellent **Kona Boys** (*konaboys.com;* p61). Most tours launch from Napo'opo'o Wharf, paddling 30 to 45 minutes across the bay to Ka'awaloa Cove. Prevailing winds are from the northwest, so returning is usually faster and easier.

Boating & Snorkeling Trips

The least strenuous way to visit Kealakekua Bay is on a boating and snorkeling trip. At the northern end, protected Ka'awaloa Cove (also known as Ka'awaloa Flats) ranks among Hawai'i's premier snorkeling spots. Protected from ocean swells, its aquamarine waters are especially clear. Tropical fish and coral are brilliantly abundant, and strong swimmers can go 100ft from shore to hang over the blue abyss of an underwater cliff. If you're lucky, *honu* (green sea turtles) and spinner dolphins might join you, but remember not to approach these wild animals. By law, you must remain at least 10ft away from turtles and 50yd from dolphins, whales and seals in the water. All Hawaiian sea turtles are endangered - give them plenty of space and never try to touch them.

Relics from the Past

Stone remnants from **Hikiau Heiau**, a sacred ceremonial site dedicated to the Hawaiian god Lono, still stand along the shore of Kealakekua Bay. This was where Captain Cook was brought upon arrival, and graced with sacred *kapa* bark cloths amid the chanting of priests before things took a turn for the worse (p80). Nearby, there was once a sandy beach used to ship cattle in the 1860s, though it's now covered by boulders from the ever-changing landscapes.

CORAL RESTORATION

The coral of Kealakekua Bay has suffered from marine heatwaves caused by climate change. To help build resiliency, the local community partnered with various organizations, including the Nature Conservancy to create Kanu Ko'a, a coral restoration pilot project. The three-year program launched in 2024, and if successful, the project may serve as a model for other coral restoration projects in Hawai'i and beyond.

TOP TIPS

- Mornings are the best time to visit, as you'll have better visibility in the water and likely calmer seas. You can also beat the busier midday crowds that arrive.
- If you're hiking, make sure you have ample water and sun protection, as little of the trail has shade. You'll also want good shoes and a walking stick for extra support on steep sections.
- If you lack gear, you can rent quality snorkeling equipment from **Snorkel Bob's** (p53) and other outfitters.
- Pick up snacks and picnic fare before making the trip. **Kainaliu Fresh** (p85) is a great spot for tropical fruits and cold drinks.

BILLY MCDONALD/SHUTTERSTOCK

Great Wall

TOP EXPERIENCE

Pu'uhonua o Hōnaunau National Historical Park

One of the most evocative places to connect you with ancient Hawai'i, Pu'uhonua o Hōnaunau combines a seminal historic site with some of the most impressive wildlife-spotting on the island. The tongue-twister name simply means 'place of refuge at Hōnaunau,' because this park once served as a sanctuary where *kapu* (taboo)-breakers and warriors could have their lives spared.

DON'T MISS

- Visitor center
- Royal grounds
- Great Wall
- Hale o Keawe Heiau
- Keone'ele Cove
- 1871 Trail
- Two-Step

Visitor Center & Royal Grounds

The visitor center (open 8:30am to 4:30pm) provides a brochure map with cultural information and a half-mile walking tour encompassing all the major sites. After picking it up, you'll enter the park in the village-like royal grounds, where Kona *ali'i* (chiefs) and their warriors lived. The spiritual atmosphere is enhanced by gently breaking waves and wind-rustled palms. Throughout the grounds are wooden *ki'i* (deity images) standing up to 15ft high.

PRACTICALITIES

● nps.gov/puho ● vehicle/pedestrian $20/10 ● 8:15am-sunset

Hale o Keawe Heiau

A reconstruction of the 'temple on the point of the cove' is located a few hundred yards past the main park entrance. The original was built around 1650 and contained the bones of 23 chiefs. It was believed that the *mana* (spiritual essence) of the chiefs remained in their bones and bestowed sanctity on those who entered the grounds. A fishpond, lava tree molds, a hand-carved koa canoe and a few thatched huts and shelters are scattered around here.

Keone'ele Cove

Keone'ele Cove was once the royal canoe landing; today it's a tongue of sand that hooks into the waters (you might spot snorkelers at Two-Step just across the way) and a favorite resting spot for sea turtles.

Great Wall

Separating the royal grounds from the *pu'uhonua* (place of sanctuary), the Great Wall was built around 1550 and is 950ft long, 18ft wide and 12ft high. Inside the wall are two older heiau platforms and legendary standing stones – a chief slept on one, and you can supposedly see the concave depression left by his head.

1871 Trail

Back in – you guessed it! – 1871, a section of derelict coastal trail that extended south all the way to Ho'okena was cleared and opened to the public, re-establishing what had once been a main artery for coastal villages in the region. Today the 1871 Trail crosses wild stretches of South Kona countryside. As you walk along the trail, you'll be flanked by shallow water extending to the ocean on one side, and on the other archeological sites that are strictly *kapu* (forbidden to enter). Natural wonders you'll see along the way include a collapsed lava tube and a tremendous, if overgrown, *hōlua* (lava-sledding course) that *ali'i* raced down. Watch out for feral goats. They're usually benign. Usually.

Snorkeling at Two-Step

Immediately north of the national historical park, concealed within a (usually) placid bay, are a series of jaw-dropping vibrant coral gardens where the reef and marine life seem locked in a permanent race to outstrip each other with the gaudiest color palette. There's no beach here – snorkelers use a stepped lava ledge beside the boat ramp to access about 10ft of water, which quickly drops to about 25ft. Good-size reef fish and a fine variety of coral are close to shore, while the predatory 'crown of thorns' starfish can be seen feasting on live coral polyps, and every now and then, sea turtles pop by. Cool, freshwater springs seep out of the ground, creating blurry patches in the water. From above it, your only indication of the action is the presence of boats and crowds gathering at the titular two steps.

A NEW START

In ancient Hawai'i, enemy warriors and violators of the *kapu* (taboo) system were punished with death. There was one loophole, however: reaching the sacred ground of a *pu'uhonua* (place of refuge). To reach the *pu'uhonua* required swimming in the open ocean, braving currents and sharks. Once the refugees were inside the sanctuary, priests performed ceremonies to placate the gods. Refugees could then return home to start afresh.

TOP TIPS

- Bring a lunch; just south of the park's central village area, an oceanfront palm-tree grove holds one of South Kona's best picnic areas.
- Swimming and snorkeling is not permitted around the historical site owing to its cultural significance.
- To snorkel at nearby Two-Step, visitors to Pu'uhonua o Hōnaunau are not allowed to leave their vehicle in the parking lot (with limited spaces, the park needs to keep access open for others). Instead, park on the highway, just outside the entrance (be sure to pull fully off the road).
- Morning is the best time for snorkeling at Two-Step, when the waters are often better for undersea wildlife watching.

Kohanaiki Beach (also known as Pine Trees beach; p57)
GARY GILARDI/SHUTTERSTOCK

Places We Love to Stay

$** Budget **$$** Midrange **$$$ Top End

Kailua-Kona

MAP p51, p55 & p56

My Hawai'i Hostel Around 2.7 miles from downtown Kailua-Kona, this simple, clean budget option offers dorms, private rooms and a friendly vibe that draws international travelers. **$**

Kona Tiki Hotel A retro well-maintained three-story hotel 1.5 miles south of downtown Kona, with airy motel-style rooms, oceanfront views and a pool just above the crashing waves. **$$**

Mango Sunset B&B Teak furnishings and bamboo accents spruce up the snug accommodations on this family-owned organic coffee farm a 15-minute drive northeast of Kailua-Kona. **$$**

Courtyard by Marriott King Kamehameha's Kona Beach Hotel This seaside icon has pleasant modern rooms and a perfect central location. **$$**

Pacific 19 Boxy on the outside, this centrally located 1970s hotel boasts attractively renovated rooms with balconies and a relaxing pool fringed by greenery. **$$$**

Royal Kona Resort Perched over the sea, this breezy, 1970s Polynesian fantasy has 400 rooms (all with balconies), ample amenities and lovely grounds that include a protected saltwater lagoon. **$$$**

Outrigger Kona Resort & Spa The family-friendly 500-room resort in the Keahou Resort Area has lovely grounds, daily cultural activities and a massive pool. **$$$**

Honu Kai B&B A plush, romantic four-room B&B set amid tropical gardens just an eight-minute drive from downtown Kailua-Kona. **$$$**

North Kona

Kohanaiki Beach Park Pitch a tent on the sand and fall asleep to lapping waves at this spot 6 miles north of town. Reserve online; closed Tuesday and Wednesday. **$**

Kona Village (p65) Hawai'i's classiest stay is powered by 8000 solar panels, and its plush rooms come with oversized lānai and outdoor rain showers, along with bikes, spa treatments, water activities and more. **$$$**

Four Seasons Resort Hualālai (p65) The luxurious address stretches across 860 acres and offers top-flight service and bountiful amenities with pools, a golf course and spa. **$$$**

Hōlualoa

MAP p69

Hale Maluhia Country Inn A jungle mountain retreat imbued with Japanese, Hawaiian and bohemian style and sensibility, surrounded by coffee plantations. **$**

Hale Hualalai B&B Set amid a 4-acre coffee farm, you'll find ocean-view suites with lānai and breakfast prepared by the friendly host-chef, sourced from his garden. **$$**

Holualoa Inn From the eucalyptus floors to the river-rock showers to the carved furnishings, beauty abounds in every detail of this exquisite B&B and working coffee farm. **$$$**

Kealakekua & Captain Cook

MAP p78

Ho'okena Beach Park (p79) A chilled-out seaside campground popular with families, with spacious sites for tents on the grey-sand beach. Book at least 72 hours ahead via hookena.org. **$**

Gingerhill Farm An eco-friendly option in a tropical 5-acre setting, Gingerhill makes an ideal zenlike retreat, whether you opt for a beautifully furnished cottage, spacious sunset suite, comfy glamping tents or rustic cabins. **$$**

Ka'awa Loa Plantation Channels Hawai'i's beauty with wraparound lānai, sweeping coastal views and cheerfully decorated rooms. **$$**

A Beautiful Edge of the World B&B Comfy, carpeted rooms with wonderful views and a tropical, secluded setting. **$$**

Aolani House Stunning vacation rental house and/or cottage with a saltwater infinity pool, spa and outdoor shower, ensconced in coffee country. **$$$**

Researched by
Jade Bremner

Hilo & the Hāmākua Coast

THUNDEROUS WATERFALLS, HISTORIC TOWNS AND RAINFORESTS

The lush green hillsides and wind-ravaged coastline of the east were once home to thriving sugar plantations and towns. Explore their faded glory.

Hawai'i Island's wild northeast starts in the island's capital, the once-thriving sugar town of Hilo, before extending up to the untamed and sacred Waipi'o Valley. Between these points sit rushing waterfalls, pounding surf on black lava beaches, and little historic plantation communities.

Hilo is about as far from the tourist circuit as you can get for a prominent Hawaiian town, and that's its appeal. Often referred to as 'authentic Hawai'i,' with its weatherworn historic buildings it's not glitzy or attractive, but what it lacks in polished facades it makes up for in charm. Visitors can delve into a surprising local food scene with an emphasis on local fresh produce, and meet a diverse mix of residents, including Hawaiian, Japanese, Filipino, Portuguese and Chinese locals. Superb museums are scattered around town, showcasing Hawai'i's culture and biodiversity, but drive northwest for just a few minutes, and the landscape goes dramatically tropical. Small-scale farms grow cacao, vanilla, tea, and all manner of fruit on the slopes of Maunakea, and locals cool off at hidden pools next to tumbling cascades. Further north are only plantation towns and a sacred emerald valley untouched by the modern world.

RITU MANOJ JETHANI/SHUTTERSTOCK

South of Hilo, the opportunities for shore snorkeling are surprising, with a chain of beach parks offering aquamarine waters alive with psychedelic marine life. In the island's southeast is Puna, home to free-spirited characters who enjoy living dangerously – it sits in the path of an active eruption zone, and has become home to hippies, funky artists and alternative healers; it's also a place to discover lava tube caves and black-sand beaches.

THE MAIN AREAS

HILO
Vibrant food scene. p96

PUNA
Beaches and apocalyptic lava. p114

HONOMŪ, HAKALAU & LAUPĀHOEHOE
Waterfalls and lush rainforests. p118

HONOKA'A
Western-style shop fronts. p126

WAIPI'O VALLEY
Verdant emerald cliffs. p132

For places to stay in Hilo & the Hāmākua Coast, see p135

SODAPURETRAVEL/SHUTTERSTOCK

Left: 'Akaka Falls State Park (p118); Above: Waipi'o Valley cliffs (p132)

Find Your Way

Northeast Hawai'i Island is a roughly 50-mile slab of scenic road, rainforest and coastline that finishes in vibrant Hilo, Hawai'i Island's largest town and the island's capital.

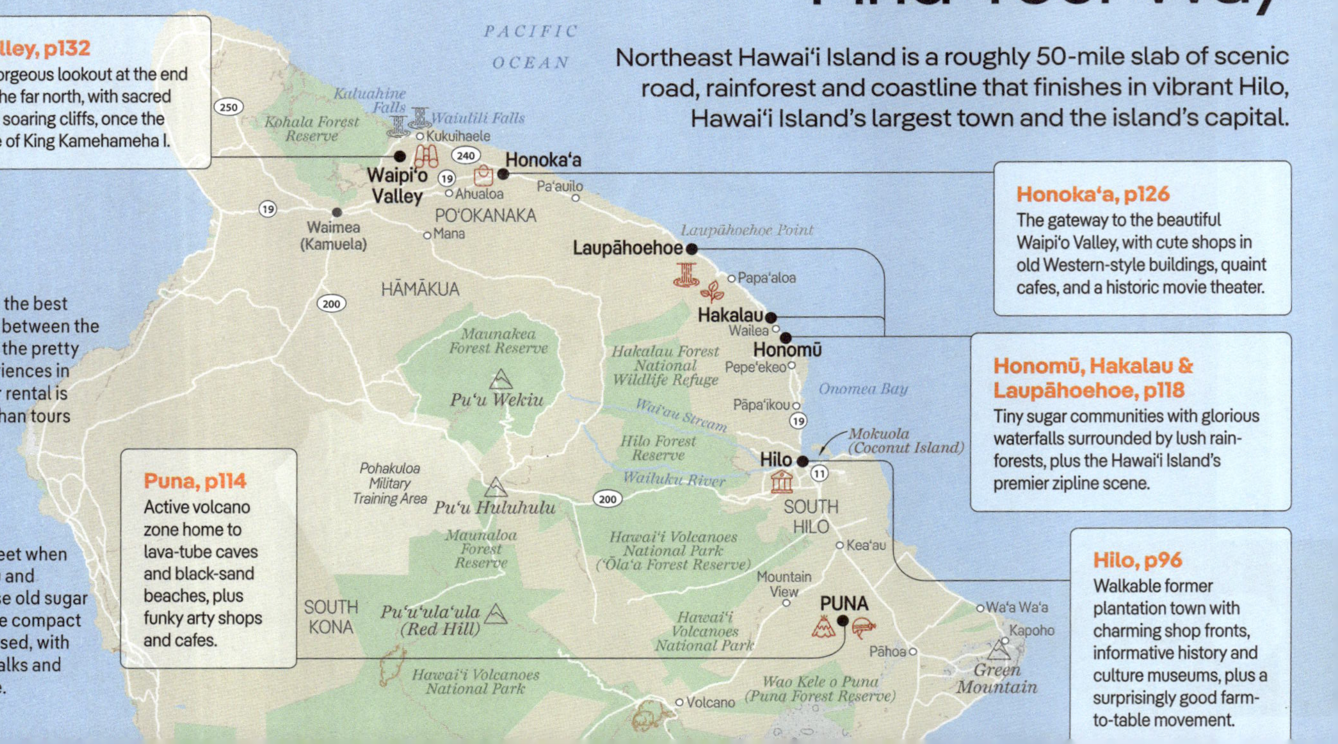

Waipi'o Valley, p132

Staggeringly gorgeous lookout at the end of Hwy 240 in the far north, with sacred emerald-green soaring cliffs, once the boyhood home of King Kamehameha I.

Honoka'a, p126

The gateway to the beautiful Waipi'o Valley, with cute shops in old Western-style buildings, quaint cafes, and a historic movie theater.

Honomū, Hakalau & Laupāhoehoe, p118

Tiny sugar communities with glorious waterfalls surrounded by lush rainforests, plus the Hawai'i Island's premier zipline scene.

Puna, p114

Active volcano zone home to lava-tube caves and black-sand beaches, plus funky arty shops and cafes.

Hilo, p96

Walkable former plantation town with charming shop fronts, informative history and culture museums, plus a surprisingly good farm-to-table movement.

CAR

Four wheels are the best way to navigate between the main areas, and the pretty drives are experiences in themselves. Car rental is much cheaper than tours and taxis.

WALKING

Set off on two feet when in Hilo, Honomū and Honoka'a – these old sugar communities are compact and pedestrianised, with plenty of sidewalks and shops to peruse.

THE_EXPLORER/SHUTTERSTOCK

Green sea turtle, Richardson Ocean Park (p102)

Plan Your Time

Roam historical sugar towns, swim in marine-life-rich oceans, clap eyes on majestic tumbling waterfalls and savor farm-to-table food in Hawai'i Island's east.

One Day to Travel Around

- Go surfing at **Honoli'i Beach Park** (p102), before exploring magnificent **Banyan Dr** (p110) by bike. Peruse the stands at **Hilo Farmers Market** (p96), and try a heaped bowl of rice and fish at **Poke N Sides** (p96). Later search for fish and sea turtles at **Richardson Ocean Park** (p102).

Two Days to Travel Around

- Wander among orchids and fruit trees at **Hawai'i Tropical Bioreserve & Garden** (p123). Snap a picture at rushing **Rainbow Falls** (p100) before swimming the **Wai'ale Falls** (p100). Finish with a white-knuckle rappel 120ft down the side of Kulaniapia Falls with **Island Mountain Guides**.

SEASONAL HIGHLIGHTS

SPRING

Hilo has festivals galore: **May Day Lei Day Festival** (p104), **Merrie Monarch Festival** (p104) and **King Kamehameha Day** (p104), plus the **Honoka'a Western Week** (p127).

SUMMER

August is the hottest month of the year. It can get humid, but trade winds help balance this – meaning it's usually warm and pleasant.

AUTUMN

Pleasant weather and fewer crowds. The island-wide epicurean **Hawaii Food & Wine Festival** (p104) is in October.

WINTER

The northwest's colder months bring longer rain showers. It's perfectly warm, but bring a raincoat.

Hilo

ISLAND HISTORY | FORMER SUGAR TOWN | RUSHING WATERFALLS

GETTING AROUND

Bike rental makes for an easy and affordable way to navigate the downtown Hilo area (when it's not raining). There are a handful of HiBike docking stations in Hilo, the most convenient in town near the Locavore Store on Kīlauea Ave and on Banyan Dr. A car makes it easy to visit attractions in the suburbs, but parking in downtown can be problematic on market days, with long waits for spaces. The cheapest way to travel is by bus; services run from Hilo to Kona in the west and around town for a couple of dollars.

Hilo is a charming, easily walkable town with a proud history. It is King Kamehameha's former home, and when foreigners arrived it turned into a bustling sugar town. When the plantations shut, residents dipped their toes into tourism. But make no mistake, there's no flashy tourist strip – it's a real community of Native Hawaiian, Japanese, Filipino, Chinese and white residents. As Hawaiian towns go, Hilo is on the grittier side. It has survived two tsunamis and has the highest annual rainfall in the US, but its original weather-washed century-old buildings ooze faded glory and include the oldest original wooden structure in Hawai'i. Around 275 days of rain per year helps to fuel the lush surrounding rainforests, rushing waterfalls just minutes out of town, beautiful gardens and a delicious farm-fresh foodie scene.

Meet Local Artisans

MAP P98

Community vibes and local eats

All parts of the community converge at the vibrant **Hilo Farmers Market** *(hilofarmersmarket.com)*. On one side of Mamo St, traders sell a variety of tropical delights like rambutan, noni and papaya, and on the other side of the road is an artisan market with locally made gifts. Wednesdays and Saturdays (7am to 4pm) are bustling market days, with dozens of vendors and live music, but a scattering of traders can always be found here. Look out for pop-up food trucks on main market days. Unique local crafts include the likes of tropical print clothing, or colorful art created by independent designers. **Poke N Sides** *(pokensides.com)* and **Kula Shave Ice** (p102; *kulashaveice.com)* at the market, meanwhile, are great spots for a bite, leading the *poke* and icy desserts categories on Hawai'i Island.

Learn About Tsunamis

MAP P97 & P98

Surviving two natural disasters

Two significant tsunamis have shaped the town of Hilo, and the informative **Pacific Tsunami Museum** *(tsunami.org;*

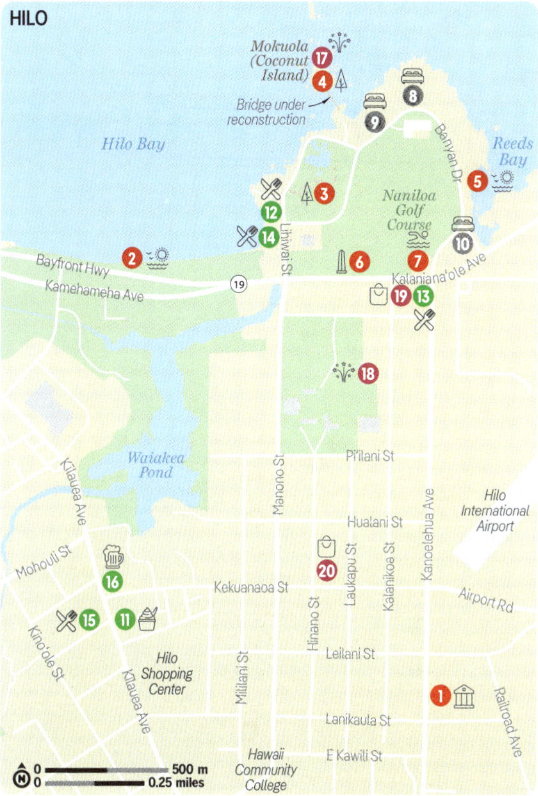

SIGHTS
1 Hawai'i Japanese Center
2 Hilo Bayfront Beach
3 Lili'uokalani Gardens
4 Mokuola
5 Reeds Bay Beach Park
6 Tsunami Memorial Clock

ACTIVITIES
7 Hilo Ocean Adventures

SLEEPING
8 Grand Naniloa Resort
9 Hilo Hawaiian Hotel
10 SCP Hilo Hotel

EATING
11 Brain Freeze Shave Ice
12 Hilo Bay Cafe
13 Ken's House of Pancakes
14 Suisan Fish Market
15 Sweet Cane Cafe

DRINKING & NIGHTLIFE
16 Ola Brew

ENTERTAINMENT
17 King Kamehameha Day Celebration
18 Merrie Monarch Festival

SHOPPING
19 Basically Books
20 Big Island Candies

adult/child $15/free) is dedicated to exploring why these and other awesome powers of nature happen. The museum (open 10am to 2pm Saturday and Sunday) recounts the shocking tales of what happened to the local community during and after these two tidal waves (in 1946 and 1960), with powerful personal stories and photos about the strength of the human spirit, and how a devastating event like this changes a community like Hilo. Display boards also inform visitors about the most lethal tsunami to ever occur, on Boxing Day 2004, hitting Thailand, Sri Lanka and India and killing more than 230,000 people.

Visitors can learn the warning signs and what to do in the event of a tsunami, plus why, crucially, you should never stand and watch a tsunami. Kids will love creating their own tidal wave, by dropping a weight into a display case filled with water, and watching the displacement create a huge surge, powerful enough to knock over a house on land. Inquisitive minds can also pick up an activity book and complete a quiz to see if they're prepared for a potential natural disaster. Passionate museum staff are on hand to offer extra tsunami knowledge.

TOP TIP

Don't let Hilo's rain dissuade you. It comes in short bursts in the summer, with longer downpours in the winter – do as the locals do and carry a rain jacket or umbrella. Many of Hilo's sights, including museums, waterfalls and botanical gardens, are arguably better in the rain.

HIGHLIGHTS	8 Kaipalaoa Landing Park	16 Makani's Magic Pineapple Shack	**DRINKING & NIGHTLIFE**
1 Hilo Farmers Market	9 Surf Cottage	17 Moms Hilo	25 Hidden Nēnē
2 Pacific Tsunami Museum	**SLEEPING**	18 Nector Cafe	26 Hilo Bottle Shop
SIGHTS	10 Howzit Hostels	see 12 Paul's Place	27 Temple Bar
3 Mokupāpapa Discovery Center	11 Lotus Garden Hilo	19 Pineapples	**ENTERTAINMENT**
4 S Hata Building	12 Pakalana Inn	20 Poke N Sides	28 KWXX Ho'olaule'a
ACTIVITIES	**EATING**	21 Puna Chocolate Company & Cafe	29 Palace Theater
5 Bayfront Boards	13 Booch Bar	22 Sugar Coast Candy	**SHOPPING**
6 Big Island Climbing	see 4 Café Pesto	23 Two Ladies Kitchen	30 Locavore Store
7 Hulakai Hawaii	14 Chillville LLC	24 Wilson's By the Bay	31 Seaweed Snack & Shop
	15 Jackie Rey's Ohana Grill		32 Turn the Page
	see 20 Kula Shave Ice		

A short drive away is **Mokuola**, commonly called Coconut Island, off Banyan Dr. It's connected to land (near Lili'uokalani Gardens) by a 250ft bridge, which was out at the time of research. Temporarily, the only way to reach it is by boat or swimming. On the island you can see, in reality, how big tsunami waves from the 1960s reached - almost as high as the palm trees! Look out for the markings on the trees indicating the wave height. The tsunami destroyed all the homes on the island. It is now a county park with beautiful ocean views.

Japanese Immigration History

MAP P97 & P98

Hawai'i Island's multicultural DNA

Hidden off Kanoelehua Ave, in an unassuming white and brown building, is the **Hawai'i Japanese Center** *(jcchawaii.org; adult/child/child under 6 $10/7/free)*, a fascinating exhibit about the Japanese immigrant community of Hawai'i Island. Around 30% of the island's population is Asian, many of whom arrived from 1885 as contract laborers for sugar plantations. Considered exhibitions recount how the Japanese community arrived and how they've shaped the culture – including the food scene, with must-visit hole-in-the-wall joints like **Two Ladies Kitchen** (serving authentic handmade *mochi* desserts in downtown Hilo), and hugely influential local businesses, including chocolate manufacturer **Big Island Candies** (p104).

Other exhibits are on plantation workers' clothes, historic local sports teams (like the Waiakea Pirates, which famously played a team with guest star Babe Ruth in 1933 and won), and how early Japanese immigrant families lived, with a large selection of vintage furniture and children's toys on show. There are early copies of the *Kona Echo* paper, created by Dr Harvey Saburo Hayashi in 1897, and the original 1884 Horii Myriagraph printing press used to create editions, plus traditional clothing and artwork. The adjacent room hosts local Japanese-inspired exhibitions. Stop by the good gift shop at the exit for textiles and Japan-inspired crafts, plus vintage dishware at reasonable prices. The museum is open 11am to 3pm Wednesday to Saturday.

Wonderful Waterfalls

MAP P103

Cascades to view and swim in

Moments from downtown Hilo, several waterfalls plunge along the Wailuku River, Hawai'i's second-longest river at 18 miles. This tributary dates back more than 10,000 years and flows along the lava lines where Maunakea and Maunaloa meet.

JAPANESE CULTURAL ARCHITECTURE TOUR

Arnold Hiura, Executive Director of the Hawai'i Japanese Center, offers places of architectural wonder to visit in and around Hilo. *@jcchawaii*

S Hata Building This striking blue and green building in downtown Hilo was envisioned by Japanese businessman Hata Sadanosuke in 1912. It's a reminder that immigrants not only worked in the sugar industry but also made significant contributions to commercial life.

Hamakua Jodo Mission Japanese immigrants built the first sanctioned Buddhist temple in Hawai'i in 1896 on the Hāmākua Coast. It's also the site of the **Katsu Goto Memorial** (p128), commemorating an outspoken human rights campaigner lynched by plantation owners.

DRINKING IN HILO: OUR PICKS

MAP P97 & P98

Ola Brew: Creative local crafts like *liliko'i* lime milkshake IPA, plus hard juice, cider, tea and seltzer in a modern taproom. *11am-10pm Mon-Sat, 10am-8pm Sun*

Hidden Nēnē: Sophisticated undergound lounge serving craft cocktails using local ingredients, from fresh *liliko'i* juice to Hawaiian chili pepper. *noon-midnight*

Hilo Bottle Shop: Superb selection of Hawai'i Island craft brews, Hawai'i brews and curious international imports at reasonable prices. *11:30am-6:30pm Mon-Sat*

Temple Bar: One of the coolest spots for a cocktail, craft beer or wine in Hilo, with space inside a smart heritage building. *11am-11pm Fri-Wed, to 10pm Thu*

WATERWORLD

Hawai'i Island has many waterfalls; there are an estimated 500 of them. Many sit on private land, but easily accessible, spectacular cascades can be found just outside Hilo's town. There are many waterfalls to discover, swim in, and hike around, with no danger of them drying up like in other warm climates. Cascades are primarily fed by the abundant rainfall on Hawai'i Island's lush northeastern side. Hilo and the Hāmākua Coast get the most rain. Hilo averages around 80in to 160in annually, making it the wettest city in the United States. This weather is heavily influenced by trade winds and the large central high volcanoes (Maunakea and Maunaloa), which create a strong orographic effect, causing rain to form from air masses rising over high topography.

Start with the free, short and snappy 80ft plunging **Rainbow Falls**, maintained by Hawai'i State Parks. The falls are a stone's throw from a parking lot, and an easy-access lookout platform offers a direct view of the cascade surrounded by lush rainforest as it pours into a turquoise pool. The best angle from which to see the rainbow, however, is at the first railing on the way to the platform; colors appear in the mist at the bottom of the falls when the sun hits it in the morning, on sunny days. (Waiānuenue, 'rainbow seen in water,' is the Hawaiian name for these falls.) During a drought or on overcast and rainy days, you'll likely be outta luck for rainbow-spotting. A small walk left of the cascade up a flight of stairs offers a view from the top of the falls; peek into the undergrowth on the way up for some magnificent banyan trees, complete with spindly roots.

Two miles up the road from Rainbow Falls is natural site **Boiling Pots**, with a series of cascades of various sizes, including **Pe'epe'e Falls**, plunging into a cauldron-like pool, which bubbles and fizzes during and after big storms. It looks inviting, but don't attempt to take a dip here – this spot is dangerous. Under the water are several lava flow tunnels, and many people have died while attempting to swim in these waters.

If you want to get wet, head further upstream to the free **Wai'ale Falls**. Park across the bridge on Waiānuenue Ave, and skip the smaller lower falls for the short 0.3-mile trail next to the riverbank, through overgrown jungle, which leads to a huge deep pool, a pebbly beach, and a plunging 55ft waterfall. Be aware that although this is a popular swimming spot, there are no lifeguards and the trail is unmaintained. The area can be prone to flash floods – check the weather forecast before you visit, and swim at your own risk.

Climb into a Lava Tube

MAP P103

Self-tour caving

Estimated to be more than 21 miles long, the **Kaumana Caves** *(free)* were created by a lava flow from Maunaloa in 1881, and offer a rugged, unlit spelunking adventure right off Kaumana Dr. There are two main paths to explore, making for a dark, eerie adventure, with narrow sections and various lava formations. Descend by a dramatic staircase into the rocky fern- and plant-filled cave entrance, like something from a fantasy flick, and you'll see the two openings to the caves. Most people arrive with a phone, and as the light quickly fades

EATING IN HILO: BEST BREAKFASTS & COFFEE

MAP P97 & P98

Booch Bar: Healthy veggie brekkies, from omelets to smoothie bowls, in a colorful downtown cafe. *8am-9pm Mon-Sat, to 3pm Sun* $

Ken's House of Pancakes: Vintage diner with good-priced all-American breakfast classics and strong drip coffee. Open early. *6am-9pm* $

Nector Cafe: Two sleek modern Hilo counter joints serving espresso drinks, smoothies and toasties. *9am-5:30pm* $

Paul's Place: Super-cute mom-and-pop cafe with retro chintzy decor. Home-style waffles, eggs Benedict, lox bagels. *7:30am-2pm Wed-Fri, 7am-2pm Sat* $

into complete darkness (around 100ft in) they turn back, realizing their torch is nowhere near strong enough. The most accessible section, on the right, usually takes 60 minutes to explore before it becomes impenetrable; the left cave is longer. Take your time on the rocks, which are uneven and slippery at the entrance. Bring proper flashlights (including a backup), plus hiking shoes with grip, gloves, and water. The caves are open 8am to 8pm.

Hawai'i's Ecosystems

MAP P98

Family-friendly nature center

Inside the century-old Koehnen Building, the welcoming **Mokupāpapa Discovery Center** *(papahanaumokuakea.gov; free)* offers exhibits on natural science and the surrounding marine life and history around the northwestern Hawaiian Islands. Open 9am to 4pm Tuesday to Saturday, it's ideal for families during rain showers. It's filled with all sorts of interpretive boards in Hawaiian and English, including on how coral reefs are formed; the Laysan albatross (99.7% of which live in the northwestern Hawaiian Islands); and endangered Hawaiian monk seals (of which there are 1500 left in the wild) and tiger sharks (which favor the shallow waters around the archipelago).

The showpiece, however, is a giant 3500-gallon saltwater aquarium with various species collected from the Papahānaumokuākea Marine National Monument, the largest marine protected area in the world, home to 7000 marine species. See some of them in the giant tank, including Hawaiian yellow anthias, stripy orange and white opae ula shrimp and bandit angelfish, plus the orange margin butterflyfish, which lives nowhere else on Earth.

On the 2nd floor are exhibits on ancient voyaging, with many historic artifacts used at sea.

East-Coast Waves

MAP P97, P98 & P103

Best beach parks for surfing

Hilo's free beaches aren't the postcard-perfect white sandy beaches many imagine when visiting Hawai'i. They're typically rugged, with black sand (if any), and dotted with volcanic rocks. However, the rocks often form natural break walls for safe swimming and marine-life viewing.

TSUNAMI ZONE

Tsunamis in Hilo are rare but taken seriously. Hawai'i sits in the Pacific Ring of Fire, meaning distant earthquakes can generate powerful swells that reach the islands. Early-warning systems include sirens across the islands, most cell phones should receive text alerts, and TV and radio stations will broadcast warnings and evacuation orders.

If a tsunami warning is issued, move immediately to higher ground or inland. Follow marked evacuation routes (which are all over town); avoid coastal roads and river valleys. If this is not possible go to the 4th floor or higher of a reinforced concrete building. If you feel a strong earthquake, self-evacuate without waiting for instructions. Be aware that the first wave of a tsunami is not always the largest, and waves may keep coming for hours.

EATING IN HILO: BEST SWEET TREATS

MAP P98

Makani's Magic Pineapple Shack: Try the seriously good *ube* (purple yam) soft-serve ice cream. *10am-5pm Sun-Fri, to 4:30pm Sat* $

Puna Chocolate Company & Cafe: Selling 100% Hawai'i-grown cacao chocolate bars. Try the liquid hot chocolate. *7am-11pm Thu-Sat, to 10pm Tue & Wed, to 9pm Sun & Mon* $

Two Ladies Kitchen (p99): *Mochi* fans flock to this hole-in-the-wall joint. Its rainbow-colored treats have island-inspired flavors. *10am-4pm Tue-Sat* $

Sugar Coast Candy: Kids lose their minds in this old-fashioned Willy Wonka-style shop, with barrels of taffy, jars of nostalgic sweet and chocolates. Samples are plentiful. $

BEST WATER SPORT RENTALS

Hulakai Hawaii For stand-up paddleboard, bodyboard, surfboard and snorkel rental, plus other beach equipment (chairs, umbrellas, lifejackets). Also runs organized tours.

Hilo Ocean Adventures Friendly family-run center renting out diving gear, snorkels, foamie surfboards, kayaks and paddleboards. Offers dive and whale-watching trips, plus PADI courses.

Bayfront Boards Surf shop with friendly advice on surf spot hazards. Sells gear and rents a limited number of surfboards.

Inn at Kulaniapia Falls Rents single kayaks for waterfall exploring. Note that an additional day pass is required to enter the site.

Surf Cottage Rents out SUPs, surfboards and kayaks. Book via phone (808-756-8388), as the address is an office with irregular hours.

Kaipalaoa Landing Park (known as the Bayfront by locals), recognizable by its mini white lighthouse, sits at the edge of the Wailuku River mouth, meaning the water is much murkier than elsewhere. This is a popular break for local intermediate surfers, but it's not a beginners' spot; locals can be protective of their break. Inside, waves break onto rocks, so paddle out to the right of the lighthouse. **Hulakai Hawaii** *(hulakai.com)* on Kamehameha Ave rents out a small selection of boards (from $20 per hour).

Two miles north of downtown Hilo is **Honoli'i Beach Park**, a picturesque tropical enclave with lifeguards, showers and some of the best waves in the area. It sits at the mouth of the Honoli'i Stream, so currents can be strong – check conditions before paddling out. **Hilo Bayfront Beach** is the big sprawling black sandy beach, popular with locals and lined with canoe clubs. Further east is **Reeds Bay Beach Park**, which has a calm, shallow cove ideal for paddleboarding and kayaking, plus picnic areas.

Fish & Turtle Spotting

MAP P103

Beach parks for snorkeling

If you want to go snorkeling, go south of Hilo, where the water turns glassy and turquoise. The shallow and crystal-clear waters of **Onekahakaha Beach Park** are protected from tumultuous seas by a rock wall, and have some of the safest around, including a 'baby beach' for kids, with grassy lawns and lifeguards. Rocky **Carlsmith Beach Park** offers a safe, lagoon-like swimming and snorkeling area, thanks to a protective reef, and is usually less crowded.

Richardson Ocean Park is another draw for families, due to the great snorkeling and frequent sightings of green sea turtles, with healthy coral and lots of marine life (such as zebra moray, butterflyfish and squid). There's a little patch of black sand, grassy nooks and rock ponds, plus lifeguards, restrooms, showers and picnic areas.

The **Wai'olena & Wai'uli Beach Parks** (also known as Leleiwi Beach Park) are a hotspot for marine life, with a good shore-entry dive spot (it's a tricky entry – not suitable for novice snorkelers or divers; local dive shops can offer advice). The park has shaded pavilions for picnics. When swimming in rocky pools, be aware of needle-sharp *wana* (sea urchins) underfoot. Ideally, avoid putting your feet down at all when snorkeling (to protect the reef) and wear wetsuit booties (to protect feet).

EATING IN HILO: BEST SHAVE ICE

MAP P97 & P98

Kula Shave Ice: Hawai'i desserts don't get better than this artisan shave ice, made with organically grown local fruit and organic cane sugar. *noon-4:30pm Tue-Thu* $

Brain Freeze Shave Ice: Classic shave ice, in rainbow-colored fruity flavors served in a kitsch old-school joint. Sugar-free options too. *11am-5pm Tue-Sat* $

Wilson's By the Bay: For homemade syrups and shavings done right, with trimmings including Snow Caps (condensed milk on top) and nutty azuki beans. *noon-5pm Tue-Sun* $

Chillville LLC: Rolled ice cream and fluffy, snow-like *bingsu* (Korean shaved ice). *noon-6pm Tue, Wed & Sun, to 9pm Fri & Sat* $

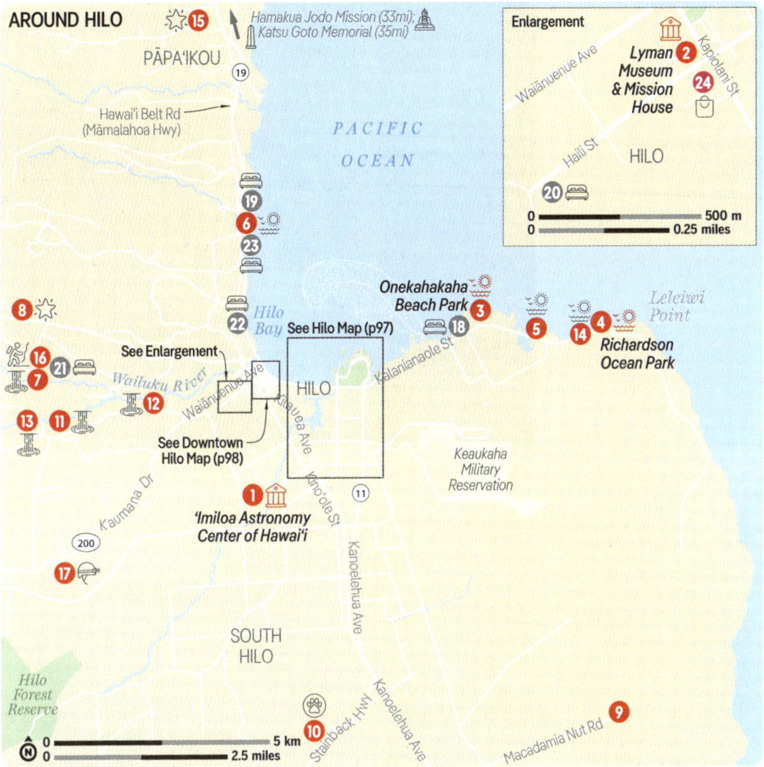

HIGHLIGHTS

1 'Imiloa Astronomy Center of Hawai'i
2 Lyman Museum & Mission House
3 Onekahakaha Beach Park
4 Richardson Ocean Park

SIGHTS

5 Carlsmith Beach Park
6 Honoli'i Beach Park
7 Kulaniapia Falls
8 Lavaloha
9 Mauna Loa Macadamia Nut Visitor Center
10 Pana'ewa Rainforest Zoo & Gardens
11 Pe'epe'e Falls & Boiling Pots
12 Rainbow Falls
13 Wai'ale Falls
14 Wai'olena & Wai'uli Beach Parks

ACTIVITIES

15 Hamakua Chocolate Farm
16 Island Mountain Guides
17 Kaumana Caves

SLEEPING

18 Arnott's Lodge
19 Hale Kai Hawaii
20 Hilo Honu Inn
21 Inn at Kulaniapia Falls
22 Lo'i B&B
23 Orchid Tree B&B

SHOPPING

24 The Knickknackery

Show Time

MAP P98

Hilo's retro theater

Hilo's historic **Palace Theater** *(hilopalace.com)*, dating back to 1925, was the grandest spot in town when it opened as a palace of silent movies. Unlike other local theaters, this Davis & Fishbourne-designed place (built entirely of redwood) survived two tsunamis. It's now the center of Hilo's cultural offerings. Visitors can have an atmospheric night watching a Broadway musical or arthouse film, or a traditional silent movie (accompanied by the original evocative house organ), plus music and dance concerts – all inside its striking beaux arts-style auditorium. Booking ahead is essential.

HILO FESTIVALS

Merrie Monarch Festival On Easter week, this huge hula celebration is named for King David Kalākaua. Competitions take place at Edith Kanakaole Tennis Stadium.

May Day Lei Day Festival Celebrated on May 1 by exhibiting flowers. Hilo's Kalākaua Park has lei-making demonstrations, music and hula.

KWXX Ho'olaule'a Local radio station KWXX (94.7FM in Hilo) hosts east Hawai'i's biggest music festival every fall/winter, with several Bayfront stages, and local venues hosting performances.

King Kamehameha Day A public holiday in honor of the monarch who first united the Hawaiian Islands, with communities doing traditional hula, music, food and crafts on June 11.

Hawai'i Food & Wine Festival This island-wide epicurean festival sees guest chefs come to town for talks, cooking classes and tastings in October.

GARY GILARDI/SHUTTERSTOCK

Kulaniapia Falls

Climbing in all Weathers

MAP P98 & P103

Indoor and outdoor thrill-seeking

Hawai'i Island's first climbing gym, **Big Island Climbing** *(bigislandclimbing.com; day passes from $15)* in downtown Hilo, with 700 sq ft of bouldering space on 14ft-high walls, is the ideal physical activity for restless children (and adults) on a rainy afternoon (Hilo has six times more rainfall than London). Regular clinics offer an introduction to climbing and include how to boulder and fall safely on padded floors without ropes. Family members can watch from an observation deck. Once you've learned the moves indoors, companies such as **Island Mountain Guides** *(islandmountainguides.com; half-day climbing from $199)* offer guided rock climbing day trips around east Hawai'i Island, plus an awesome 120ft rappelling experience down **Kulaniapia Falls** at Hawai'i's largest privately accessible waterfall ($248 per person), which is followed by waterfall swimming and hiking in the grounds of the lush **Inn at Kulaniapia Falls** (p135).

Sugar Highs

MAP P97 & P103

Big treat producers

It comes as no surprise that the former sugar town of Hilo has a sweet tooth, and numerous handcrafted specialties can be tried around town.

Big Island Candies *(bigislandcandies.com)* was established in 1977 by Japanese immigrants, who started with just a chocolate melter and a shrink-wrap machine. Husband-and-wife team Allan and Irma Ikawa created chocolates and cookies using 100% Hawai'i-grown macadamia nuts. Their enormous showroom factory and shop in Hilo used to offer the chance to peer through a windowed wall and watch saliva-inducing sweet creations being made, but the factory wasn't running during our last visit. However, the signature chocolate-dipped shortbreads and brownies, bars of chocolate macadamia nut crunch, Hawaiian red chili toffee and many more are still available to buy and sample in the gift shop (8:30am to 5:30pm), which is stuffed with Hawai'i Island gifts and toys. A snack bar here also serves good savory mac-nut salads and sandwiches.

Meanwhile, the **Mauna Loa Macadamia Nut Visitor Center** *(hawaiianhost.com; free)* tells the story of how this historic mac-nut producer, dating to 1949, followed suit and got into candy-making in the 1980s – with chocolate-covered nuts. Samples are generous for visitors at the plantation and working factory, while the gift shop sells packaged nuts at reasonable prices, plus exotic-flavored ice cream. Don't leave without a self-guided nature walk through the orchard's fruit trees; guests are allowed to take home fallen fruits, and bounties might include starfruit, pineapples or breadfruit. Look out for Hawaiian goose, zebra dove, yellow-billed cardinal and Java sparrows among other birds in the tranquil grounds.

Artisanal Chocolate

MAP P103

Go on a farm tour

Learn the history and process of how Hawaiian chocolate is made from tree to bar at two extraordinary and scenic farms, **Hamakua Chocolate Farm** *(hamakuachocolate.com; tours & tastings per person from $99)*, and **Lavaloha** *(lavaloha.com; tours per person from $43)*, both around 6 miles from downtown Hilo in the lush countryside. At Hamakua (open 9am to 5pm) you can try making it, before devouring your creations and other chocolate samples from around Hawai'i and the world. A Californian-Australian couple started planting cacao and a good number of exotic fruit and spice trees here on their 6.5 acres of land; they produce more than a dozen varieties of chocolate and offer tours, workshops and tastings, and monthly harvest parties, plus farm stays in eco rooms with garden and sea views. At Lavaloha (open 9am to 5pm Monday to Saturday), get whisked around by electric shuttle to vibrant cacao orchards, see how cacao is processed from bean to bar, and sample a selection of artisanal chocolates, all of which are made using 100% Hawaiian, single-origin chocolate.

SWEET TOOTH

Sugar plantations dominated Hawai'i's agricultural landscape for more than a century, providing jobs, shaping communities, and attracting workers from Asia, Europe and beyond, but the industry has now vanished. At its peak in the mid-20th century, Hawai'i produced roughly a million tons of raw sugar a year, supplying around 10% of US consumption and making the islands world-renowned for cane production. Post-sugarcane, the state's love affair with sweet treats has remained, with new, smaller, farming industries (from growing macadamia nuts to cacao and tropical fruits). It's easy to find a whole host of locally made sugary delights, from small-batch artisanal chocolate to well-known treat producers, including Mauna Loa and Big Island Candies, both of which can be visited on the island.

EATING IN HILO: BEST POKE & SUSHI

MAP P97 & P98

Suisan Fish Market: Take-out *poke* bowls are served with fish from the adjacent ocean – about as close to the source as you can get. *9am-3pm Mon, Tue & Thu-Sat* $

Hilo Bay Cafe: Exceptional contemporary Japanese dining, plus *poke* bowls, in a sleek modern space, with views of Hilo Bay. *11am-2:30pm & 5-8:30pm* $$$

Poke N Sides (p96): Outstanding *poke* bowls with super-fresh fish from this counter joint with outside seating. *10am-3pm Sun-Tue, Thu & Fri, 8am-3pm Sat & Wed* $

Moms Hilo: For fresh sushi rolls done right, with local fish. Nigiri sets and mouthwatering udon hit the spot. *4:30-8:30pm Tue-Sat* $$

BEST SHOPS IN HILO

Basically Books Hawai'i-specialty books on everything from sea life and surfing to cooking and history, plus an excellent selection of maps and travel guides, gifts, toys and souvenirs.

The Knickknackery Go digging for Hawaiiana and retro collectibles at this vintage and eclectic store.

Locavore Store Selling 100% locally grown or made food products, this tidy little health food market has most things you need.

Turn the Page Bright and airy bookshop with a great vibe and reading nooks. Packed shelves contain books on almost every subject.

Seaweed Snack & Shop Mainly a cute gift shop, selling things produced by local artisans, also has a great selection of Hawai'i-inspired children's books and fun games such as Kazoo That Tune.

RITU MANOJ JETHANI/SHUTTERSTOCK

Pana'ewa Rainforest Zoo & Gardens

Wildlife in Lush Surrounds

MAP P103

Explore a rainforest zoo

Pana'ewa Rainforest Zoo & Gardens *(hilozoo.org; adult/child/child under 3 $12/5/free)* is the only zoo in the US located inside a rainforest – and it's a delight. Children love exploring the 12 acres of paved pathways, which lead to alligators, tropical birds, a two-toed sloth, marmosets, a giant anteater, monkeys, frogs and a pair of Bengal tigers – an orange one named Sriracha and a white one named Tzatziki. These are just some of the 80 species at the zoo. On Saturdays (between 1:30pm and 2:30pm), guests can go giddy at the cute overload at the petting zoo – offering hands-on encounters with a miniature horse, donkey and pigs, plus chickens, guinea pigs, rabbits and chinchillas. Ask about the snapper, snake and alligator feeding sessions, which happen on Sunday, Tuesday and Thursday (at 11am).

EATING IN HILO: ISLAND-INSPIRED EATS

MAP P97 & P98

Sweet Cane Cafe: Casual farm-to-table. Locally sourced meat-free health food – think mac nut pesto sandwiches and breadfruit burgers. *9am-4pm* **$$**

Café Pesto: Asian-Hawaiian fusion (from Korean garlic bread to coconut calamari) in a large dining room in a historic downtown building. *11am-8:30pm* **$$**

Pineapples: Popular open-air dining room with island-inspired plates, such as coconut-crusted fresh catch and lemon macadamia chicken. *11am-9pm Tue-Sun* **$**

Jackie Rey's Ohana Grill: *Kālua* pork spring rolls, coconut-crusted brie and lobster ravioli with Hawaiian prawns in a chic interior. *11:30am-8:30pm Sun-Fri, from 3pm Sat*

TOP EXPERIENCE

'Imiloa Astronomy Center of Hawai'i

On the University of Hawai'i Hilo campus, the $28-million 'Imiloa Astronomy Center of Hawai'i is housed in an impressive building with conical roofs, containing a museum and planetarium. Exhibits show what we've learned from the stars and night sky throughout history, from ancient Polynesian to modern astronomy on Hawai'i Island's Maunakea summit today. Leave a couple of hours to explore.

Planetarium

The highlight of a visit is a show at the immersive planetarium, where you crane your neck up and watch the mysteries of the night sky unfold as a resident astronomer tells tales of the universe. Shows typically start on the hour and films rotate, including Cosmic Perspectives, covering subjects like the vast scale of the universe and why other lifeforms are most likely out there, but it could take light-years to find them (one light-year equals 10,068 years). Messengers of Time and Space, meanwhile, is a 4K show explaining how observatories monitor the night sky. Check show timings on the website before visiting.

Museum

Exhibitions span ancient Hawaiian traditions to the universe beyond. Learn how Polynesians navigated using the night sky and the historical significance of Maunakea, Hawai'i's highest volcano and a sacred peak with world-class observatories at its summit. Then learn about the story of the sun, how planets change over time, and about recent discoveries in the astronomical world, such as a new distant black hole. Also try hands-on exhibits – build a carbon nanotube, look at a real piece of moon rock launched by an asteroid, and do a puzzle of planets.

TOP TIPS

- Smaller children love the reading corner, filled with games and storybooks about Hawai'i life and the night sky.
- Stop by the terrific gift shop for freeze-dried space food and educational science experiments to take home.
- Next door, the Lehua Restaurant is a smart place for lunch or dinner, serving steaks, fish plates, soba noodles, and 'ahi (yellowfin) katsu.

PRACTICALITIES

- imiloahawaii.org
- adult/child/child under 4 $19/12/free
- 9am-4:30pm Tue-Sun

WALKING TOUR

Stepping Back in Time

Polynesians settled the Hilo area around 1100, and were followed centuries later by Christian missionaries, whalers, and then an influx of immigrants who worked on plantations. Sugar was the biggest industry here for decades. When the plantations closed, Hilo made a tourism push. On this easy 1.2-mile walking tour you'll see several galleries and museums housed in some of the town's historic buildings.

1 S Hata Building

Built by a Japanese businessman in 1912, the S Hata (p99) has a distinctive Renaissance revival style. A row of arched windows bordered with red and blue paint remain on the 2nd floor. The 1st floor contains several independent shops, plus the very good **Café Pesto** (p106).

The Walk: Stroll left around the corner some 500ft along Furneaux La to the AOF Building.

2 AOF Building

Dating to 1925, the AOF Building was named for the Ancient Order of Foresters, a friendly society or brotherhood that invests the funds of its members (King Kalākaua was a member). The striking building with its decorative columns and balcony survived two tsunamis and now houses **Perfect Harmony Boutique & Tea Room**.

The Walk: Head north on Keawe St and turn right on Haili St to the Palace Theater.

3 Palace Theater

Dating from 1925, Hilo's cultural hub (p103) beams with resplendent original features, including a beaux arts–style auditorium and a refurbished organ (still used for silent movie screenings).

DOUGLAS ZIMMERMAN/SHUTTERSTOCK

Pacific Tsunami Museum

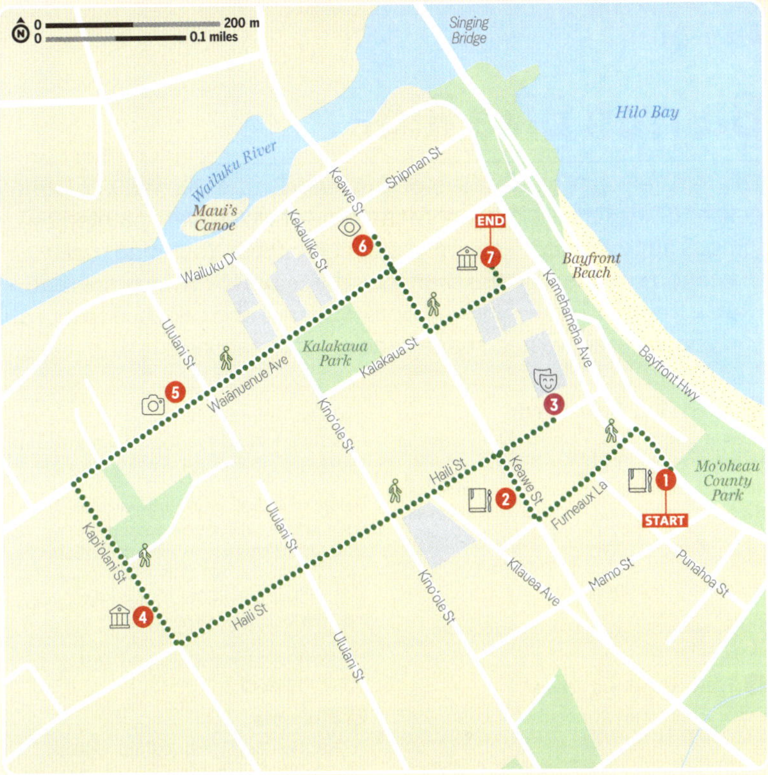

The Walk: Go west up the hill on Haili St for a third of a mile to Mission House.

❹ Mission House

Hawai'i's oldest remaining wooden structure, a two-story plantation-style house (p112), dates to 1839. The original layout has been painstakingly renovated with rich wood floors and antique furniture. The terrific Lyman Museum next door is not to be missed; it offers tours of the house.

The Walk: Turn left at the Lyman Museum on Kapi'olani St and turn right on Waiānuenue Ave before stopping at Hilo Public Library.

❺ The Naha Stone

Legend holds that the person who could move this 3.5-ton stone would be strong enough to defeat (and unite) the Hawaiian Islands. The revered King Kamehameha did exactly this when he was in his 20s, and the prophecy was set.

The Walk: Head east on Waiānuenue Ave for 1000ft to the next stop.

❻ Kaikodo Building

Dating to 1908 and built with then-high-tech 'fireproof' steel beams on reinforced concrete, this was home to Hilo's first Masonic Lodge. It's now **Jackie Rey's Ohana Grill** (p106), but a huge bank vault remains inside the restaurant.

The Walk: Wander right on Keawe St before turning left on Kalakaua St to reach the Pacific Tsunami Museum.

❼ Pacific Tsunami Museum

The Bishop National Bank building – a solid hunk of cast stone and reinforced concrete with an art deco edifice and fluted columns (designed by Hawaiian architect Charles W Dickey) may not be the prettiest place in Hilo, but it sure does its job. It was built to withstand great force in 1930 and has survived two tsunamis, despite being in their direct path on the beachfront. There's no better place for the Pacific Tsunami Museum (p96) to be located.

BIKE TOUR

Banyan Bike Ride

This leisurely 2-mile bike ride along Banyan Dr, the Hilo Walk of Fame, passes 50 distinctive banyan trees (many of which were planted by famous authors, local Hawaiians and celebrities). You'll ride under the canopy of trees, whose branches drape down towards the road. Dating from 1933, they survived both tsunamis and continue to morph and change their twisted shapes and root formations.

1 Reeds Bay Beach Park

Rent a bike at Big Pacific Wheels or via HiBike, Hawai'i's bike-sharing scheme. Start at Reeds Bay Beach Park (p102) on the southeastern side of Banyan Dr, a lovely hangout spot with grassy nooks and picnic benches overlooking a calm water enclave good for paddleboarding.

The Route: Begin cycling counter-clockwise along Banyan Dr.

2 Trees Glorious Trees

Cycle under the atmospheric canopy of sprawling prop roots, which dangle towards the road, almost touching cyclists as they pass. Stop to read the plaques on trees planted by musician Louis Armstrong, baseball legend George Herman 'Babe' Ruth and adventurer Amelia Earhart.

Detour: Hula Grill, inside the Grand Naniloa Hotel, serves cocktails overlooking the bay in a retro space (live music Wednesday to Saturday from 7pm). To the right of the lobby, visitors can book a future waterfall or Maunakea stargazing tour with KapohoKine Adventures.

The Route: Continue on Banyan Dr to Coconut Island off Kelipio Pl.

3 Mokuola

Mokuola, commonly called Coconut Island (p99), is a tranquil county park with picnic tables and beaches for swimming,

GARY GILARDI/SHUTTERSTOCK

Lili'uokalani Gardens

but it was once a residential area named Waiakea Town. Tragedy struck in 1960 when a tsunami producing waves almost as high as palm trees crashed over the island, destroying the houses. Luckily, residents evacuated in time.

The Route: Dock/lock your bike to explore the neighboring Lili'uokalani Gardens.

4 Lili'uokalani Gardens

Possibly Hilo's most beautiful green spot, these sprawling 24-acre Japanese gardens were built as a tribute to immigrants who worked in the sugar industry. The charming footbridges, rock gardens, pagodas, statues and ornamental ponds are free to wander.

The Route: For ocean views, take the back road along Liniwai St towards Hilo Bay Cafe and Suisan Fish Market.

5 Hilo Bay Cafe

Don't miss a meal at the Hilo Bay Cafe (p105), serving uber-fresh sashimi with delicious yuzu sauce, creative sushi rolls and crispy salads in a smart modern dining room with views over the bay. Or get a heaped bowl of mouth-watering takeout *poke* from **Suisan Fish Market** (p105) to enjoy at Lili'uokalani Gardens.

The Route: Finish the loop by turning left along Kamehameha Ave (or skip the traffic and walk on the sidewalk for a few minutes to the next stop), at the mouth of the Wailoa Boat Harbour.

6 Tsunami Clock of Doom

Traveling east along Kamehameha Ave, stop at this historic clock face, which once told the time at the Waiakea School. It now stands here, hands frozen in time, at 1:04am, marking the early-morning tsunami that decimated Hilo in 1960, killing 61 people.

TOP EXPERIENCE

Lyman Museum

The Lyman Museum is the only Hawai'i Island museum dedicated to Hawaiian history, telling the story through the natural world and its inhabitants. It was envisioned by the relatives of New England missionaries David and Sarah Lyman, who lived in Mission House next door, now the oldest remaining wooden structure in Hawai'i.

RICHARD CUMMINS/ALAMY

TOP TIPS

- Book the Mission House tour ahead of time via the website. Only five people are allowed on tours at a time.
- Stop at the museum shop to avoid the replicas and fake Hawaiian crafts often found in tourist shops. It has curated pieces by local artisans, who receive the proceeds.

PRACTICALITIES

- lymanmuseum.org
- adult/child $7/2
- 10am-4:30pm Mon-Fri

Earth Heritage Gallery

Walk through a lava tube with displays of all the different types of lava forms on Hawai'i Island, and explore a seriously impressive tropical shell collection, pulling open drawers lined with the spiky, knobbly, colorful former mollusks' homes. Equally astounding is the mineral, crystal and gemstone collection, with hundreds of items arranged by their raw shapes atop hexagonal display columns. Exhibits also explain the geological makeup of Hawai'i Island, the youngest island in Hawai'i's chain, formed by volcanoes to create mountain alpine, subalpine, montane, rainforest, plus beach and reefs habitats.

Island Heritage Gallery

The museum's 2nd floor is dedicated to the people of Hawai'i and their culture, from the food brought by Polynesian settlers to Hawai'i's great ocean voyages. A section on Hawai'i's monarchs tells the story of the kings and queens who ruled Hawai'i, and you can learn how the plantation era drastically changed it.

Mission House

Next to the museum is the oldest remaining wooden structure (1839) in the state of Hawai'i. The striking veranda-wrapped white-and-green house was built by missionaries David and Sarah Lyman, who traveled from New England to Hawai'i in 1832. Tours run three times a day (adult/child $3/1) through the property's fabled rooms.

PUNA DISCOVERY DRIVE

Mini arty villages sit in one of the island's most active rift zones, where tropical plant life grows between rugged lava and turquoise ocean meets jet-black sand.

START	END	LENGTH
Hilo	Kaimū Black Sand Beach	32 miles; 3hr

Drive south from ❶ **Hilo** past a series of former sugar plantations. Paradise is sweetest when earned, so detour off the main road east, along Kaloai Rd, and onto Beach Rd, get out of the car, and embark on a demanding trek to the pristine Hā'ena Beach in a protected cove. Access is via the 2.5-mile muddy, jungly ❷ **Puna Trail**. You'll likely have this slice of perfection to yourself (best enjoyed at low tide).

Further south, the popular ❸ **Maku'u Farmers Market** *(makuu.org)* takes place on Sunday mornings. Enjoy live music while sampling fresh Hawaiian, Mexican and Thai *grinds*. Further south on Pohoa Bypass Rd, ❹ **Pāhoa** has a colorful bohemian edge with a ramshackle main street, gift shops and cafes to visit. Not far from here, ❺ **Leilani Estates** was a community destroyed by volcanic activity in 2018. Book a local tour of Fissure 8 *(f8va.com; entry $15)*, where lava rose from the earth, and hear stories from a resident whose house was swallowed up by the molten magma. Further on, the rocky, picturesque ❻ **Pohoiki Beach** (Isaac Hale Beach Park) was once a popular local surf spot, but thanks to the Puna eruption, it is now a dramatic black-sand beach. Waters here are too rough for swimming, so instead of swimming at beautiful black-sand ❼ **Kehena Beach**, tucked beneath a cliff, drive south and walk the tropical path to the quiet new ❽ **Kaimū Black Sand Beach**.

Puna

LAVA TUBES | ARTIST COMMUNITY | BLACK BEACHES

GETTING AROUND

The Hele-On Bus network goes south from Hilo along Rte 11, but having your own wheels allows you to discover the furthest corners of the area.

TOP TIPS

It's incredibly rare for anyone to be harmed by lava flow in this area, due to volcanic activity being predicted in advance, areas being cordoned off early, and the lava being very slow-flowing (meaning plenty of time to evacuate). Still, it pays to be aware that you're travelling in a volcano zone and to pay attention to local news about foreseeable activity. Bring sturdy footwear if you're planning on hiking over natural lava formations or visiting lava tubes, as it can be sharp.

Hawai'i's isolated eastern corner is home to a free-spirited community of artists, alternative healers, activists, *pakalōlō* (marijuana) organic farmers and those who like living off-grid. 'Punatics' is the local nickname for these folks, which they affectionately embrace. Puna has some of the more affordable real estate on the island, thanks in part to it sitting in one of the most dangerous lava hazard zones, the rift zone of Kīlauea and Maunaloa. Eruptions have devastated residential zones on numerous occasions; in 2018 the gated residential community of Leilani Estates had 24 active volcanic fissures, spewing red hot lava, and destroying around 700 properties. The cooled lava can be seen all over the landscape. This lesser-visited area of Hawai'i Island is a chance to explore lava tubes, visit empty black sandy beaches and discover an artistic community.

Journey into the Longest Lava Tube

Going underground

Descending into the 500-year-old Kazumura Cave, measuring more than 41 miles long, is an otherworldly experience, especially with local guide Steve Krucker, who has gone to areas of the cave where no other humans have ventured, and spent more than two decades exploring and studying the peculiar formations inside the tube. On his **Kīlauea Caverns of Fire** tours *(kilaueacavernsoffire.com; per person from $39; pre-booking essential),* visitors can choose from three types of adventure – an easy Walking Tour into a section of the tube (around 500ft; one hour); the Adventure Tour (around 1 mile; three hours), which requires using a 16ft ladder, climbing up stacks of lava and ducking under small sections; or the Day in the Cave Tour (5 to 6 miles) for full immersion and a long walk into the pitch black with the chance to see all kinds of

JADE BREMNER

Kīlauea Caverns of Fire

lava-tube configurations in the cave, which impresses both in its scale and its naturally chiseled perfection. Visit an area Steve has named Willy Wonka Lava, which appears like melted chocolate. And see 'Shark Tooth' ceilings and geological features like the 'Rock Lobster,' which looks like a creature from the deep, and 'Big Pile,' a giant heap of volcanic rock you have to climb to get into the next section of lava tube. Each tour starts by entering a *kipuka* (light hole) surrounded by tropical foliage. Wear long pants and walking boots.

HELP ME PICK:

Waterfalls of the East

Welcome to one of the most waterfall-rich regions in the Hawaiian archipelago, where lush rainforests, dramatic cliffs and year-round rainfall create hundreds of cascades. Some waterfalls invite you to take a dip, others are best admired from scenic lookouts, while others offer full-on adrenaline-filled activities.

Where to Go if You Like...

Swimming

Set in a tropical, less-developed area, the free-to-visit **Wai'ale Falls** (p100; pictured below) is the one for confident swimmers looking for a natural, refreshing dip. Reached by a short jungle hike (sometimes a little wading through a river, depending on water levels), it's suited for all levels of swimmers – those who just want a paddle or those who want to feel the rush of the voluminous cascade up close. There are no lifeguards here, so don't swim beyond your ability and always check for flash flood warnings before you visit. You may see locals climbing the rocks and jumping in here; refrain from joining them – it's dangerous.

JOE FERRER/SHUTTERSTOCK

MARYNAG/SHUTTERSTOCK

Views

For sheer visual impact, **'Hi'ilawe Waterfall** (p134), set in the sacred Waipi'o Valley, is one of Hawai'i's tallest, dropping around 1450ft. It's best admired after rainfall and can only be reached with a local or during a shuttle tour into the valley (which needs to be booked ahead of time). **'Akaka Falls** (p118), meanwhile, is accessed by a short, well-maintained loop trail (pictured above) inside a state park and plunges dramatically into a gorge for a classic waterfall view. Don't forget to pause to admire the jungle of tropical plants en route.

Water Activities

The vertigo-immune can take the adrenaline up a notch by donning a hard hat and a harness and rappelling 120ft down the **Kulaniapia Falls** (p104), set on pristine jungle-filled private land. Those who join the thrilling rappelling tour can also go swimming in the pool below, do a lush river hike, or try paddleboarding at the same waterfall. Nearby triple-tier **Umauma Falls** (p121) adds more fun with kayaking, ziplining and scenic trails.

Photos

The dramatic Kamae'e Falls hidden on the grounds of **Botanical World Adventures** (p123) is fed by a lava tube, and creates a stream that meanders through an emerald-green valley among giant boulders and dynamic lava-rock formations. From the viewing platform, capture fast-moving water compositions. Come early to snap a picture of the arc of colors at the aptly named **Rainbow Falls** (p100), as the light hits the falls in the morning – it's an easy waterfall to visit and find outside Hilo town.

Rainbow Falls (p100)

HOW TO

Avoid the crowds
Visit early in the morning for fewer tourists and better light, especially at Rainbow and ʻAkaka Falls.

Swim safely
Check the rainfall levels; heavy rain boosts flow (great for photos) but can make swimming less safe.

Book ahead
Many Hawaiʻi Island waterfalls require pre-booking and access fees. Activities may cost extra and require guides.

Bring the right gear
Bring reef shoes if you plan on swimming or hiking; bring insect repellent, sunscreen and a light rain jacket year-round.

Self-Guided or With a Tour

Tours can quickly add up in Hawaiʻi, taking up a significant chunk of your vacation budget. Many of Hawaiʻi Island's most tropical waterfalls are on private land – meaning there is likely an entry charge or they are only accessible via a guided tour.

For those on a budget, go self-guided, but you may have to battle with crowds; these sites are popular for a reason, due to their iconic, accessible cascades. ʻAkaka and Rainbow Falls are budget-friendly, easy to combine with scenic drives, and good for short visits, though you'll mostly miss out on experiences like swimming and water activities. Those who are a little more adventurous can visit the free Waiʻale Falls, which requires a little hiking and wading to reach, but when there, you can swim, and on weekdays will likely have the place to yourself.

Adventure tours at Kulaniapia or Umauma suit travellers with more disposable cash who are seeking hands-on experiences like rappelling or paddleboarding. They offer a unique experience in nature and the chance to stay longer at the waterfalls. However, costs can be much higher and schedules fixed. Swimming-focused exploration is best for confident swimmers who are able to monitor weather and water conditions closely – it's a more immersive experience but there's always risk. Those wanting to take excellent waterfall pictures should allow extra time for the right light and weather conditions, especially at Rainbow Falls.

Honomū, Hakalau & Laupāhoehoe

WATERFALLS & COASTAL SCENERY | OUTDOOR ADVENTURE | HISTORY

GETTING AROUND

Hele-On Bus services run along Hwy 19, stopping at Hawai'i Island's northwest towns. For the most flexibility and to discover remoter sights a car is needed.

The towns and settlements dotted off Hawai'i Belt Rd and the Old Māmalahoa Hwy were booming during Hawai'i Island's plantation era. They operated alongside the island's railway and the once-bustling port of Laupāhoehoe, which transported sugar from the fields to Hilo. These are now tiny residential communities that happen to be near incredible scenery, including the soaring rainforest-shrouded 442ft 'Akaka Falls. The falls are moments from the little town of Honomū, with its pretty cluster of original Western-style sugar town buildings, adopted and turned into charming cafes and boutique shops. The northeast's many picturesque communities now cater to adventurers who can ride miles of ziplines through tropical forests and over waterfalls up to 250ft high, or hike and horseback on the high slopes of Maunakea to natural swimming holes fit for paddleboarding and kayaking.

TOP TIP

Book ziplining and horse-riding waterfall tours in advance (online or by phone), since these have limited spaces and book up fast in peak season. Take a rain jacket for wet weather, but don't be tempted to cancel – ziplines are faster and arguably more thrilling in the rain.

Giant Free-Flowing Waterfall

Outstanding state park

Two miles west of Honomū is the family-friendly **'Akaka Falls State Park** *(hawaiistateparks.org; $5)*, which has two rushing waterfalls – the 100ft **Kahuna Falls**, clasped by dense rainforest; and the epic 442ft **'Akaka Falls**, plunging into a moss-lined bowl and emerald pool, which some locals consider to be the highest free-flowing waterfall in Hawai'i. Both cascades are accessed by an easy half-mile counterclockwise paved loop (roughly 20-minute walk), rising and falling via several stairways through a vast array of flora, including massive monstera leaves, vines, orchids, ferns, hibiscus, *ōhelo* (native shrub), bright *pua lehua* flowers and sprawling banyan trees with mazes of vertical roots.

HIGHLIGHTS
1 'Akaka Falls State Park
2 Botanical World Adventures
3 Hawai'i Tropical Bioreserve & Garden

SIGHTS
4 Laupāhoehoe Point Beach Park
5 Laupahoehoe Train Museum

ACTIVITIES
6 Hawaii Zipline Tours
7 Umauma Experience
8 Wailea Horseback Adventures

SLEEPING
9 Akiko's Buddhist B&B
10 Hamakua Guesthouse & Camping Cabanas
11 Honomu Inn

EATING
12 Big Island Birria Boss
13 Honomu Goat Dairy
14 Mr Ed's Bakery
15 The Hive

SHOPPING
16 Annie Lou's
17 Hamakua Toffee Company
18 Vintage Hawaiian Wood

The waterfalls are caused by streams running down from the Maunakea volcano, rising 13,796ft above sea level and measuring 33,476ft from the ocean floor – technically making it taller than Everest from the base up. Water has eroded the ash and basalt slopes for thousands of years to forge deep, narrow gulches. Upon reaching ledges and steep drops they create tumbling and often spectacular cascades. The mighty 'Akaka Falls is the highest on the Kolekole Stream, which starts at lofty elevations on Maunakea and passes by the town of Honomū before spilling out into the Pacific Ocean below.

Some 200,000 people visit the park annually, and the parking lot can get busy – expect to wait in line. You can avoid paying by parking on the road just outside the parking lot. The falls face eastward – sunlight is best in the morning for photos.

FLORA & FAUNA SPOTTING

While ziplining, your Hawaii Zipline Tours guide will likely point out pineapple trees, pink lemons, mangosteen and banana trees in the foliage (with the opportunity to try sweet apple bananas en route). Instructors recount fascinating facts about Hawaiian plant and animal life. The yellow hibiscus state flower, grown on the farm, is worn by local women behind their right ear if they are looking for love, while *kō* (a perennial grass), dubbed the Hawaiian Christmas tree (due to the shape of its flower), also grows here. The latter was eaten during famines and used for its medicinal properties by ancient Hawaiians. Keep your eyes peeled for the *pua'a* (pig), first brought to the island chain by Polynesian settlers in 500 to 750 CE. When zooming over the rainforests it's also possible to spy flying endangered Hawaiian hawks, which only live on Hawai'i Island.

ELITE_PROGRESS/SHUTTERSTOCK

Jungle Thrills

Zip through the countryside

Numerous other beautiful waterfalls lie around the town of Honomū. These are dotted along the tributaries running from the high slopes of Maunakea to the Pacific Ocean, along the Kolekole Stream and Pahe'ehee Stream. The problem for visitors is access – they are often surrounded by dense rainforests and private land.

Luckily for us, entrepreneurial companies like **Hawaii Zipline Tours** *(hawaiizipline.tours; adult/child from $225/210),* on Old Māmalahoa Hwy, have struck up deals with local owners to build unobtrusive and thrilling ziplines on a nearby working agricultural farm, where visitors can zoom along seven lines or hike to three waterfalls, one with a swimming hole, as part of an exceptionally run guided tour. The finale of the zipline tour is a half-mile white-knuckle ride over dense, seemingly impenetrable rainforest above the top of the 250ft **Kolekole Waterfall**, which tips down a lime-green cliff into a deep pool. The two-hour experience starts with a couple of tame short ziplines over farmland and then more thrilling ziplines, requiring you to climb tall launch towers, as you progress – including the wire over **Wailele Falls**

Kolekole Waterfall

(another contender for the tallest free-flowing waterfall in Hawai'i, along with 'Akaka Falls – this one reportedly has a single 1201ft free-flow drop).

Nearby, the **Umauma Experience** *(umaumaexperience.com; adult/child from $249/239)* has nine ziplines over 2 miles of wire, crossing 14 rushing waterfalls, and traveling up to 65mph in the fastest sections. Zipline and kayak, rappelling, and ATV adventures are also available separately or as part of longer combo tours.

Ride Paniolo-Style

Adventures by horseback

See views of the Pacific, historic plantations, lush tropical foliage, the Umauma River, and Maunakea in the distance, as folks did in the old days, with **Wailea Horseback Adventures** *(waileahorsebackadventure.com; guided rides from $145; pre-booking required)*. This friendly operator offers two-hour adventures on private land, riding Hawaiian *paniolo*-style through the countryside. Stop for a picnic in the surroundings, then finish at Umauma Falls, where there's an option for a refreshing swim and paddleboard in the natural pool's refreshing waters at the bottom of the hidden cascade.

GHOSTS OF THE HAWAIIAN RAILROAD

Most lines were dismantled after Hawai'i Island's 1946 tsunami, and fanatics can go in search of signs of Hawai'i's sugar plantation railroad, says **Lisa Barton**, curator at Laupahoehoe Train Museum. *@laupahoehoe_train_museum*

Roundhouse Behind Kawamoto pool in Hilo, view the eight-bay structure that used to store locomotives.

Mahukona This beautiful South Kohala campground was once the location of the Hawaiian Railway terminus building.

Old trestle sites Bridge supports and foundations can be found on Belt Rd (Rte 19) near streams like Hakalau and Nānue.

Honu'apo Near Na'alehu on Hwy 11, find old pier pilings and building foundations from the plantation line.

Hāmākua Heritage Coast Driving this coast, retrace the old railway route, with bridges, lush pleated valleys, and soaring ocean views.

BEST GIFT SHOPS

Glass from the Past Thousands of vintage bottles and glass items of all shapes, sizes and colors in Honomū.

Vintage Hawaiian Wood Extraordinary collection of handcrafted koa (Hawaiian timber) pieces, from rocking chairs to weapons with jagged edges and classic bowls.

Annie Lou's Funky Western clothing shop, selling boots, bags, hats and fun gifts on Honomū's main street.

Laupahoehoe Train Museum Shop For a whole selection of train memorabilia, including toy trains, books, puzzles and games, including many vintage models.

Hamakua Toffee Company Come here to try salivatingly good Hawaiian macadamia nut butter toffee, made from a recipe dating back five generations.

ANDRE JENNY/ALAMY

Laupahoehoe Train Museum

Hawai'i Island's Doomed Railway

Trains and coastal scenery in Laupāhoehoe

On the road to Waipi'o Valley, stop in at the **Laupahoehoe Train Museum** *(thetrainmuseum.com; adult/child $10/5)* to learn about Hawai'i Island's failed railway, which met its end after the 1946 tsunami destroyed it beyond repair. Once considered Hawai'i's great engineering feat, the 34-mile railway was completed in 1913, costing a million dollars. It had 44 bridges, crossed 150 streams, and included one particularly splendid 230ft bridge – built on steel beams over the Hakalau Gulch. Riding the train was a delight, passing waterfalls, plantations, gorges, tropical trees and surf-ravaged coastlines.

The museum (open 10am to 2pm Monday to Saturday), housed in an old station agent's house, is chock-full of memorabilia and photographs from the 1900s, plus a model train room for railway aficionados. A video allows visitors to see what it would have been like aboard the fabled train.

Afterwards continue on to **Laupāhoehoe Point**. The thrilling winding road goes through dense jungle to a strikingly pretty jagged volcanic coastline, with deep blue waters crashing onto shore. The fierce surf makes it unsuitable for swimming so pack a picnic instead.

EATING IN HONOMŪ: BEST BITES

Mr Ed's Bakery: An old-fashioned counter joint filled with freshly baked pastries like guava bear claws and sweet monkey bread. *7:30am-5pm Mon-Sat, from 10am Sun* $

The Hive: Part coffee shop, part healthy cafe serving sublime flower-topped salads and chunky sourdough sandwiches. *9am-5pm Tue-Sat, to 4pm Sun* $

Honomu Goat Dairy: Working farm serving up homemade cheese and award-winning milk caramels, plus fresh goat-milk fudge. *10am-5pm Sat & Sun* $

Big Island Birria Boss: Casual joint for a taco and nacho fix after a zipline adventure or visit to 'Akaka Falls. *11am-5pm* $

TOP EXPERIENCE

Botanical Gardens

Two sprawling gardens are located a short drive outside Hilo. Botanical World Adventures covers hundreds of acres with tropical trees, shrubs and perennial plants. There's also a cactus garden, a waterfall, ziplines and a full hedge maze. Hawai'i Tropical Bioreserve & Garden, meanwhile, is a 17-acre living museum with a 1.25-mile walking trail that descends deep into a thick rainforest. Stop for orchids, butterflies, exotic fruit, waterfalls, and ocean views.

Maze, Waterfall & Tropical Gardens

The massive grounds at Botanical World Adventures include dozens of fruit trees (visitors can help themselves to fruit they find, with help from a resident 'fruit picker'), plus a self-guided walk through a shrubbery maze, and **Rainforest Trail** with up to 2mi of empty trails winding though the tropical grounds. Also a short drive from reception is the less frequently visited 100ft **Kamae'e Falls**. You can up the ante with a Segway (from $197) or go ziplining (adult/child $227/197) on a course with a suspension bridge, a Jurassic 300ft gorge and a hidden 250ft waterfall.

Lush Rainforest

At Hawai'i Tropical Bioreserve & Garden it's all about being fully immersed in the jungle, with its atmospheric raised boardwalk dropping 100ft over 500ft, with tropical trees and ferns all around. On the **Palm Jungle Trail**, coconut palms soar some 80ft up. Spy the trickling twin **Onomea Waterfalls**, surrounded by emerald moss and fern-covered rocks, then visit **Torch Ginger Trail** and **Orchid Garden**, home to some seriously vibrant plants, so vivid and wacky they could have been plucked from a fantasy flick. Nearby **Turtle Point** (also known as Crab Cove) is a nesting site for endangered green sea turtles and hawksbill turtles, and offers the rare chance to see them from a viewing platform during nesting season.

TOP TIPS

- Go on a rainy day – rainforests thrive in the rain and some say plants appear even more vibrant in wet conditions (Tropical Bioreserve has umbrellas to rent and ponchos to buy).
- Wear hiking boots or closed-toe shoes, especially in wet weather. Bring insect repellent.

PRACTICALITIES

Botanical World Adventures
● botanicalworld.com ● adult/child/child under 5 $15/5/free ● 8am-5pm

Hawai'i Tropical Bioreserve & Garden
● htbg.com ● adult/child/child under 6 $35/25/free ● 10am-6pm, last entry 5pm

DRIVING TOUR

Pāpa'ikou to Waipi'o Valley

Soak up the rugged beauty of the Hāmākua Coast on an exhilarating 43-mile drive from Pāpa'ikou, a small town just north of Hilo, to the verdant Waipi'o Valley, with its rich pleated valleys. Combine the Old Māmalahoa Hwy with the new Māmalahoa Hwy (known as Hawai'i Belt Rd) to cruise past jungles, rivers and pounding surf and through quaint towns, and stop for a host of adventures en route.

1 Pāpa'ikou to Honomū

Join the Old Māmalahoa Hwy in Pāpa'ikou as it veers off into lush narrow road with steep rainforest banks and crosses single-lane bridges and the Aleamai, Kaiee and Kalaoa streams. The foliage thickens and the air becomes moist while nearing the Onomea Bay Trail (a worthwhile mile-long ramble into the Onomea Valley with striking views of the Hāmākua Coast). Stop in at the **Hawai'i Tropical Bioreserve & Garden** (p123), before continuing the drive past coconut palms and wild fauna, crossing the Kawainui Stream over a wooden single-track bridge.

The Drive: Cross Hawai'i Belt Rd and travel 4.3 miles along the Old Māmalahoa Hwy to Honomū.

2 Honomū

Cruise through the old sugar town of Honomū with its pastel-colored storefronts and gift shops. Don't leave without a jar of local fruit jam from **Mr Ed's Bakery** (p122); popular varieties include *liliko'i* (passion fruit), banana-coconut and jackfruit flavor. From here the scenery turns from jungle and town to farmland.

The Drive: Dip back onto Hawai'i Belt Rd, head north, and join the Old Māmalahoa Hwy to the west, just beyond Hakalau Bay. Follow for 3.4 miles.

FOMINAYAPHOTO/SHUTTERSTOCK

Waipi'o Valley Lookout

3 Hakalau & Umauma

Along Hawai'i Belt Rd, look out for magnificent views of the lush hillsides flanking Hakalau Stream, where a long bridge crosses a deep ravine with beautiful valley and ocean views. Wind back onto the Old Māmalahoa Hwy to **Botanical World Adventures** (p123), where ziplines zoom over the Kama'e'e Falls. The nearby Umauma River offers more adventures.

The Drive: Continue on the Māmalahoa Hwy and rejoin Hawai'i Belt Rd at Ninole to Laupāhoehoe Point, some 10.6 miles away.

4 Laupāhoehoe Point

Sea views appear beyond the small settlements of Ninole, Papa'aloa and Weloka along Hawai'i Belt Rd towards Laupāhoehoe. Stop in at the informative **Laupahoehoe Train Museum** (p122), which tells the story of a railroad that was never to last, thanks to the 1946 tsunami. Then continue to windy, rugged **Laupāhoehoe Point** (p122).

The Drive: Rejoin Hawai'i Belt Rd for a 16.7-mile drive through thick fragrant forests towards the town of Honoka'a, where you join Ohia St.

5 Honoka'a

Reaching Honoka'a (p126) is like stepping back in time, with well-maintained clapboard shop fronts painted in subdued tones, and protected landmarks. Antique shops, cafes and restaurants with vintage fronts line tiny-but-happening Mamane St.

The Drive: The final stretch to Waipi'o Valley is an 8.7-mile cruise along an elevated section of the Waipi'o Rd (Hwy 240), with clearings in the trees offering views of the ocean some 700ft below.

6 Waipi'o Valley Lookout

A soaring view over the **Waipi'o Valley** awaits at the end of Hwy 240. The spectacular natural amphitheater covered in lush jungle forms part of seven valleys on the windward side of Kohala Mountains.

Honoka'a

HISTORIC TOWN | BOUTIQUES & ANTIQUES | FARMERS MARKETS & FESTIVALS

GETTING AROUND

Hele-On Bus services run from Hilo to Honoka'a each day. The little town is walkable with sidewalks and a vibrant main street, but further afield a car is needed.

TOP TIP

Visit Honoka'a early in the day (but not too early) – most places including restaurants and shops open around noon and close their doors by 6pm, with the exception of Honoka'a's Public House, open until at least 9pm most days.

It's hard to believe that laid-back Honoka'a, with its small cluster of old pastel-colored, wooden, Western-style buildings, was once the third-largest town in Hawai'i, after Hilo and Honolulu. This formerly thriving sugar and farming town had a diverse community of Hawaiians and Japanese, American, Chinese and Portuguese immigrants, but dwindled in size following the closing of the plantations in the 20th century – Honoka'a Sugar Company's last harvest was in 1993. Today, it serves nearby farmers and has become a charming historic tourist stop on the way to Waipi'o Valley. Its main street, Mamane St, is dotted with quirky boutique and antique shops, plus places to try farm-fresh produce. Stop for a show at the Honoka'a People's Theatre or visit during big community events, like the Hāmākua Harvest Farmers Market on Sunday mornings and the annual Honoka'a Western Week, to indulge in local life.

Honoka'a's Story

Local history museum

The go-to place to understand the little town of Honoka'a and its surrounding areas is the free **NHERC Heritage Center** *(honokaaheritagecenter.org; suggested donation per visitor $8)*. Staffed by knowledgeable, friendly volunteers, the center has detailed info boards and dozens of antique artifacts: an old Singer sewing machine, a 1940s TV, an early 1900s Victrola record player, plus original plantation tools, ornate Japanese dolls, and a full case of weapons confiscated by the local sheriff. Many historical photos date to the town's booming plantation days, complete with community events and teams (including local baseball and judo clubs).

Exhibitions remember the diverse services that kept the town running, including the lawmakers, the families running hardware stores, and the quirky Bragado Bus Service. Exhibitions also tell the story of the nearby Waipi'o Valley. The center is open 9am to 4pm Monday to Friday, and 9am to 1pm Saturday.

SIGHTS
1 Katsu Goto Memorial
2 NHERC Heritage Center

EATING
3 Cafe il Mondo
4 Fish and Things
5 Harmoni Foods

DRINKING & NIGHTLIFE
6 Andrade's Honokaa Cafe
7 Fudge'n Coffee Cafe
8 Honoka'a Public House
9 Lean-To Farm Hawai'i

ENTERTAINMENT
10 Honoka'a People's Theatre
11 Honoka'a Western Week

SHOPPING
12 Beach Dog Books
13 Big Island Grown
14 Cathy's Angelite Crystals
15 Honoka'a Trading Company
16 Revel Artistry Collection

Local Life at the Farmers Market

Fresh produce and community life

Taking place every Sunday morning (9am to 2pm), rain or shine, the terrific **Hāmākua Harvest Farmers Market** *(hamakuaharvest.org)*, around 3.5 miles east of town, is the place to dive into Hawai'i Island community life, with regular entertainment such as live music and occasional talks. A variety of local vendors tout sustainable and locally grown or made produce, including honey, jerky, goat cheese, smoked fish, exotic fruit-infused gelato, tropical tacos and whatever is ripe from residents' gardens. Free (often organic) samples are abundant.

The bigger annual **Farm Fest** takes place at the same location in spring, usually on the first Sunday of **Honoka'a Western Week** *(honokaawesternweek.org)*, with food comps, such as the Portuguese Bean Soup & Smoke Meat contest, plus activities and workshops celebrating *paniolo* (Hawaiian cowboy) culture. The Hawai'i Saddle Club rodeo, *paniolo* parade, block party, line dancing, and a saloon girl contest, plus hula and Hawaiian cultural events, are all a blast.

KATSU GOTO MEMORIAL

Katsu Goto is something of a local legend. The Japanese cane-field worker, who later opened a general store in Honoka'a, was an activist who spoke out against human rights abuses and the exploitation of Japanese field workers. Fluent in English, he often showed up for plantation employees in court. As to be expected, he was deeply unpopular with local plantation bosses, and was tragically lynched by a mob of six men after visiting a local plantation during the night to discuss working conditions with Japanese employees. He was hanged from a telegraph pole in 1889. A large plaque dedicated to Goto in the spot where his body was found can be seen on Mamane St.

DYLAN GARCIA PHOTOGRAPHY/ALAMY

Visit a Historic Pub

Try local beer

There's only one watering hole in town, but it's a goodie. **Honoka'a Public House** *(honokaapub.com)* has taken up residence inside the original wooden historic First Bank of Hilo building, dating to 1910 (although it was moved to its present location in 1927). Its cabin-like setting is brimming with local charm. The bar serves more than half a dozen craft beers, including Hawai'i tipples, cocktails, and Coconut Hiwa Porter and Hana Hou Hefeweizen on tap. Accompany beverages with a whole host of American eats – burgers, sandwiches, smoked meat and pizzas (including its roast beef *paniolo* pizza and the infamous breakfast pies, known to have been served on Sunday mornings). Open 11am to 9pm Wednesday to Sunday.

Chocolate Farm Tour

Orchard visit and cocoa tastings

A quarter of a mile into the hills above Honoka'a town is this great rainy-day activity: a two-hour orchard tour at **Honoka'a Chocolates** *(honokaachocolateco.com; from $65)* run by California transplants Mike and Rhonda Pollard. You'll

EATING IN HONOKA'A: OUR PICKS

Tex Drive-In: Specializing in hot, fresh *malasadas* (Portuguese-style donuts), *loco moco* and decent plate lunches. *6am-6pm* $

Harmoni Foods: Sensational Korean hole-in-the-wall serving up bibimbap and pork tacos with uber-local farm-fresh ingredients. *noon-7pm Fri & Sat* $

Fish and Things: Basic spot selling a menu with half a dozen items – fresh *poke*, plus tacos and bento. *11am-6pm Tue-Sat* $

Cafe il Mondo: Sit-down dinner and wine are a rarity in these parts, especially in a trattoria-style setting serving pizza and Italian classics. *5pm-7pm Tue-Thu, 11am-6pm Fri & Sat* $$

Honoka'a People's Theatre

take a look around their 5-acre cacao farm, where they grow the beans that make award-winning chocolate, and learn about how the beans are harvested, fermented and dried. At the end of the tour, you'll taste the fresh fruit of a ripe cacao pod and try five exceptional chocolate varieties. Alternatively, the Honoka'a Chocolates factory store on Mamane St sells all the current bars and offers free chocolate tastings, from the sensational pure Hawai'i 85% dark chocolate to the smooth coconut dark milk chocolate and the ridiculously moreish rum-infused chocolate.

Watch a Movie at a Vintage Cinema

Classical revival-style theater

On a rainy day or evening, there's nothing more evocative than watching a movie at the **Honoka'a People's Theatre** *(honokaapeople.com; adult/child $10/6)* a grand old-fashioned classical revival-style theater and the Hawai'i Island's largest outside of Hilo, with more than 500 seats. It was built in 1930, at the height of the Silver Screen era, when it would show Japanese, Portuguese, Filipino and Hollywood blockbuster movies for the area's immigrant populations. Today it shows independent and popular movies on a 50ft screen and turns into an occasional concert venue for local and touring musicians and artists. Check the program online.

Walk in a Secluded Forest

Off-the-beaten-track park

Six miles southeast of Honoka'a, the 100-acre public-access **Kalopa State Recreation Area** *(dlnr.hawaii.gov; free to hike, camp per night $30)* has camping facilities with three

MACADAMIA NUTS

Hawai'i's first macadamia trees were planted in Honoka'a in 1881 by William Purvis, a sugar-plantation manager who brought seedlings from Australia. For 40 years, the trees were grown mainly for ornamental purposes because the nutshells were considered too hard to crack.

Hawai'i's first large-scale commercial macadamia orchard was planted in Honoka'a in 1924. Macadamia nuts have proven to be one of the most commercially viable agricultural crops in Hawai'i, producing around 40 million pounds of them annually. Roughly 700 Hawai'i Island farms plant more than 20,000 acres. Confectionery brands Mauna Loa and Hawaiian Host have some of the largest orchards, containing hundreds of thousands of trees.

BEST HONOKA'A SHOPS

Honoka'a Trading Company Hangar-size store with some seriously cool vintage items, including plenty of Hawaiiana.

Cathy's Angelite Crystals Containing hundreds of gems and stones, including an enormous 1000lb quartz at the center of the store.

Big Island Grown Large array of locally produced gifts and trinkets such as jewelry, stuffed toys and handmade soaps.

Beach Dog Books Hand-selected books, including local gems, and history books about the area, plus a good selection of books for young readers.

Revel Artistry Collection Locally made jewelry, crafts, clothes, tableware and more in this well-curated store on Mamane St.

NANI WELCH KELI'IHO'OMALU FOR LONELY PLANET

Big Island Grown

shelters for tents, plus restrooms and barbecues (permits required) and a couple of empty trails. The very easy 0.75-mile loop **Native Forest Nature Trail** traverses figs, ferns and old *'ōhi'a lehua* forest – some giant trees have 3ft trunks. The 3.7-mile easy round-trip **Perimeter Horse Trail** (accessible for horses and hikers) climbs 450ft through forest and exotic vegetation and is utterly peaceful – it's unlikely you'll see other tourists. Pick up a trail guide at the info board in the park or at Honoka'a Heritage Center on Mamane St.

Try Everything Vanilla

Afternoon tea and farm tours

Family-run **Hawaiian Vanilla Company** *(hawaiianvanilla.com; tours from $41.50)* is the first commercial vanilla operation in the US. It offers pricey, but saliva-inducing, lunches with fresh produce that foodies go gaga over. But the real draw here is the full afternoon tea experience, with proper tiered cake stands, suitably stacked with a host of vanilla-infused treats: vanilla *lilikoʻi* (passion fruit) pound cake, vanilla banana bread, vanilla bourbon citrus chicken sliders, vanilla sweet bread, and vanilla raspberry sorbet. All washed down with a whole host of Hawaiian Vanilla Vineyard tea blends, naturally.

DRINKING IN HONOKA'A: BEST COFFEE

Lean-To Farm Hawai'i: Best place in town for a cuppa Joe, serving locally grown and roasted Papaaloa Joe coffee, with tropical notes. *7am-1pm Wed-Sun* $

Andrade's Honokaa Cafe: For strong pots of filter coffee and 'boot' beer floats (ice cream served in a hoppy pint in the shape of a boot). *11:30am-4pm Mon-Thu* $

Fudge'n Coffee Cafe: Mom-and-pop shop with coffee, chai lattes and fudge. *10am-3pm Wed-Fri, noon-4pm Sat* $

Honoka'a Country Market: Filter coffee and hearty breakfast burritos are served up at this friendly market, on the way to Waipi'o Valley. *8am-6pm Mon-Sat* $

HONOKA'A ON FOOT

Peer into the past of Hawai'i Island's sugar plantation boom days. Mamane St is lined with wooden plantation-era buildings.

START	END	LENGTH
Our Lady of Lourdes Catholic Church	Hotel Honoka'a Club	.5 miles; 1hr

Begin at ❶ **Our Lady of Lourdes Catholic Church**, a 1927 landmark that traces Honoka'a's roots. A short stroll east along Lehua St is the ❷ **Antone Luce Ferreira Building**, erected in 1927 by Japanese carpenter Kiyoichi Irie. The site once housed a store owned by AS Cleghorn, father of Princess Ka'iulani.

Across the road is ❸ **B Ikeuchi & Sons Hardware**, the oldest continually run family business in town. It still feels like a classic plantation-era hardware store. Continue south to the 1930-built ❹ **Honoka'a People's Theatre** (p129), a still operational grand cinema that became the heart of town life. Films from America, Japan and the Philippines played here.

Just along the road is the ❺ **MS Botelho Building and Garage** (now the Honoka'a Heritage Center). Built in the 1920s by Judge Manuel Silva Botelho, it once housed a Ford and Lincoln showroom. Nearby stands the ❻ **former First Bank of Hilo** building, relocated here in 1927 (now the Honoka'a Public House). It has served as a bank, a law office, a tailor, a bar and even a duplex.

Finish at ❼ **Hotel Honoka'a Club**, a hotel until recently and once a haven for sugar workers, *paniolo* and visiting Marines Laurence Rockefeller reportedly drove over from Kona just to eat its famous *teishoku* meals and lobster dinners.

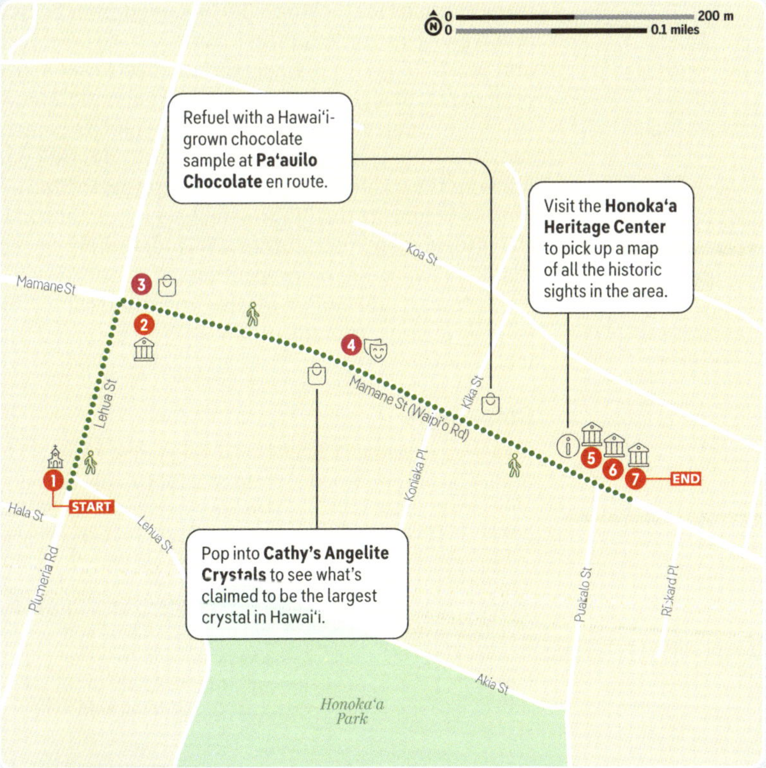

Waipi'o Valley

SCENIC VIEWPOINT | HAWAIIAN SACRED SITE | REMOTE HIKES

Sacred to Native Hawaiians, the 'Valley of the Kings' is a jaw-dropping natural amphitheater, scalloped into verdant emerald cliffs, offering a stunning viewpoint and a challenging (and hard-to-reach) hike. In the 1700s, it was home to King Kamehameha, who was brought to this secluded tropical refuge as a boy to protect him from threats from warring chiefs. In 1791 he led a successful canoe battle, known as the Battle of the Red Mouth Guns, off the coast here, using cannons for the first time (obtained from British and American traders); the invaders were defeated, and fled to Maui. In 1946, a tsunami destroyed many of the ancient sights here, including a temple, structures and ancient taro patches. But Waipi'o's beauty remains intact, luring the curious into an area cut off from the modern world, and tempting adventure seekers to hike its thrilling switchbacks and waterfall-rich gulches. In 2022, authorities indefinitely closed Waipi'o's Valley Rd for 'precautionary safety' reasons. Visitors can no longer access the valley floor by vehicle or foot, though it can still be accessed via local shuttle tours.

GETTING AROUND

Hele-On Bus runs services along Hwy 19, stopping at Hawai'i Island's northwest towns, but these do not connect with the Waipi'o Valley, so a car is needed for the most flexibility and to discover remote sights.

TOP TIP

Plan ahead if you want to do anything more than look at the view. Shuttle tours are the only way in for nonresidents, overnight camping on the hikes requires permits, and the weather can change dramatically.

Epic Views

Clap eyes on Hawai'i Island's most staggering valley

At the end of Hwy 240, the **Waipi'o Valley Lookout** (p125) offers a stunning view of Waipi'o's emerald amphitheater, black-sand beach and pounding surf. Feast your eyes on one of Hawai'i's iconic images. Don't attempt to drive into the valley unless you are with a local with local ID – the single-track Waipi'o' Valley Rd is one of the nation's steepest, with grades reaching up to 45%, and is closed to nonresidents due to safety issues. The car park at the viewpoint is free (some bays have maximum stays of up to 30 minutes); you may have to wait as bays are limited. Views are best during golden hours.

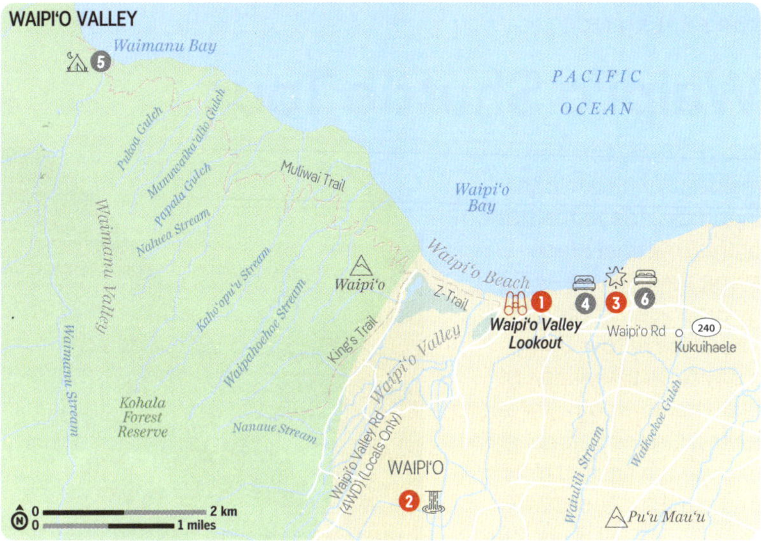

★ **HIGHLIGHTS**
1 Waipi'o Valley Lookout

SIGHTS
2 'Hi'ilawe Waterfall

ACTIVITIES
3 Waipi'o Valley Shuttle Tour

SLEEPING
4 Hale Kukui Orchard
5 Waimanu Valley Campground
6 Waipi'o Lodge

Hike the Valley

Tackle the Muliwai Trail

While the 8.5-mile difficult backcountry Muliwai Trail from Waipi'o Valley to Waimanu Valley is open, it's logistically very difficult to reach if you're not with a local who owns a 4WD – Waipi'o Valley Rd (going down the valley from Waipi'o Lookout) is closed to visitors on foot. One way down to the beach (the trailhead is at its northern end) is to arrange a ride with a local or take the shuttle service.

Due to the trail's lower footfall, prepare for a steep, slippery 1200ft ascent, zigzagging up the side of Waipi'o's western wall, crossing around a dozen gulches (some with waterfalls), through dense tropical plants, and up to a plateau with soaring views. Start very early; it's around a seven-hour hike one way. Otherwise, bring equipment to camp at one of the nine pitches with basic restrooms at the **Waimanu Valley Campground** *(camping.ehawaii.gov; pre-arranged permit required, per night $30)*. Don't attempt the hike before or after it rains.

TOP EXPERIENCE

Waipiʻo Shuttle Tour

The only way for non-residents without local friends to ride to the bottom of this mystical place along Waipiʻo' Valley Rd is by organized shuttle tour. These leave four times a day from the village of Kukuihaele, south of Waipiʻo Valley. On them, local guides explain the sacred history of the valley. Tours vary, but visitors will likely meet wild horses, drive through water-filled roads, and see the 1450ft ʻHiʻilawe Waterfall and beaches below.

JOSHUA WHITCOMB/SHUTTERSTOCK

Wild horses, Waipiʻo Valley

Road into the Valley

The tour takes visitors down the 45%-grade hairpin road (reportedly the steepest of its length in the US) with a cumulative drop of around 1400ft. At its base expect to see herds of wild horses, which are docile and roam free in this unpopulated, naturally contained area free of traffic. In the 1700s, roughly 5000 Hawaiians lived in this fertile valley, sustained by farming, abundant rain and fish. There are fewer than 100 people living here now, in houses entirely off-grid and separated from the modern world. Most residents are taro farmers.

Mysticism of the Area

Shuttle tours cross rivers and follow flooded roads into remote sacred corners. Waipiʻo Valley is considered supernatural for many reasons. Not only was this where the god Lono wooed his beautiful maiden Kaikilani and King Kamehameha I received the war god Ku, but there are numerous other legends. Shuttle guides explain how Waipiʻo's **ʻHiʻilawe Waterfall** is also shrouded in Hawaiian folklore. Forbidden lovers Hiʻilawe and Hakalaoa fled to the remote back Waipiʻo cliffs and prayed for help from the gods to keep them together. The gods answered by transforming Hiʻilawe into a towering 1450ft waterfall and Hakalaoa into the large rock formation at its base. The flow of the water is said to represent Hiʻilawe's eternal tears for her lost love.

TOP TIPS

- Hikers can organize to be dropped off at the bottom of the valley, spend a few hours hiking, then catch a later shuttle back up the mountain.
- Bring rain clothes; it rains more often than not here – the reason it's so lush.
- Pick up Hawaiian timber pieces (from bowls to rocking chairs) plus snacks at Waipiʻo Valley Artworks at the starting point of the tour.

PRACTICALITIES

- waipiovalleyshuttle.com
- adult/child $67/36.50
- departures 9am, 11am, 1pm & 3pm

Places We Love to Stay

$ Budget $$ Midrange $$$ Top End

Hilo

MAP p97, p98 & p103

Arnott's Lodge Best value in Hilo, with safe, clean rooms (private and semi-private) and shared kitchen areas, plus laundry. There's the option to camp on the grounds too. Guests get discounts on Arnott's adventure tours. $

Howzit Hostels The only hostel in Hilo's town, this comfortable hostel has a shared lounge and kitchen, plus free chocolate-chip pancakes and coffee in the mornings. Choose from six- or eight-bed dorms (including one female dorm). $

SCP Hilo Hotel Hilo's best adventure base with motel-turned-boutique rooms, plus free paddleboards, bike rental, a small gym and yoga around the pool. Watch out for the hidden 'amenities fee.' $$

Hale Kai Hawaii B&B with breezy sea views near Honoli'i Beach Park, with one- to three-bedroom condos with kitchens. $$

Hilo Honu Inn Quaint residential house close to Hilo's downtown area, with three tropical and ocean-themed vintage rooms. $$

Pakalana Inn Hidden delight near Hilo Farmers Market, with clean, spacious queens and kings, plus a colorful proprietor, who used to be a guitar virtuoso. $$

Lotus Garden Hilo Jungle chic two-story cottages in downtown Hilo with full kitchens and lots of light. Choose the Mauna studio for stunning design, vaulted ceilings, and a gold-colored standalone tub. $$

Orchid Tree B&B Elegant rooms in a wooden house overlooking surf spot Honoli'i Beach Park Cove. The tropical grounds have a koi pond and swimming pool. $$

Inn at Kulaniapia Falls Immaculate, lush tropical grounds around 5 miles north of Hilo town, with a private waterfall with a natural pool to swim in, walking trails, adventure activities, and farm-to-table dinner. $$

Lo'i B&B One mile out of town, stay amid a tropical jungle, with a waterfall and swimming pond on the grounds. Offers two spacious studios with high ceilings and hardwood floors. $$

Grand Naniloa Resort Hilo's plushest hotel has hundreds of rooms and is a DoubleTree by Hilton hotel, with oceanfront views and lots of facilities, including a restaurant and a lively lobby bar. $$$

Hilo Hawaiian Hotel Adjacent to Lili'uokalani Gardens, with panoramic views of Hilo Bay, this grand dame has operated for half a century and has around 300 well-maintained rooms with touches of kitschy Hawai'i. $$$

Honomū & Hakalau

MAP p119

Hamakua Guesthouse & Camping Cabanas Rustic off-grid guesthouse with B&B rooms in neighboring properties with panoramic Pacific and river views. Two rooms include a king and one with two queen beds (one raised with ladder access). There's also a shared kitchen and barbecue available, plus a shared TV room. $

Akiko's Buddhist B&B No-frills rustic but charming B&B rooms 13 miles north of Hilo, with low Japanese-style beds and shared baths, plus two off-grid studio cottages. $

Honomu Inn Set on a quiet village street, 10 miles north of Hilo, this boutique guesthouse, housed in a historic wood-fronted property, has beautiful well-styled rooms with natural light and airy interiors. There's a communal kitchen, and self-serve breakfasts include bagels, cereal, yogurt and coffee. Some rooms have balconies. $$

Waipi'o

MAP p133

Hale Kukui Orchard One of the few places to stay with actual views of the dramatic Waipi'o Valley. Choose from three cottages with waterfall views from the bed and all amid citrus, banana and papaya-tree-filled grounds. The two-bed cottage has a hot tub on the deck. $$

Waipi'o Lodge Our choice for a place to stay near Waipi'o Valley, this sustainable guesthouse in Kukuihaele has two plush safari-like tents, with wooden decks looking to the Pacific, plus a main house with very comfortable kitsch rooms circling a shared kitchenette and TV room. Bathrooms are shared. Barbecue available. $$

For places to stay in Hawai'i Volcanoes National Park & Ka'ū, see p167

PARA_DISE_PHOTO/SHUTTERSTOCK

Above: Kīlauea volcano (p140); Right: Punalu'u Black Sand Beach Park (p162)

Researched by
Ashley Harrell

Hawai'i Volcanoes National Park & Ka'ū

EXPLOSIVE VOLCANOES, MULTICOLORED BEACHES AND UNDEVELOPED COUNTRYSIDE

For a dramatic reminder that the planet remains under construction, dare to visit Hawai'i's most active volcanoes and the surreal landscapes born of their wrath.

With steaming craters and emerald rainforest, majestic coastline and unearthly deserts, windblown ranches and eccentric artist enclaves, the southern region of the Hawai'i Island is a land of extremes and untamed adventure. At the center, two of the world's most active volcanoes regularly explode into fiery lava fountains and red-hot flows, striking awe (and terror) into the hearts of all who behold them. Whether the lava will be flowing during your visit is difficult to predict, but one aspect of Hawai'i Volcanoes National Park – an International Biosphere Reserve and UNESCO World Heritage Site – remains certain: the mapmakers' jobs are secure.

BILL MCCAY/SHUTTERSTOCK

Over the last few years, the volcanoes have been cranky. Kīlauea (4091ft), the world's youngest volcano and one of its most active, erupted dozens of times in 2024, 2025 and 2026, shooting lava hundreds of feet in the air. Maunaloa (13,679ft), the world's largest active volcano and a beast of a hike, last sprang into action in 2022 after a 38-year hiatus, spewing lava down its flanks and nearly taking out Saddle Road. With some 1.5 million people descending on the volatile national park each year, and a diminished staff due to Trump administration cuts, safety has become a concern. Check for alerts on the park's home page, and consider a detour to the far-flung beaches and rural enchantments of Ka'ū.

THE MAIN AREAS

Find Your Way

Stretching over more than 500 sq miles, the vast Hawai'i Volcanoes National Park is nearly the size of O'ahu. With each eruption there's more new ground to cover, literally, so you're in for quite the adventure.

CAR

You'll need wheels for Hawai'i Volcanoes National Park and Ka'ū, as public transport is extremely limited (and nonexistent inside the park). The park is 30 miles (45 minutes) from Hilo and 95 miles (2¾ hours) from Kailua-Kona via Hwy 11.

BUS

Although geared towards service workers and locals, Hele-On Bus services do reach Volcano, Hawai'i Volcanoes National Park and Ka'ū. They travel between these destinations several times a day, and schedules can be found at heleonbus.hawaiicounty.gov.

Ka'ū, p156
Large ranches and macadamia nut plantations abut forested highlands, and sparse windswept shores punctuated with scenic coves make up the longest uninhabited coastline on the island.

Hawai'i Volcanoes National Park, p140
Captivating hiking trails take in lava flows and tubes, steam vents and wild beaches, while a long, winding downhill drive leads past several major sights.

IV-OLGA/SHUTTERSTOCK

Chain of Craters Road (p145)

Plan Your Time

Prioritize the volcanoes, but build in some downtime for beach-hopping, art appreciating, farm-stand sampling and casual strolling in the rainforest.

Pressed for Time

- Base yourself at a sweet B&B in **Volcano** (p150) and hit up the national park's highlights, including a tour along **Crater Rim Dr** (p146), a crater trek down the **Kīlauea Iki Trail** (p141), and a scenic drive via **Chain of Craters Road** (p145) all the way to the sea. If time allows, take a detour around to **South Point** (p160) to see **Green Sand Beach** (p156).

Five Days to Travel Around

- Hike up the long flanks of **Maunaloa** (p208) or do some more easy-going **volcano park hikes** (p141), then spelunk through a lava tube at **Kula Kai Caverns** (p158). Take the scenic drive along **Ka'alaiki Rd** (p164) and stop in for a food forest tour at **Manadina Farm** (p166).

SEASONAL HIGHLIGHTS

SPRING

The national park is at its rainiest, but in the late spring, sleepy Pāhala is ramping up for the **Ka'ū Coffee Festival** (p158).

SUMMER

The park is crowded in July and *'ōhi'a lehua* trees are in full bloom. The clearest days are in August and September.

AUTUMN

Fewer crowds in October, but rain is fairly low. Tour art studios during the **Volcano Village Artists Hui** (p153) in late November.

WINTER

In December, the rainfall is minimal in Ka'ū and the winter crowds haven't started showing up yet.

Hawai'i Volcanoes National Park

EPIC LANDSCAPES | ACTIVE VOLCANOES | SCENIC DRIVES

GETTING AROUND

You'll need your own wheels to get around Hawai'i Volcanoes National Park, as there is no transportation or shuttle service inside. Cyclists are permitted on paved roads, and a handful of dirt ones, including the Escape Rd, but not on most trails.

Hele-On Bus, a public bus service operated by Hawai'i county, does have routes connecting the national park with Hilo, Volcano and Ka'ū. The bus picks up and drops off at the intersection of Volcano House and the second entrance to Kīlauea Visitor Center, but schedules often change and delays are common. A car will make it much easier to get around.

From the otherworldly summit of the world's most massive volcano Maunaloa, to the windswept coastline where lava poured into the sea for decades, Hawai'i Volcanoes National Park is a micro-continent of dripping rainforests, bizarre desertscapes, high-mountain meadows and coastal plains, with plenty of geological marvels in between. At the heart of it all is Kīlauea – the planet's youngest and most active shield volcano – which erupted dozens of times in 2024, 2025 and 2026 and at the time of research was continuing to spew lava.

Once you've paid your respects to the Hawaiian deity Pele, who is said to live in Kīlauea's Halema'uma'u crater, it's worth checking out the Kahuku Unit, a former ranch whose 116,000 wild and undeveloped acres became part of the park in 2003. And just beyond park boundaries, the misty village of Volcano is an ideal base for exploring the region, with art galleries, nature walks and cute restaurants galore.

Volcanoes 101

Meet some rangers

So, you've paid your $30 per vehicle entrance fee, which is good for seven days, and cruised through the park's gates. Next stop? The new **visitor center** *(nps.gov/havo)*, which was under construction during this guidebook's research period but slated to open in late 2026. It's here that you can ask for advice about volcanic activity, air quality, road closures, trail conditions and how best to spend your time. You can also find out which ranger-led hikes and education programs are on offer during your visit, and plan around these key opportunities to learn about the landscape from the people who know it best.

Take note, though, that because of staffing cuts across the National Park Service, fewer programs than usual may be on offer, and the remaining staff members may be stretched thin.

To avoid adding to their workload and stress level, keep yourself informed about conditions and follow all safety guidelines throughout your time in the park.

Before you set off to see the sights, browse some of the newly installed exhibits (which were moved over from the famously demolished Jaggar Museum), and head next door to the **Volcano Art Center** *(volcanoartcenter.org)*, a sharp local gallery housed in the historic 1877 Volcano House hotel. It spotlights museum-quality pottery, paintings, woodwork, sculpture, jewelry, Hawaiian quilts and more in a series of rotating exhibits.

Trails of Lava

Must-do day hikes in the park

The park's 150 magical miles of trails offer suitable options for every level of athleticism (and some wheelchair-accessible paths). Regardless of the hike, be prepared for rapidly changing conditions: a hot sunny stroll can turn cold and wet in an instant, and when eruptions are imminent or happening, large swaths of the park can close without warning for safety reasons.

If you can only do one day hike, make it **Kīlauea Iki Trail**, and do it counter-clockwise. The 4.5-mile loop traverses an astounding microcosm of the park, descending through fairy-tale *ʻōhiʻa lehua* forests to a mile-wide, still-steaming crater that was filled by a fiery fountain that turned it into a lava lake. The eruption took place over five weeks at the end of 1959, filling the crater and forming the cinder pile above, which reached 1900ft (the highest ever recorded in Hawaiʻi). To fully appreciate this hike, first watch the vintage film *Eruption of Kilauea 1959–1960* (found on YouTube) and download the brochure from the park website (*nps.gov/havo/index.htm*). Hit the trail before 8am to beat the crowds and follow the *ahu* (stone cairns) for navigation and safety purposes.

Another rightfully popular path in the heart of the park is the **Halemaʻumaʻu Trail**, which begins at the visitor center and proceeds down through forested terraces to the Kīlauea caldera. Although the section of the trail that crosses the caldera has been closed for several years due to activity at the other end, the ranger-led hike 'Into the Volcano' takes visitors over this area then back up the Byron Ledge and Crater Rim trails.

Other worthwhile and relatively easy paths include the **Devastation Trail** (0.5 miles of wheelchair-accessible path through a hellscape buried beneath falling cinder during a 1959 Kīlauea eruption); the **Haʻakulamanu Trail** (an easy 1.2-mile roundtrip from the visitor center that takes in a volcanic thermal area's multicolor deposits and billowing **vapors**); and the **Nāhuku Trail** (a 1.5-mile round trip through the rainforest and the 500-year-old **Thurston Lava Tube**). Casual hikers who drive the Chain of Craters Road should also hike the **Puʻu Loa Petroglyphs Trail**, an easy 1.4-mile round-trip path to ancient petroglyphs chiseled into rock, including abstract designs and animal and human figures.

WHAT HAPPENED TO THE JAGGAR MUSEUM?

Formerly the second-most-visited museum in the state, the Jaggar Museum once contained exhibits on volcano science and Hawaiian culture. It perched precariously on the rim of the Kīlauea Caldera, and suffered significant structural damage during the 2018 eruption cycle, which included tens of thousands of earthquakes, towering ash plumes and a collapse of the caldera. The museum's foundation was destabilized, so park officials demolished it and two other buildings (including a USGS field station) in 2023 and restored the area to its natural state. The salvaged exhibits were expected to be on display at the visitor center by late 2026.

TOP TIPS

For updated information on Kīlauea and its eruptions, visit the USGS webpage *(usgs.gov/volcanoes/kilauea/volcano-updates)* and the crater's live webcams on YouTube. Whether or not the volcano is erupting, try to get an early start. The park is open 24 hours but tour buses and crowds start arriving around 10am.

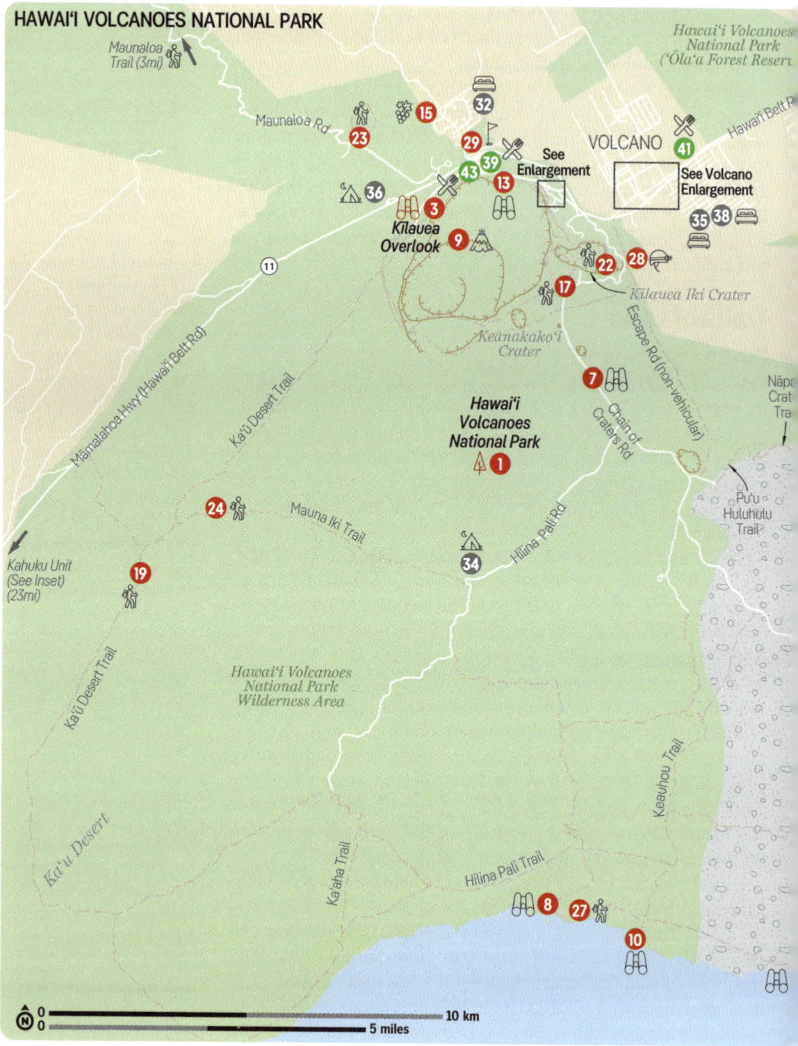

HIGHLIGHTS

1 Hawai'i Volcanoes National Park
2 Kahuku Unit
3 Kīlauea Overlook
4 Kīlauea Visitor Center & Museum

SIGHTS

5 Akatsuka Orchid Gardens
6 'Apua Point
7 Chain of Craters Road
8 Halapé
9 Halema'uma'u
10 Keauhou
11 Niaulani Campus
12 Pu'u Loa Petroglyphs
13 Steam Vents & Steaming Bluff
14 Volcano Art Center
15 Volcano Winery

ACTIVITIES

16 Backcountry Office
17 Devastation Trail
18 Halema'uma'u Trail
19 Ka'ū Desert Trail
20 Kazumura Cave Tours
21 Kilaeua EcoGuides
22 Kīlauea Iki Trail
23 Kipuka Puaulu Trail
24 Mauna Iki Trail
25 Nāpau Crater Trail
26 Pit Crater Trail
27 Puna Coast Trails
28 Thurston Lava Tube
29 Volcano Golf Course

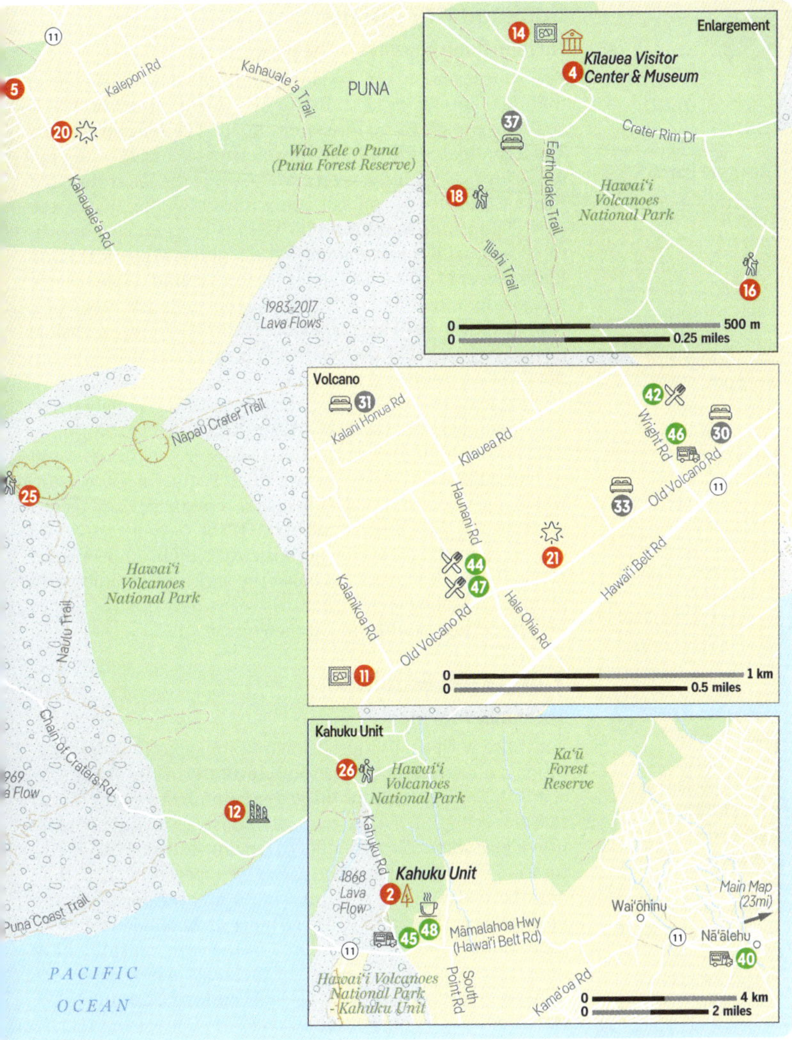

SLEEPING
30 Hale 'Ohu Bed & Breakfast
31 Holo Holo In
32 Kilauea House of the Five Blessings
33 Kilauea Lodge
34 Kulanaokuaiki Campground
35 Lava Pond Lodge
36 Namakanipaio Cabins & Campground
37 Volcano House
38 Volcano Rainforest Retreat

EATING
39 10 Pin Grill
40 Aloha Mixed Food Truck
41 Café Ono
42 Cooper Center
43 Crater Rim Cafe
44 Eagle's Lighthouse Cafe
45 El Encanto Food Truck
46 Hopper's BBQ & Smokehouse
see 33 Kilauea Lodge Restaurant
47 Lanikai Brewing Company
see 37 Rim Restaurant
see 29 Tuk Tuk Thai Truck

DRINKING & NIGHTLIFE
48 Miranda's Farms Coffee Shop
see 37 Uncle George's Lounge

BEST VOLCANO TOURS

Friends of Hawai'i Volcanoes National Park Private scientist/naturalist-led tours including Sunday Walks in the Park every second Sunday of the month. Visit fhvnp.org.

Bike Volcano Informative guided e-biking tours of the park, along with self-guided audio tours. The three- to five-hour trips are mostly downhill along Crater Rim Dr and Chain of Craters Road.

Kilaeua EcoGuides Professional guides who offer customized foot tours for small groups, mainly focused on the Kīlauea Volcano and the park's geology.

Blue Hawaiian Helicopters Fly above waterfalls, valleys and coastline and for a tour of active volcano Kīlauea.

Ranger Programs National Park Service rangers lead a mix of tours exploring areas around the Kīlauea Caldera, including the summit, the craters and various viewpoints.

Backcountry Bound

Further-flung journeys in the park

For experienced hikers spending multiple days in the park, there are lots of good trails further afield, many of which you'll access off Crain of Craters Road. The **Nāpau Crater Trail** undulates for 14 miles (round trip) over rugged terrain past a lava shield and several craters, while the **Keauhou** and **Puna Coast** trails connect you with the wilder side of the park. The Hilina Pali Rd brings visitors to a savagely beautiful desert wilderness where the challenging **Mauna Iki** and **Ka'ū Desert** trails (each about 14 miles round trip) traverse a desolate, moon-like environment that tells the story of a 1790 eruption. On a short offshoot leading to (and accessible from) Hwy 11, you'll find scattered ancient footprints left in the ash and preserved in sediment.

These long, exposed trails – along with the extremely strenuous and bucket-list-worthy **Maunaloa Trail** (p209) to the volcano's summit – are most often tackled by visitors who aim to spend the night. All overnight hikes require a $10 permit, which must be purchased online via recreation.gov and picked up from the park's **Backcountry Office** *(808-985-6178)* up to a week in advance. One permit covers up to 12 people for seven nights. Be sure to download the park's backcountry trip planner covering potential hazards with safety tips and advice for protecting wildlife and archeological sites.

Rainforest Rambles

Short hikes for kids

For those with small kids or looking for something less ambitious, one great option is the **Kipuka Puaulu Trail**. The shady, 1.2-mile hike loops through a rainforest *kipuka* (oasis) that has rebounded after years of intensive grazing turned it into a grassland. Now, thanks to fencing and aggressive restoration this parcel has more native tree species per acre than anywhere else in the park, making it a haven for birds and birdwatchers. The trailhead is 1.5 miles up Maunaloa Rd at the turnaround, and is best explored in the early morning or at dusk, when you'll be enveloped by the songs of honeycreepers.

Just outside the park, over at the **Niaulani Campus** (p155; *volcanoartcenter.org)* of the Volcano Art Center, there's also an easy path through an old-growth *'ōhi'a lehua* rainforest, which can be hiked anytime and takes about an hour. If you show up at 9:30am on Mondays, a guide will lead you through, covering the ecological importance of koa and *'ōhi'a lehua* forests, traditional Hawaiian uses of plants, and the key role of birds. The Niaulani Nature Walk is free, but donations are appreciated.

MORE MAUNALOA

For in-depth coverage of Maunaloa's eruption history, lookout, hiking trails and backcountry cabins, along with some tips for exploring its flanks and summit, see p208.

CRUISING CHAIN OF CRATERS ROAD

Scenic Chain of Craters Road winds down the southern slopes of Kīlauea, punctuated with viewpoints, trailheads and ancient sites.

START	END	LENGTH
Crater Rim Dr turnoff	Hōlei Sea Arch	20 miles; 1hr

Begin at a turnoff from Crater Rim Dr, where the ❶ **Devastation Trail** (p141) also begins (if you've got time to spare, hike the 0.5-mile trail through the wasteland of Kīlauea Iki's 1959 eruption). From there, you'll cruise down the road past a series of pit craters including ❷ **Pauahi Crater**, the site of three eruptions whose name means 'destroyed by fire.'

Continue driving past formations from a 1969 lava flow and descend a series of *pali* (cliffs) to reach ❸ **Kealakomo**, a viewpoint with picnic tables overlooking the sea (and possibly the windiest lunch spot in the park). Below the switchbacks, imagine the smoking red lava pouring down the hillsides, consuming the road, and bulldozers making a new one after that lava cooled. When you reach the ❹ **Pu'u Loa Trailhead**, hop out and hike the gentle, 1.4-mile round trip to one of Hawai'i's largest concentrations of ancient petroglyphs, some over 800 years old.

Continue the drive to the ❺ **End of the Road**, where there's a small ranger shack, pit toilets and a small concession stand at the turnaround. Constantly brutalized by unrelenting surf, the coast here has sharply eroded lava-rock *pali*, including the ❻ **Hōlei Sea Arch**, an ephemeral rock carved by crashing waves.

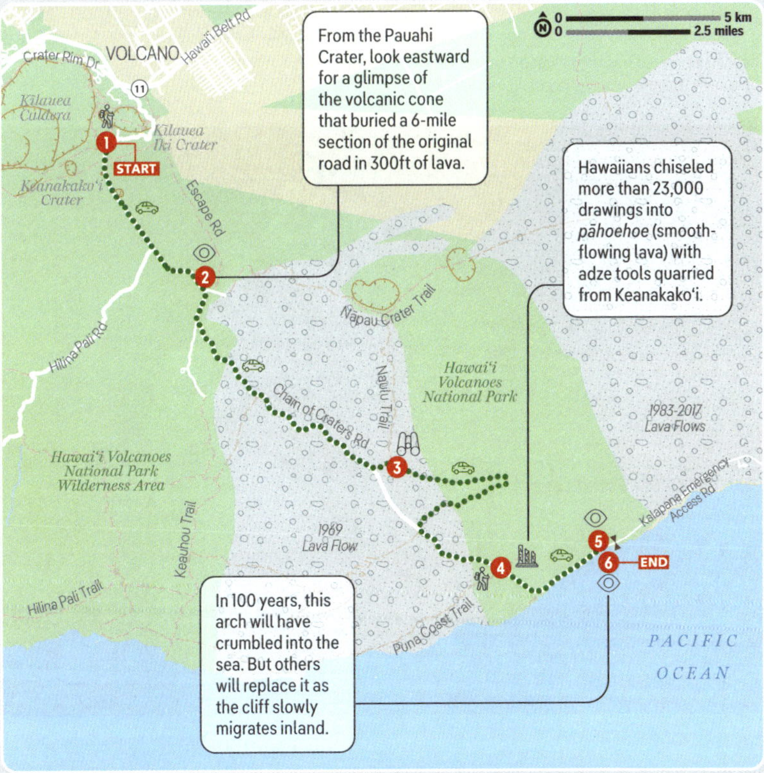

DRIVING TOUR

Touring the Crater's Edge

At the center of activity in Hawai'i Volcanoes National Park, 11-mile paved loop Crater Rim Dr starts at Kīlauea Visitor Center and skirts the rim of Kīlauea's summit caldera. The trail passes steam vents and rifts, hiking trailheads and amazing views of the smoking crater. You can do this by car or on two wheels, but expect to spend some time on foot as well.

1 Steam Vents & Steaming Bluff

At this **viewpoint**, plumes billow in the cool early morning. Hot rocks below the surface boil rainwater as it percolates down, producing the steam. The vents at the parking area are fine, but even more evocative is Steaming Bluff, found along a short walk out to the rim. Here curtains of steam frame the cliffs above a post-apocalyptic landscape.

The Drive: Head 1.5 miles west on Crater Rim Dr, past a turnoff to some lava tree molds (deep wells that formed when flows engulfed the rainforest) to the main event.

2 Kīlauea Overlook

More than just a pause-worthy panorama, this overlook is a front row seat for one of the most active volcanoes in the world. Kīlauea was erupting about once every two weeks in 2026, and its massive steaming crater-within-a-crater, **Halema'uma'u**, has spewed lava for much of the last 25 years.

BILDAGENTUR ZOONAR GMBH/SHUTTERSTOCK

Thurston Lava Tube (p141)

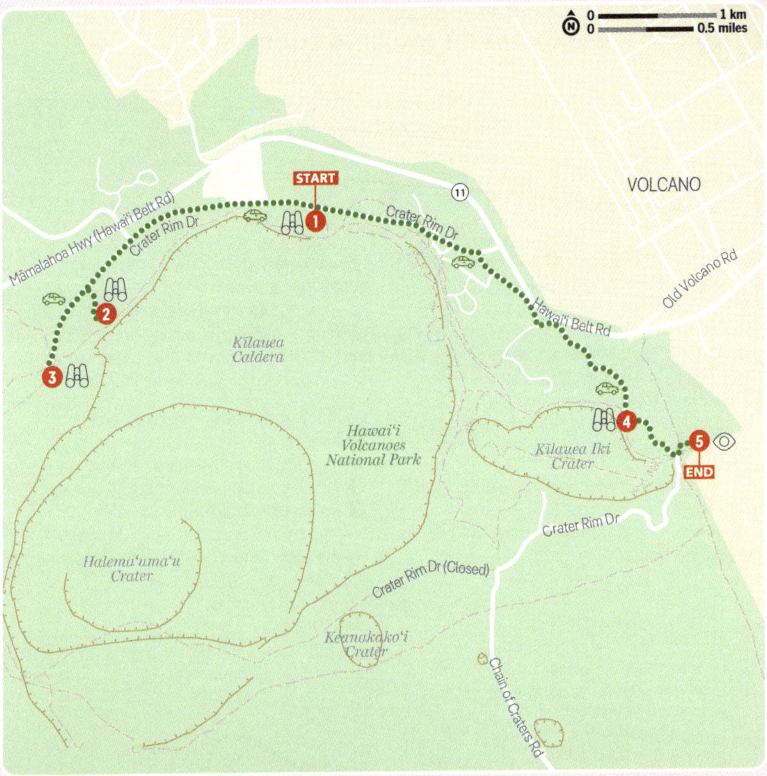

The Drive: Go 0.7 miles west on Crater Rim Dr and park in the Uēkahuna lot. Walking out to the observation deck, you'll notice newly replanted native shrubs, grasses and trees.

3 Uēkahuna

At the former site of the Jaggar Museum, the footprint of the building is marked with stones from the original columns. At the highest point of the caldera, this spot is considered a *wahi pana* (sacred place) by Native Hawaiians, and remains ideal for viewing the crater's drama and the soaring tropicbirds that nest in the crater walls.

The Drive: Double back past the visitor center and continue along Crater Rim Dr, tracing Kīlauea's eastern side until you see the Kīlauea Iki parking lot on your right.

4 Kīlauea Iki Overlook

When 'Little Kīlauea' burst open in a fiery inferno in November 1959, it filled the crater with a roiling lake of molten rock fed by a 1900ft fountain that lit up the night sky with 2 million gushing tons of lava per hour at its peak. It took over 30 years for the lake to completely solidify. From the overlook, you'll see the spectacular mile-wide crater and astonishing trail traversing the middle.

The Drive: It's only 0.3 miles to reach the Thurston Lava Tube, so feel free to drive, bicycle or, better yet, hike through the rainforest.

5 Nāhuku

The 0.3-mile loop through the **Thurston Lava Tube** (also known as Nāhuku Trail) starts in an *'ōhi'a lehua* forest filled with birdsong, then heads underground through a gigantic (but short) artificially lit lava tube. Nāhuku, as this tube is called in Hawaiian, was 'discovered' by controversial figure Lorrin Thurston, the newspaper baron who was instrumental in overthrowing the Kingdom of Hawai'i.

OLD KAHUKU RANCH WALKING TOUR

A leg-stretching glimpse into Ka'ū's past, with highlights including native forest, a historic airstrip and an obliterated ranch.

START	END	LENGTH
Visitor Contact Station	Pu'u o Lokuana Trailhead	1 mile; 1hr

Begin at the Kahuku Unit's ❶ **Visitor Contact Station**, where you'll find helpful posters and rangers (or volunteers) who can answer questions. From here you'll meander through old-growth native *'ōhi'a lehua* trees and cross the main road, then follow the ranch road across the ❷ **1868 lava flow**, which spared the pasture ahead and formed a ❸ ***kipuka***, an oasis, of older land surrounded by new lava.

Exit the *kipuka* and enter Captain Robert Brown's nightmare. Having just started ranching at Kahuku less than three years before, Captain Brown was reluctant to vacate when a series of earthquakes devastated surrounding communities in 1868. On the night of April 7, however, the ❹ **fissure eruption** here began gushing lava above his home, forcing his family to flee for higher ground. There they watched as their house and cattle were incinerated.

Continue up the lava flow and along the ❺ **historic airstrip** that once serviced the ranch lands. Cross the main road again to ❻ **Pu'u o Lokuana** cinder cone. Return to the ❼ **Pu'u o Lokuana Trailhead** via the switchbacks on the cone's south face – or channel your inner child and somersault down the soft grass.

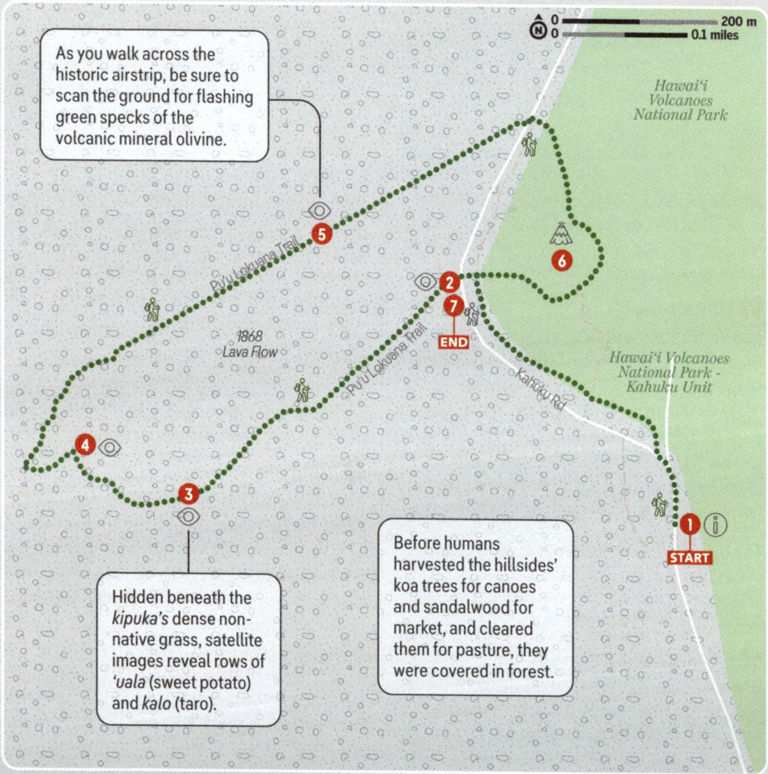

A Scenic Drive & Some Hikes

Exploring the Kahuku Unit

For those who simply want to sightsee, there's the 6-mile (round trip) scenic drive through the **Kahuku Unit** *(nps.gov/havo/planyourvisit/kahuku.htm)*, which traverses steep, open pastures juxtaposed against fissures and lava flows from the devastating 1868 eruption. The road is unpaved but passable in a standard car for about 2.5 miles, while the upper reaches require a high-clearance 4WD. The drive connects to most of the unit's eight hiking trails, which lead through green pastures to volcanic cinder cones, lava tree molds, rainforests and lava flows.

You can explore these trails on excellent ranger-guided hikes that take place around twice a month, depending on staffing levels (see nps.gov/havo/planyourvisit/calendar.htm), but you can also enjoy them by yourself Thursday to Sunday (8am to 4pm). Double-check opening hours online as they have been known to change.

The most popular trail is the **Pu'u o Lokuana Trail**, a 2-mile loop following historic ranch roads through verdant pasture lands. After passing lava tree molds, the route wanders around spatter ramparts from Maunaloa's 1868 eruption. Follow an abandoned airstrip back to the road and climb the cinder cone that gives this trail its name for some spectacular views. If you don't want to do the whole trail, join the trail across the street from the landing strip and get to the crater in a few hundred feet (cheater!).

The real highlight of the park, though, is the **Pit Crater Trail**. This strenuous 4.8-mile jaunt (round trip) up an old pasture road culminates at a huge pit crater, a deep bowl full of pristine rainforest looking like the entrance to the underworld. Hikers on this trail must brush off their shoes at the decontamination gate to avoid spreading the spores that cause Rapid Ōhi'a Death.

Although part of the national park, the Kahuku Unit is 42 miles southwest from the main park entrance on Hwy 11. There's no food available for purchase here, but nearby, **El Encanto Food Truck** *(instagram.com/elencantofoodtruckllc)* offers affordable Mexican and Salvadorean staples, and neighboring **Miranda's Farms Coffee Shop** *(mirandasfarms.com)* serves excellent local coffee drinks.

MORE ON RAPID ŌHI'A DEATH
Learn more about Rapid Ohi'a Death, and what you can do to prevent it, on p244.

HISTORY OF THE KAHUKU UNIT

In 2003, the Hawai'i Volcanoes National Park and the Nature Conservancy jointly bought historic Kahuku Ranch in the biggest conservation land purchase in the state's history (adding 116,000 acres to the park and increasing its size by over 50%). Previously, Hawai'i's ranching heritage was centered here. It haphazardly began in 1793 when King Kamehameha I received a gift of 12 Texas longhorn cattle. They ran rampant throughout the land eating everything they could reach, and future landowners experimented with goats and mouflon sheep, which prolonged the destructive legacy. The ranching continued through several owners, including Captain Robert Brown. Today the Kahuku Unit remains a largely wild, undeveloped and under-visited playground for history buffs and nature lovers.

WHAT'S UP WITH KĪLAUEA MILITARY CAMP?

Kīlauea Military Camp (KMC; *kilaueamilitarycamp.com*) is an active US Army recreation facility occupying about 50 acres within Hawai'i Volcanoes National Park. Established in 1916, it was originally envisioned as a National Guard training ground and an Army vacation spot. And although early conditions were rough, the enchanting setting soon made it a favorite retreat for service members. Today, overnight stays are limited to those accompanied by a military sponsor, but civilians can eat at KMC's restaurants and bowl at its six-lane alley (reserve well in advance). If you get an eerie feeling walking around, you aren't alone. During WWII, more than 100 Japanese Americans were imprisoned here for several months, and that dark chapter has fueled rumors of hauntings.

ZUMA PRESS, INC./ALAMY

Ash plume, Volcano Golf Course

Aloha Central

Stay at a Volcano B&B

The rainforest setting and kind, creative residents of Volcano Village make this an ideal place to stay a few nights in a B&B. The crème de la crème is **Volcano Rainforest Retreat** *(volcanoretreat.com)*, a property that feels straight out of some tropical Zen fairy tale. Its four unique and elegant cottages have more windows than walls, and are well secluded among the dense ʻōhiʻa hāpuʻu rainforest. Two of them feature private outdoor Japanese-style soaking tubs while the other two share an outdoor hot tub. The smallest (but our favorite) is the Sanctuary, a hexagonal oasis of 360-degree windows. For added romance, in-room massage can be arranged, and a breakfast basket is delivered each morning.

For the fine hospitality and cozy fireplace, we also recommend **Lava Pond Lodge** *(lavapondlodge.com)*. The high-ceilinged living area and small library make for relaxing common spaces, and guests stay in four modern and clean rooms in the main house. An above-garage studio with separate lānai (balcony) is a good option for light sleepers who need more privacy, and the front-porch hot tub is a welcome amenity during cooler evenings. The breakfasts are outstanding, and the host has a wealth of knowledge about the area.

EATING & DRINKING IN THE NATIONAL PARK: OUR PICKS

Rim Restaurant: Crater-front dining with modern cuisine made from local ingredients. Don't miss the seared Kona kampachi. *7-10:30am, 11am-2:30pm & 5-8:30pm* **$$$**

Uncle George's Lounge: Small bar serving salads, burgers, sandwiches and pizza. Volcano views all day, along with local craft brews. *11am-9:30pm* **$$**

10 Pin Grill: Kīlauea Military Camp's bowling alley offers affordable diner grub that does the trick: we can vouch for both the *loco moco* and the chicken katsu. *11am-10pm* **$**

Crater Rim Cafe: This cafeteria-style restaurant serves standard American fare, plus prime rib specials on Saturday nights. *7-11am & 5-8pm Fri & Sat* **$$**

Just up the street, **Hale 'Ohu Bed & Breakfast** *(haleohu.com)* sits on a historic 5-acre property tucked into the rainforest. The adults-only stay was painstakingly renovated and opened by twin sisters in 2017, and the pair live on-site in the main house. In a building beside it, three rooms feature private entrances, spa-inspired bathrooms, breakfast nooks, patios and TVs (with Netflix), and a walk through a nearby botanical garden culminates in a rainforest viewing lounge equipped with coffee and snacks. A healthy in-room continental breakfast is included.

Finally, for visitors with deep interest in wildlife, look no further than **Kilauea House of the Five Blessings** *(kilaueahouse.net)*, located in a quiet neighborhood just behind the Volcano Golf Course. One of the owners is a bird and bat expert, and the two plush rooms are avian themed: one celebrates the endemic and endangered nēnē goose, the other is an homage to the scarlet honeycreeper. Both rooms feature king beds, private backyard patios equipped with electric firepits, and breakfast tables where local coffee, pastries and fresh fruit is served in-room daily.

Tee Off

Golf with a volcano view

With a lush setting at the foot of Maunaloa, the straightforward 18-hole, par-72 **Volcano Golf Course** *(volcanogc.com)* is a local favorite. The island's beloved and endangered nēnē geese can usually be spotted on these putting greens, and when the volcano is erupting, its fiery fumes are usually visible from the course. At 4000ft above sea level, it has the thinnest air of any course on the island, which some people say makes their drives fly further. Weekday/weekend rates are $78/82 for nonresidents (one or two people) and a set of rental gear costs $45.

Spelunk Through Lava

One crazy cave tour

After learning his property straddled **Kazumura Cave** *(kazumuracave.com)* – one of the world's longest lava tubes – Harry Schick tirelessly worked to become an expert on this geologic phenomenon. Although 30 years of tours has made his delivery a bit rote, the abundant information and unique sights still make for a fascinating adventure through this ancient tube system that was created during the 'Ailā'au eruption in the 15th century.

There are three tours on offer. The Lava Falls tour ($60 per person) lasts two hours and involves venturing about a third of a mile into the cave, with Schick explaining the many features and the geology of the place. The Pit Room tour ($120 per person) is a bit more challenging, with uneven floors and some ladder climbs as visitors venture a mile inside the cave. Finally, a Maze tour ($140 per person) is for experienced cavers and climbers only. You'll be scaling ladders, using ropes and crawling over loose, rocky terrain to reach what Schick has dubbed 'the wow formation,' which defies explanation.

BEST BACKCOUNTRY CAMPSITES

Gwendolyn Hill is the founder and president of bikevolcano.com, which offers e-bike rentals and tours (including a self-guided audio tour) in Hawai'i Volcanoes National Park. She shares some of her favorite backcountry campsites.

Halapé This is my favorite place to camp. There are freshwater ponds created by the 1979 earthquake and tsunami, and you can bathe in them (no soap, though!).

Keauhou (p144) The snorkeling here is just amazing. There's so much coral (never stand on it, please) and endangered hawksbill turtles nest along the coast.

'Apua Point This is a pretty spot where very few people go. The surf is great because of the south swell, and there's powerful ocean energy.

WHY I LOVE HAWAI'I VOLCANOES NATIONAL PARK

Ashley Harrell, Lonely Planet writer

I had been chasing lava my whole life, but I never saw it with my own eyes until I did the research for this book. On one of my last days on the island, January 24, 2026, the Kīlauea volcano exploded into one of its most dramatic eruptions in years, and I jumped in my rental car and drove straight to the park. By the time I arrived, lava was shooting 1600ft into the air and volcanic rocks were raining down, denting cars and striking the occasional visitor. It was total chaos, and the National Park Service ended up having to evacuate the park. But I felt incredibly lucky to have witnessed the eruption, and that massive red wall of lava is forever seared into my memory.

PHILLIP B. ESPINASSE/SHUTTERSTOCK

If you are afraid of tight spaces, the underground, heights or the dark, this tour isn't for you, and it's worth considering that the cave entrance is locked during the tour for the cave's protection. Make reservations at least a week ahead; directions to the site are given upon reservation.

Hit the Markets

Community gatherings around local products

At the heart of Volcano Village, the **Cooper Center** *(thecoopercenter.org)* serves as a community hub, hosting weekly markets for locals to eat, shop, talk story and celebrate the island's farmers and artisans. For travelers, stopping by the Cooper Center markets offers a glimpse of everyday life in Volcano.

The most well-known event is the Sunday morning Volcano Farmers Market, one of the longest-running markets on the island. Held from 6am to 10am, this market is famous for local breakfast favorites like wholegrain pancakes, homemade bagels, fresh cheese, baked goods and made-to-order juices.

EATING IN VOLCANO VILLAGE: OUR PICKS

Lanikai Brewing Company: This taphouse opened in 2025 to rave reviews for its brick-oven pizza and small-batch brews. Great ramen, too. *11am-9pm* $$

Eagle's Lighthouse Cafe: Fresh and hearty sandwiches, salads and wraps are served out of a small kitchen fronted by picnic tables. *7am-2pm Tue-Sat* $

Kilauea Lodge Restaurant: High-end breakfast buffet. Seafood, steak and pasta for lunch and dinner. Reservations required. *7-10:30am, 11am-2:30pm & 5-8:30pm* $$$

Café Ono: Organic vegetarian and vegan comfort food served in the garden and sunroom behind Volcano Garden Arts. Do not miss the carrot cake. *11am-2pm Thu-Sun* $$

Volcano Art Center (p141)

You'll also find standout local vegetables and tropical fruits, along with fresh breads, pastries, toffees, flowers, coffee and handicrafts.

More recently, the Cooper Center began hosting the Volcano Thursday Market from 3pm to 6pm. It features food vendors, barbecue, Thai dishes, sandwiches and locally made goods. In addition, on the third Saturday of each month, the center hosts an 'anything goes' swap meet.

Celebrate Art & Culture

Open studios, demonstrations and performances

The savviest of travelers time their visits to Volcano Village with cultural events, art shows and performances. The **Volcano Art Center** *(volcanoartcenter.org)* hosts free Hawaiian craft and cultural demonstrations year-round, along with concerts, dance shows and plays at both its location inside the park and at the **Niaulani Campus** (p155) in Volcano.

For those looking to mingle with local artists and buy their pieces at reasonable prices, there's the **Volcano Village Artists Hui** *(volcanovillageartistshui.com)*. It takes place over a three-day weekend in late November, when local working artists open their studios to visitors and display new creations including pottery, fiber work, wood sculpture, ceramics, woodblock prints, glass blowing and photography.

BEST FOOD TRUCKS

Eli Schonbrod is the head chef for Lanikai Brewing Company, a brewery that opened in the summer of 2025 and has become the talk of Volcano Village. He's lived in the area for years, though, and watched with interest as local food trucks have proliferated. Eli has tried them all, and these are his personal favorites:

Tuk Tuk Thai Truck Great Thai food truck located at the Volcano Golf Course. Good spot to grab lunch before heading down the road to Volcano Winery.

Aloha Mixed Food Truck Located across the street from Punalu'u Bake Shop in Nā'ālehu, it's a must stop if traveling that part of the island.

Hopper's BBQ & Smokehouse Delicious barbecue that runs pop-ups all over the region, but can reliably be found at the Thursday Market in Volcano.

DRIVING TOUR

Volcano Village Art, Nature & Wine Tour

In between hikes through lava tubes and around volcanic craters in the national park, take a leisurely drive through fern-festooned and artful Volcano Village next door. Along the way, you'll breathe the scent of orchids, browse local galleries and sample wine birthed on the slopes of Maunaloa, and encounter the artists at the village's creative heart.

1 Akatsuka Orchid Gardens

Begin your Volcano Village adventure at this long-standing family-owned **nursery**, where hundreds of blooming orchids make for a visual and olfactory feast of floral hybrids. Don't miss the extensive collection of Cattleya orchids, which resemble corsages, the 'volcano queen' hybrids, and the $20,000 Lady Slipper Orchid.

The Drive: Turn left on Kahauale'a Rd then left on Hwy 11, and it's just a short drive along the 'Ōla'a Forest Reserve before you reach the signed turnoff at Old Volcano Rd.

2 2400 Fahrenheit

The glass sculptures of Michael and Misato Mortara can be found in private collections and museums all over the world, and you can also see them here at the working **studio and gallery** in Volcano, along with newer endeavors such as one-of-a-kind epoxy-and-hardwood tables and fine jewelry. Gallery hours are 10am to 3pm Thursday through Sunday.

The Drive: Take Old Volcano Rd back to Hwy 11 and head west along the edge of 'Ōla'a Forest Reserve. Turn right on Pearl Ave, then left on Volcano Rd. Volcano Garden Arts will be on the left.

CREATIVE TOUCH IMAGING LTD/NURPHOTO VIA GETTY IMAGES

Lady Slipper Orchid, Akatsuka Orchid Gardens

❸ Volcano Garden Arts

Tucked into an old farmhouse within a fern forest, this **art gallery and studio** is the place to do your Hawai'i Island art shopping. Walls and tables overflow with paintings, handicrafts and jewelry produced by dozens of regional creatives. The space is surrounded by quiet, elaborate gardens, and you can get lunch from the neighboring and fabulous Café Ono (p152).

The Drive: Make a right out of the parking lot onto Volcano Rd and continue through the heart of the village. You'll pass a few restaurants and inns before the art center comes up on the right.

❹ Volcano Art Center: Niaulani Campus

On the edge of an old-growth *'ōhi'a lehua* forest, the center's Niaulani Campus (a satellite of the main Volcano Art Center gallery in Hawai'i Volcanoes National Park) showcases spillover and related exhibits unencumbered by the park's thematic requirements. A monthly changing schedule of workshops and events features local artists.

The Drive: Head west on Hwy 11, edging the national park until you reach Piimauna Dr. Hang a right, pass the golf course and soon the winery will appear on the left.

❺ Volcano Winery

Grapes from Maunaloa's volcanic soil may never erupt onto the world stage, but this unusual winery produces delectable infusions with local fruits, nuts, honey and tea. Tastings ($20 per person) include six pours, and the Hawaiian Guava-Grape and Macadamia Nut Honey Wine are particularly delightful. There are also vineyard tours ($40 per person, six pours) and tea field experiences ($60 per person, three steeps).

Kaʻū

RURAL TOWNS | SPRAWLING FARMS | REMOTE BEACHES

GETTING AROUND

While Hele-On Bus services do circumnavigate the island, around here the schedules are infrequent and inconvenient for visitors. A standard car will get you most places you want to go, but a 4WD expands your exploration options considerably. One great option is **Ready Rigs** *(readyrigs.life)*, a company that rents off-roading vehicles with pop-up tents and other outdoor gear.

'This was the beginning of Hawaiʻi, and it will be the end.' That's what they say of Kaʻū, the archipelago's southernmost district, where Polynesians are thought to have first landed in the 13th century, and where locals have thus far resisted large-scale development.

This lesser-visited region is defined by macadamia and coffee plantations, forested highlands and an uninhabited stretch of rugged, windswept coastline. Secluded and independent, Kaʻū may be a little rougher around the edges than some visitors are accustomed to, but those with the right attitude and sense of adventure will deeply appreciate this destination.

Come to Kaʻū for the long drives through wide-open countryside, the bountiful farm stands brimming with tropical produce and the beaches layered in unique volcanic sands. Stay for the understated, quiet beauty of the rural towns of Nāʻālehu and Pāhala, the abundant historical sites and the off-the-beaten track adventures to even more remote beaches.

TOP TIPS

Don't rush through. The highlights of Kaʻū take a little more time to reach, and are best appreciated with a picnic and plenty of time to spare. Also, when driving the scenic and remote roads out here, be sure to bring anything and everything you might need.

An Olivine Dream

Explore Green Sand Beach

Tinted by volcanic forces, this secluded, rugged and legendary stretch of sand is less green than you might expect, but infinitely more beautiful. The olive-colored sand of **Green Sand Beach** (officially known as Papakōlea) on Mahana Bay sparkles in the sun, while the surrounding cliffs resemble stacks of pancakes, having been eroded over time by relentless wind and turquoise waves. As with many of the world's rare and beautiful places, getting here is definitely a challenge – but also part of the draw.

You'll drive in on a lonely two-lane road through Hawaiʻi's undeveloped and rural southern outskirts. Take the left (east) fork of South Point Rd, some 10 miles from Hwy 11, to the old barracks. Park here (don't leave any valuables in your car) to begin the 2.5-mile hike to the beach. It's dusty, hot and exposed the entire way, so you'll need plenty of water and sun protection. You should strongly consider going early or late in the

HIGHLIGHTS
1 Green Sand Beach
2 Punalu'u Black Sand Beach Park

SIGHTS
3 'Ailani Orchards
4 Edge of Chaos
5 Henry Opukaha'ia Chapel
6 Ka Lae (South Point)
7 Kalalea Heiau
8 Kamaoa Wind Farm
9 Kane'ele'ele Heiau
10 Kāwā Bay
11 Manukā State Wayside & Natural Area Reserve
12 Mark Twain Monkeypod Tree
13 Morse Field
14 Pali'okūlani Overlook
15 Road to the Sea
16 South Point Satellite Station
17 Whittington Beach Park
18 Wood Valley Temple

ACTIVITIES
19 Kula Kai Caverns
20 Manadina Farm

SLEEPING
see 3 'Ailani Orchards
21 Green Sand Oasis
22 Kalaekilohana
23 Keola Retreat
see 20 Manadina Farm
24 Pele's Eye
25 Punalu'u Beach Park Campground
26 Sea Mountain
see 18 Wood Valley Guesthouse

EATING
see 3 'Ailani Orchards
27 Hana Hou Restaurant
28 Ka-Lae Garden
29 Nameless Farm Stand
30 OKK Farmer & Artisan Market
31 Paradise Meadows Orchard & Bee Farm
32 Punalu'u Bake Shop
33 Taco Tita
34 Tai Shan Farms

DRINKING & NIGHTLIFE
35 Honua's Coffee House
36 Ka Lae Coffee
37 KaiLoki's
38 Ka'u Coffee Mill

ENTERTAINMENT
see 38 Ka'ū Coffee Festival

SHOPPING
see 31 Paradise Meadows Orchard & Bee Farm

day or when it's overcast; this will not only help prevent dehydration but help you beat the crowds as well.

Start the hike by heading south to the Kaulana boat ramp, then veer left (east) following the coastline. The unceasing winds will sandblast your face, making the trip feel twice as far as it is. Upon arrival, you'll be rewarded with panoramic views over Mahana Bay. After an exciting scramble down a steep stairway built into the cliff, you can scoop some of the green sand up and contemplate its origins: the olivine crystals formed around 49,000 years ago with the eruption of Pu'u Mahana, a cinder cone volcano whose lava spewed down into the sea. Then, powerful waves eroded the hardened lava over thousands of years, and the relatively heavy element olivine stayed behind on the beach.

LEARN MORE ABOUT GREEN SAND BEACH

To learn more about how visitors and residents have created illegal roads to the Green Sand Beach, scarring the land in this ecologically sensitive area, see p247.

In the parking lot and along your hike, you will notice some locals shuttling tourists to and from the beach in the backs of their trucks. This off-road driving is illegal and destructive to the coastal ecosystems, along with ancient cultural sites. Deep ruts and dirt paths created by the vehicles have harmed sensitive dune plants such as *'ōhai,* a native shrub with orange and red blossoms. In addition, loose dirt kicked up by vehicular traffic eventually makes its way to the ocean, where it prevents coral reefs from obtaining needed sunlight. The region is sacred, for the dunes contain *iwi kūpuna* (ancient Hawaiian bones) that aren't meant to be disturbed. Don't take the ride.

Don't take any sand, either, and think twice before swimming at the beach. It's OK if the surf is calm, and extremely dangerous when it's not. People have died here.

Hawaiian History 101

Journey into a lava tube

Led by conservationists and scholars with deep passion for Hawaiian history and ecology, the compelling tours at **Kula Kai Caverns** bring visitors on journeys through 1000-year-old lava tubes within the Kipuka Kanohina Cave System, one of the longest enterable cave systems in the world. The subterranean caverns are owned by theCave Conservancy of Hawai'i and contain fascinating artifacts, including stone tools, *kukui* nut lamps and *poi* pounders (rocks for beating taro root into a paste). Exploring these caves feels like a form of time travel, and guides are skilled at describing the ways ancient Hawaiians made use of them.

DRINKING IN KA'Ū: OUR PICKS FOR COFFEE

Ka Lae Coffee: An institution in downtown Nā'ālehu specializing in 100% Ka'ū coffee grown locally on the owners' family farm. *Mon-Fri 8am-4pm*

Ka'u Coffee Mill: A down-to-earth coffee farm that harvests, processes and roasts its own award-winning beans and gives free tours at 11am and 1pm on weekdays. *9am-4pm*

Ka'ū Coffee Festival: In late May, Pāhala wakes up with a strong brew of music, coffee, hula and coffee-farm tours. Expect cooking contests and coffemaking demonstrations.

Honua's Coffee House: Locally owned coffee house known for innovative flavors and seasonal treats. *6:30am-4pm Sun-Thu, from 7am Fri*

You'll need to reserve in advance to receive the code and enter the Ocean View neighborhood where tours are held. Options include a basic 'lighted trail tour' *(adult/child $35/20)*, which lasts about an hour and requires scaling or descending 75 stairs, but is suitable for children. The 'extended wild tour' *(adult/child $98/68)* lasts two hours and involves helmets, lights, kneepads and gloves (all provided). There's also an 'archeological tour' *(adult/child $45/25)*, which emphasizes how ancient Hawaiians used lava tubes as shelter while traveling, and brought in hollowed-out gourds to catch water that dripped from the ceilings.

There's ongoing scientific research in the caves and guides emphasize respectful stewardship of these 'living museums.' Over the last two decades, the Cave Conservancy of Hawai'i *(hawaiicaves.org)* has purchased and protected more than 141 acres and mapped dozens of miles of lava tubes.

Superlatives in the South

Hit all the southernmost US landmarks

Beyond the obvious **South Point**, the southernmost tip of Hawai'i Island and also the US, there are several other destinations that travelers sometimes visit in a nod to their geographical uniquity. A stop in tiny Nā'ālehu, the southernmost town in the US, is all but mandatory if you're road-tripping through Ka'ū. While here, you can also knock out the country's southernmost bakery, **Punalu'u Bake Shop** (p164; *bakeshophawaii.com*).

Up until early 2026, you could also visit the country's southernmost restaurant in Nā'ālehu, the 1940s family diner **Hana Hou Restaurant** *(eathanahou.com)*. That restaurant still exists and remains worthwhile, but a newcomer further south has usurped the claim to fame. At the time of research, there was a new vegan restaurant opening within the 23-acre grassland expanse known as **Pele's Eye** (p166; *808-443-7057*), a collection of off-grid cabins in South Point. Delicious fruit juices, smoothies, salads and Filipino dishes are lovingly prepared with fresh ingredients mostly grown on-site.

To throw back a beer in the country's southernmost bar, you'll have to head west to Ocean View, a 10,000-acre subdivision built atop scrubby lava flows. This is where, right off Hwy 1, you'll find **KaiLoki's** *(facebook.com/KaiLokis)*. Friendly staff serve burgers, sandwiches and a rotating selection of daily specials to a mix of local characters and visitors, while the horseshoe bar buzzes with the latest Ocean View gossip. There are paint-and-sip nights on Thursdays, and on Friday nights, karaoke is the most 'happening' thing between Kona and Hilo.

THE BIG ISLAND'S BIG ONE

The largest earthquake in Hawai'i Island's recorded history took place on April 2, 1868. After several days of tremors and an eruption on Maunaloa's summit, the southeast flank of the island slipped toward the ocean, causing a 7.9 magnitude earthquake. The quake flattened every building in Ka'ū and triggered a 50ft tsunami that swept coastal fishing villages out to sea, killing some 46 people. A massive mudslide near Wood Valley traveled 3 miles seaward, burying 30 people and their homes and livestock. Aftershocks from the quake continued until April 7, when a 2-mile-long crack opened along Maunaloa's Southwest Rift Zone, releasing fissure eruptions. Lava poured down the mountainside, reaching the ocean 10 miles away in less than three hours.

EATING IN KA'Ū: BEST RESTAURANTS

Hana Hou Restaurant: Family diner in Nā'ālehu serving up American and Hawaiian comfort food in a cozy indoor space or out on the patio. *8am-8pm* $$

Taco Tita: A Mexican joint in Nā'ālehu serving up tacos, burritos, nachos and taco salads. Salsa varies from mild Chipotle to scorching Scorpion, yowza! *11am-3pm* $

Tai Shan Farms: Lovingly prepared farm-to-table grub in an open-air pavilion on a dragon fruit farm in Ocean View. *4-7pm Mon-Wed* $$

Ka-Lae Garden: Dishes are made-to-order with ingredients fresh from the organic garden out back, and the food comes with world-class views. *11am-6pm Fri-Tue* $$

DRIVING TOUR

South Point Drive

It's worth making this drive for the bracing sea air and cliff-top views alone (and the wind turbines, for the renewable energy nerds). But it also comes with bragging rights: you've gone as far south as is possible before you fall off the edge of the US. Start your odometer where South Point Rd turns off of Hwy 11, in a semi-forested area where residents continue a long tradition of agriculture.

1 Paradise Meadows Orchard & Bee Farm

This 75-acre farm packs a lot in, including an art gallery and free samples of locally produced coffee, honey and macadamia nuts (and chocolate-covered versions). Do the guided tour ($30 per person) for a look at engineered sustainability, or a more casual self-guided one. You'll meet rescue parrots and there are rotating taco and pizza pop-ups for lunch.

The Drive: Cruise 10 miles south over the easternmost finger of the infamous 1868 lava flow, past a satellite tracking station and a couple of wind farms.

2 Ka Lae

Park at the end of the road and hike the rest of the way to the southernmost tip of Hawai'i Island, Ka Lae. 'The Point' appropriately feels like the end of the Earth, and it was here that the first Polynesian sailors likely made landfall. Although archeologists believe it was consistently occupied for centuries, today it's a mostly vacant landscape with a lofty cliff that foolish tourists sometimes leap from. (Don't do it.)

The Drive: Double back to the north and then turn right where South Point Rd forks. Soon you'll reach the parking lot for the Green Sand Beach.

RADOSLAW LECYK/SHUTTERSTOCK

Green Sand Beach (p156), Ka'ū

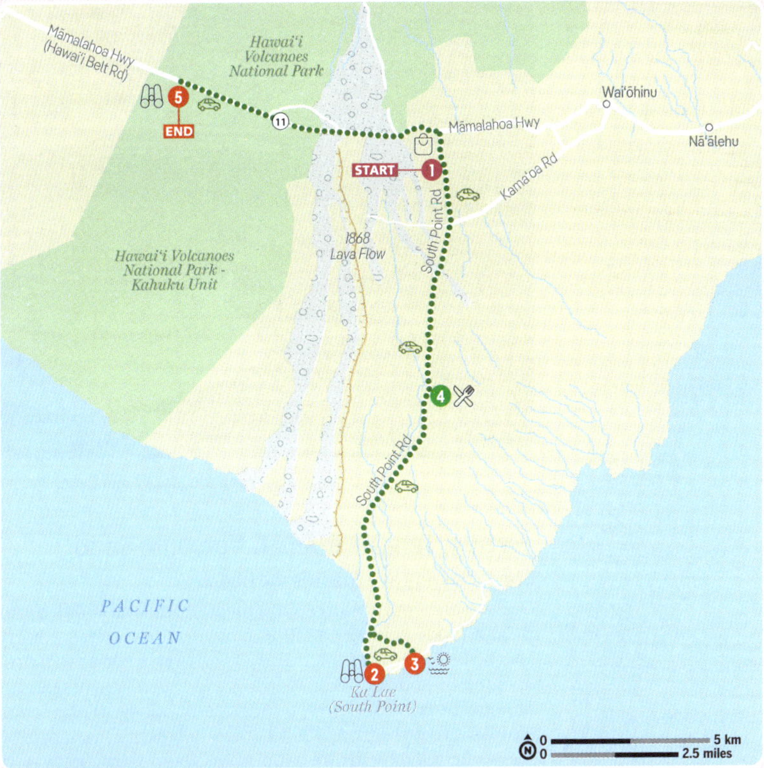

③ Green Sand Beach

Hawai'i's famous and rare Green Sand Beach (p156; also known as Papakōlea) is absolutely worth seeing. But to do it right, you'll need to leave your vehicle behind, and also pass on the convenient ride in the back of a local truck. The coastal dune ecosystem out here is fragile. To behold these volcanic sands, which are green thanks to the mineral olivine, hike (instead of driving) to the beach.

The Drive: Head back north the way you came, back past the wind farms and the satellite tracking station, and this time stop in at the farm stand.

④ Farm Stand

Don't be alarmed at the cow skulls displayed on a post out front – this nameless farm stand at 93-1280 South Point Rd rules. They've got Spam *musubi* (grilled spam over rice), coconut water, banana bread, hot dogs, sodas and more, and the service is pure aloha. Hours vary.

The Drive: Continue the rest of the way north to Hwy 11 and hang a left toward the ocean view. Soon you'll approach a pullout where other cars are parked; go there.

⑤ Pali'okūlani Overlook

Complete the drive at Hwy 11 mile marker 75 with this overlook and its commanding view of the escarpment that forms the southernmost tip of Hawai'i. Pali'okūlani (*pali* means 'cliff') was formed when the land west of the Kahuku fault either slid into the ocean, or possibly just sunk in place (geologists disagree). At the base, fishhooks left behind by the ancient settlement of Wai'ahukini suggested that the earliest settlers came from the Marquesas Islands.

HISTORICAL SITES

Kamaoa Wind Farm The rusty carcasses of 37 windmills from the failed Kamaoa wind farm lie next to their foundations along South Point Rd.

Morse Field The landing strip here was a fuel stop for a trans-Pacific air ferry route until the attack on Pearl Harbor. Barracks foundations and a runway scar remain.

Henry Opukaha'ia Chapel A small rock chapel above Kāwā Bay dedicated to Punalu'u resident Henry Opukaha'ia, whose conversion to Christianity inspired a wave of missionaries.

Kane'ele'ele Heiau Also referred to as Punalu'u Nui, 800-year-old Kane'ele'ele Heiau was the region's *luakini*, or place of human sacrifice.

Kalalea Heiau This ancient temple and shrine is where Hawaiians left offerings in return for a bountiful catch.

TADA IMAGES/SHUTTERSTOCK

Green sea turtle, Punalu'u Black Sand Beach Park

Turtles, Temple Ruins & Volcanic Sand

Start your day at a black-sand beach

Once an ancient Hawaiian settlement, **Punalu'u Black Sand Beach Park** *(808-961-8311)* is now an uninhabited county beach flanked by temple ruins. The windswept area is frequented by endangered hawksbill and green sea turtles and famous for its black sand: pulverized basalt from Maunaloa eruptions that absorb and reflect the sunlight in a mesmerizing scene encircled by tilting palm trees. The rough, cold waters and undertows frequently make swimming undesirable, but a lifeguard is posted and when it's calm, snorkeling is a treat.

The name Punalu'u means 'spring dived for,' and according to legend, in times of drought Hawaiians would collect fresh water bubbling up beneath the bay by plunging under the waves with empty upturned gourds. The northern part of the beach is backed by a duck pond and the remains of an old resort: a rotting testimony to local economics and the antidevelopment movement. Near the park restrooms, a small rock wall protects easy-to-miss petroglyphs. The ruins of the Pahala Sugar Company's old warehouse and pier lie on the northeast edge of the bay. The pier was intentionally destroyed during WWII to prevent the Japanese from landing on the unguarded coast. Above it, **Kane'ele'ele Heiau** keeps a watchful eye over the land.

Come in the early morning since the beach park quickly fills with picnickers and tour buses. Camping is allowed with an advance county permit. There are two signed turnoffs for Punalu'u between mile markers 56 and 57 on Hwy 11.

The Spiritual Side of Ka'ū

Temples, shrines and heiau

It's impossible to explore the rural district of Ka'ū without stumbling on some seriously spiritual places, be it a Buddhist temple, a shrine to the sea or a place of human sacrifice. Just outside Pāhala, you'll find the cheerful **Wood Valley Temple** *(nechung.org)*, a Buddhist structure and 25-acre forested retreat center. Visitors can join a chanting session (10am Sunday) or just visit the temple and gift shop. A meditative guesthouse lets you stay a few nights.

Down on South Point, the **Kalalea Heiau** is a testament to the area's important fishing grounds. Ancient Hawaiians left offerings here in return for a bountiful catch. Some still do today, although their angling methods have changed. Look for salt pans in the area: depressions carved in the rocks where fishermen would evaporate ocean water then use the remaining salt to cure their catch.

Finally, the **Kane'ele'ele Heiau** (also referred to as Punalu'u Nui and located at Punalu'u Black Sand Beach) is an 800-year-old *luakini* (place of human sacrifice). A large flat stone below the southwest corner of the temple walls is believed to have served this purpose, and a pit full of bones discovered during construction of nearby sugar warehouses seemed to confirm that. Reach the heiau by following a short steep trail up above the warehouse foundations at the northeast corner of the beach park. It's not easy to spot. Look for a path heading east from the heiau paved with smooth gray stones set to ease the journey of barefoot warriors over the *'a'ā* (rough, jagged type of lava).

An Off-Roading Beach Adventure

Take the Road to the Sea

At the end of a rugged 6-mile drive, remote black- and green-sand beaches set before looming cliffs and cinder cones are beacons for true adventurers. The high-clearance 4WD road may cross enough *'a'ā* to shake your fillings loose – and you may find after all the trouble of getting here that the sea is too rough to swim and the beach too windy to enjoy. Still, this trip into the volcanic 'great beyond' is worth it for the scenery alone, and you should drive it now because there's talk of someday paving the road.

To find the **Road to the Sea**, turn *makai* (seaward) off Hwy 11 at the row of mailboxes between miles 79 and 80. From there it's 6 miles of rudimentary, seemingly neverending lava which most high-clearance vehicles can handle, but you'll want a 4WD at mile 3.1 where the road drops off a lava bench. It takes about 45 minutes or so to reach the first green-sand beach, depending on how rough you like your ride. Another 0.5 miles to the east (hike it unless you have a rock-crawler), an incongruous tree provides shade over a bleached coral beach. To the west, a series of littoral cones (mounds of tephra formed as hot lava explosively boils in to the ocean), coves and fishponds provide unending coastal exploration. Bring as much water as you can carry because it can be a mercilessly hot and shadeless walk in any direction.

NATURAL ATTRACTIONS

Manukā State Wayside & Natural Area Reserve A 13-acre reserve offering a pleasant 2-mile nature trail through transitional forest to a volcanic crater.

Mark Twain Monkeypod Tree Legend has it that the author originally planted this tree near Wai'ōhinu city park. A hurricane claimed it, but this beauty re-sprouted from its roots.

Whittington Beach Park Northeast of Nā'ālehu, this small park has tide pools, an ancient Hawaiian fishpond frequented by birds, and the ruins of a historic pier.

Edge of Chaos Just north of Whittington Beach Park, turning right through a yellow gate leads to this jagged, otherwordly shoreline. Only 4WD vehicles can drive it; otherwise, just go on foot.

Kāwā Bay A quiet, pebbly cove deeply important to Native Hawaiians. Park at the yellow gate at mile 58.5 on Hwy 11 and walk half a mile down to the cove.

DRIVING TOUR

Cruising Kaʻalaiki Road

For an elevated look at central Ka'ū's quiet, pastoral side, take what locals refer to as the 'high road' from Nā'ālehu to Pāhala. Its real name is Ka'alaiki Rd (or Old Cane Haul Rd), and the paved two-laner crosses rocky cascades between verdant hills with commanding sea views. You'll find coffee farms, macadamia nut plantations and a eucalyptus farm.

1 Nā'ālehu

Begin in tiny Nā'ālehu, the island's southernmost town. Although the name means 'volcanic ashes,' Nā'ālehu is a greenscape filled with sprawling trees, pastel-colored plantation houses and the beautiful but boarded-up Nā'ālehu Theatre that, giving a lost-in-time rural feel. The town is central Ka'ū's commercial hub with a few markets, restaurants and services.

The Drive: After taking in the town and working up an appetite, head west on the Māmalahoa Hwy and hang a right on Puluala St. The Punalu'u Bake Shop is on your right.

2 Punalu'u Bake Shop

The town's biggest attraction is this bakery. Order the *malasada,* Portuguese fried sweet pastries that come in delicious flavors like guava, *liliko'i* (passion fruit) and mango. Enjoy with a smoothie or coffee in the picnic area out back, which sometimes doubles as a space for cultural events. Then browse the Hawaiiana in the gift shop and take some baked goods to-go.

The Drive: Turn right out of Punalu'u Bake Shop onto Puluala St and then right onto Ka'alaiki Rd, heading north. You'll pass the Nā'ālehu Cemetery on your left, then the ridgetop Nā'ālehu Radar Station, which provides weather data, on the right.

NIKO NATSUKI/SHUTTERSTOCK

Punalu'u Bake Shop

3 Manadina Farm

Soon after the radar station, a dreamy food forest (p166) comes into view. Call ahead to book guided tours that meander through its thriving permaculture oasis, where you'll learn about dozens of varieties of tropical fruits, medicinal herbs and canoe plants – the species Polynesian settlers brought to the islands centuries ago. You'll also visit 'food islands,' sniff unique plants, sample edible flowers and leave the tour with plenty of goodies. The tour is $25 per person, with a minimum of two people.

The Drive: As you continue along Ka'alaiki Rd past the private, unattended Ka'alaiki Airstrip, the views of the coastline out the passenger-side windows will become increasingly epic.

4 Ninole Hills

Glance to the north for a view of the eroded Ninole Hills, oddities from Maunaloa's geologic past that long puzzled scientists for their relatively old age – which you can see by the gulches and creeks not normally found in younger, porous lava rock. Recent studies of the gravity around here have determined that the 125,000-year-old hills once made up the Southwest Rift Zone.

The Drive: Continue along the road over narrow bridges and stream beds, past coffee plantations and eucalyptus forests. Views toward the ocean remain stunning.

5 Pāhala

Pāhala's quiet streets are mostly lined with unrestored early-20th-century plantation houses occupied by former sugar plantation workers. While Hawai'i's sugar boom was coming to an end, the lands around here still managed to produce record yields – but that only helped for so long. In the mid-1990s, forced to choose between pay cuts or the mill closing, the workers chose the latter.

KĀWĀ BAY'S SURF HISTORY

Once disputed territory plagued with coastal-access and land-rights issues, **Kāwā Bay** (p163) is now a quiet, pebbly cove protected as public land. It's bounded by a creek and cliff-top heiau (temple) on one side, and Ka'alaiki, the island's second-largest freshwater spring system and fishpond estuary, on the other. It's a peaceful place to picnic, and because surf breaks are hard to come by in Ka'ū, this spot (sometimes called Windmills) is the local go-to. Go with a local. Or channel Nu'uanupa'ahu, the Ka'ū chief who honed his legendary surfing skills here. Those same skills allowed him to survive shark attacks and win the respect of his rival, Kalaniōpu'u (though the latter did later die from his wounds).

Overnight at a Farmstay

Lodgings less usual

One of the best ways to fully immerse in Ka'ū is to live close to the land, if only for a night or two. And there are a few wonderful options.

Off rural Ka'alaiki Rd, **Manadina Farm** *(manadina.com)* offers three off-grid cottages within an 8-acre food forest bursting with tropical fruits, herbs and vegetables. Colorful and boho, the accommodations are all solar-powered and feature outdoor showers, private decks and sweeping volcano and coastal views (sunrises are killer). The kind co-owner Jasmine leads food forest tours, and occasionally her upimg daughter joins.

For something still more remote, veer off South Point Rd and down the gravel path toward **Pele's Eye**, an off-grid collection of lodgings on 23 windswept, grassy acres offering wide-open skies and panoramic ocean views. The artist-owner Ruebón built all three accommodations, including the downstairs apartment with a spectacular garden bathroom and two cozy glamping cabins adorned with his paintings. Ruebón's wife Mei prepares delicious vegan and Filipino meals, and additional highlights include quiet trails and stargazing.

And finally, off Hwy 11 a bit west of Nā'ālehu, California transplants Barney and Elizabeth have raised their family at **'Ailani Orchards**, an organic farm and orchard brimming with macadamia nuts, avocados and citrus. Guests can rent spacious homes on the property and join the rhythm of daily farm life, but at least a month-long stay is required.

EATING IN & AROUND KA'Ū: FARM STANDS & MARKETS

OKK Farmer & Artisan Market: A small farmers market selling handicrafts, fresh produce and prepared foods. *8am-2pm Wed, 10am-3pm Fri* $

'Ailani Orchards: Open-air farmers market selling macadamia nut products, Ka'ū coffee, avocados and citrus fruits from the surrounding 5-acre property. *1-5pm Mon-Fri* $

Cooper Center (p152): The whole community comes to this long-standing Sunday market to buy farm-fresh produce, local crafts and snacks. *6-10am Sun* $

Paradise Meadows Orchard & Bee Farm: This farm stand offers samples of locally produced coffee, honey and macadamia nuts, as well as self-guided farm tours. *9am-5:30pm* $

Places We Love to Stay

$ Budget **$$ Midrange** **$$$ Top end**

Hawai'i Volcanoes National Park

MAP p142

Namakanipaio Cabins & Campground Tent camping and small A-frame cabins in a meadow near the highway, managed by Volcano House. Sites have water, picnic tables and barbecues. $

Kulanaokuaiki Campground This minimal campground down Hilina Pali Rd has walk-in sites tucked into the *'ōhi'a lehua*. Expect pit toilets and picnic tables, but no water. $

Volcano House Perched on the rim of Kīlauea caldera, this is the park's only hotel, with 33 spacious (if plain) rooms. Ask for a volcano view. $$

Volcano

MAP p142

Holo Holo In Reliably clean and comfortable hostel with dorm beds and cabin-like private rooms, and a friendly vibe in a quiet location. $

Lava Pond Lodge (p150) Cozy home where guests sit by the fireplace or in the hot tub, and socialize with each other and the knowledgeable host over excellent breakfasts. $$

Hale 'Ohu Bed & Breakfast (p151) Adults-only rainforest retreat with spa-like rooms, private entrances, botanical garden access, lounge amenities and healthy in-room breakfasts. $$

Kilauea House of the Five Blessings (p151) Wildlife-focused B&B with avian-themed rooms, private patios, well-informed hosts and locally sourced in-room breakfasts. $$

Kilauea Lodge A renovated 1930s YMCA camp supplements history with luxury: chic rooms come with gas fireplaces and Hawaiian quilts, and there's a garden hot tub. $$$

Volcano Rainforest Retreat (p150) Top-notch B&B ensconced in the rainforest, with four secluded, window-filled cottages, soaking tubs, romantic touches and daily breakfast baskets. $$$

Ka'ū

MAP p157

Punalu'u Beach Park Campground Pitch a tent on the grass at this accessible beach campground offering grills, showers, tables and water. Permit required. $

Wood Valley Guesthouse A meditative, rustic guesthouse at Wood Valley Temple primarily caters to retreat guests, but welcomes anyone seeking peaceful accommodations. $

Green Sand Oasis Rustic, colorful cabins featuring tropical decor, tucked into the Hawaiian countryside. They're not fancy but they come with aloha. $

Pele's Eye (p166) An artist-built, off-grid compound on windswept grasslands near South Point, with quiet trails and a tasty vegan kitchen. Try for the apartment with the garden bathroom. $

Manadina Farm Three colorful, solar-powered cottages tucked into an 8-acre food forest, with outdoor showers, private decks and sweeping volcano and ocean views. $$

Keola Retreat Hidden in foliage off Hwy 11, these tasteful geodesic dome tents offer lofted beds, outdoor soaking tubs, grills and fire pits. $$

Sea Mountain Timeshare condo complex blissfully located in walking distance of Punalu'u Beach. The whole place has ocean views, including the relaxing pool and hot tub. $$

'Ailani Orchards A working organic orchard west of Nā'ālehu, where spacious rental homes available for extended stays sit among macadamia, avocado and citrus groves. $$

Kalaekilohana A sophisticated, away-from-it-all inn with a wide porch, a library and music room, and luxe rooms featuring private lānai. Wonderful hosts. $$$

Researched by
Catherine Toth Fox

Kohala & Waimea

ANCIENT HAWAIIAN CULTURE, RESORTS AND WINDSWEPT VISTAS

Stark contrasts characterize this northerly region – seaside resorts give way to rural towns amid rolling ranchlands, and vertiginous vistas are interspersed with the remnants of significant Native Hawaiian sites.

Dormant Kohala, the oldest of the island's five volcanoes, has an enticing split personality. Along the coast, dry, hot lava deserts mingle with velvety white sand and fulfill the stereotypical Hawaiian beach scene. Waterfall-backed deep valleys line its northernmost tip. In the interior, elevated terrain reveals the grassy hills of cattle country – the wind picks up, the air is cooler and yet the sun still bakes, and the white-capped waves of the Pacific unspool in the distance.

South Kohala's palm-fringed oases amid black-lava desert are where you'll find most of the island's amenity-laden resorts and neighborhoods of multi-million-dollar homes. A significant (if a bit unsightly) industrial port in the coastal crook at Kohala's base connects West Hawai'i with the outside world. It's within sight of Pu'ukoholā Heiau, a towering 18th-century temple base built to fulfill a wartime prophecy.

MGAMBILL/SHUTTERSTOCK

In the central uplands, the town of Waimea (Kamuela) straddles the wet/dry ecosystem divide, and beckons visitors into the rural north with its unique *paniolo* (Hawaiian cowboy) culture. The quaint, community-oriented villages of the northern coast, steeped in the sugar plantation style of the region's more recent past, are the gateway to the island's show-stopping coastal valleys. This wild and agricultural region hides remnants of some of the isl5and's oldest and most significant cultural sites including the homelands of King Kamehameha, training grounds for seagoing voyagers, and sacred heiau (temples) where blood sacrifices were offered to the gods.

THE MAIN AREAS

WAIKŌLOA RESORT AREA
Accommodations, shopping, beaches and bars. **p172**

WAIMEA (KAMUELA)
Paniolo and art culture and first-rate dining. **p182**

HĀWĪ
Tiny town en route to Pololū Valley. **p192**

For places to stay in Kohala & Waimea, see p197

BONITA R. CHESHIER/SHUTTERSTOCK

Left: Maunakea Beach (p175), Kohala; Above: ‘Aaneho‘omalu Beach Park (p172)

Find Your Way

Despite Kohala's considerable size – most of O'ahu could fit in its nearly 500 sq miles – there are few roads and large swaths remain inaccessible. Most resorts sit on the coast some 20 miles north of Kona International Airport; from there Hāwī and Waimea are each a 40-minute drive.

CAR

A car is required to explore this remote region; rent one from the Kona airport. Don't miss the verdant Kohala Mountain Rd, connecting Hāwī and Waimea; its high-elevation ocean views comprise some of the island's most scenic vistas.

BUS

The infrequent Hele-On Bus connects population centers (Puakō, Waikōloa Resort Area, Waikōloa Village, Waimea and Hāwī) in a pinch. Within Waimea, a flex-connector offers custom pickups within one mile of the main bus route (call to schedule at least one hour in advance 808-961-8744, option 1).

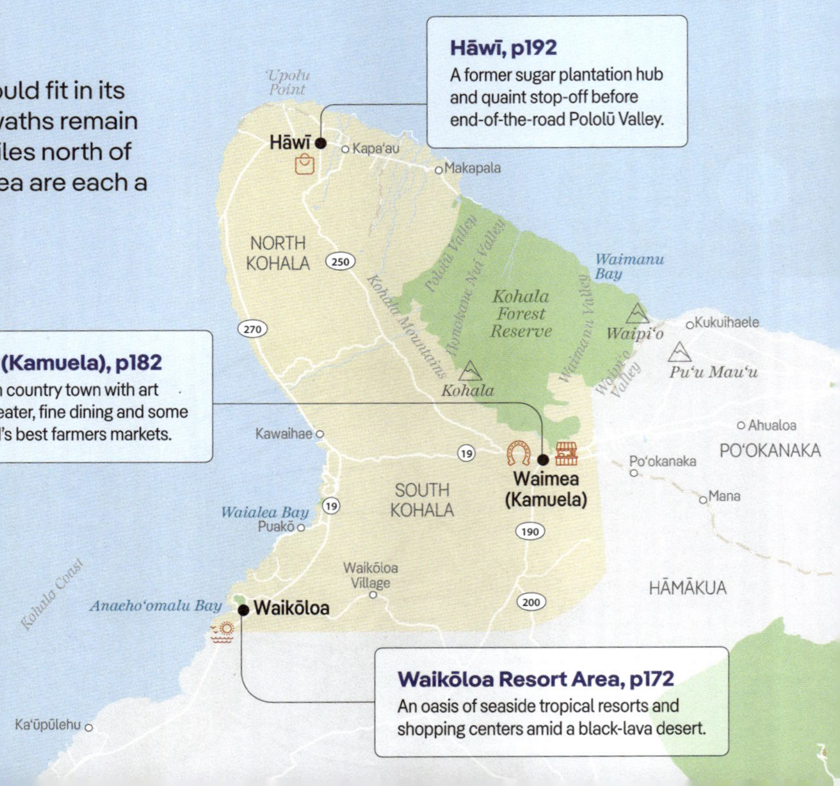

Hāwī, p192
A former sugar plantation hub and quaint stop-off before end-of-the-road Pololū Valley.

Waimea (Kamuela), p182
Inland ranch country town with art galleries, theater, fine dining and some of the island's best farmers markets.

Waikōloa Resort Area, p172
An oasis of seaside tropical resorts and shopping centers amid a black-lava desert.

Kohala Mountain Road (p190)

Plan Your Time

Kohala's scenic highlights can be explored in a single day. Tack on more time to hunt for temple ruins, dive deeper into lesser-visited towns, and swim in the clear waters off the island's largest white-sand beach.

With Just One Day

- Stop at **Pu'ukoholā Heiau** (p179) en route to **Hāwī** (p192). Snap a photo with the formerly sunken **statue of King Kamehameha** (p196). The road ends at **Pololū Valley** (p194), where a mile-long trail descends to its black pebble and driftwood strewn shore. Return via **Kohala Mountain Rd** (p190) to **Waimea** (p182), where abundant dining options await.

Two or More Days

- Spend time deciphering the massive array of mysterious rock etchings within **Puakō Petroglyph Archeological Preserve** (p174), sunbathing at **Hāpuna Beach** (p176) and dining, toes in the sand, at **Lava Lava Beach Club** (p174). Catch one of the local or international acts on the program at the **Kahilu Theatre** (p187).

SEASONAL HIGHLIGHTS

SPRING
Whale watching in Pu'ukoholā Heiau and cherry blossoms in Waimea with an annual heritage **festival** (p189).

SUMMER
Warm, dry and windy. Trade winds reach peak this time of year and are strongest in Kohala.

AUTUMN
Endemic *wiliwili* trees display showy orange flowers in Kohala's lowland **dry forest** (p177); and it's tiger shark mating season, a good time to skip surfing.

WINTER
High tourist season. Resorts and towns celebrate the festive season with decorative lights, parades and musical performances.

Waikōloa Resort Area

RESORT LIVING | FAMILY FUN | SANDY BEACHES

GETTING AROUND

Free resort shuttles connect points within the immediate vicinity; book with an independent operator for transfers to and from Kona International Airport. Unless you're on an organized tour, rental cars make the most sense to explore the region but plan to pay to park at the resorts.

As you leave the Ellison Onizuka Kona International Airport at Keāhole, you come to an intersection. Right leads you to Kailua-Kona. But left takes you to another world on Hawai'i Island. Follow Hwy 19 – aka Hawai'i Belt Road – for about 20 miles and you'll see a palm-tree-lined oasis among the black lava fields. The Waikōloa Beach Resort Area is home to the bulk of the island's large resorts, high-end condos and timeshares, with a handful of more upscale resorts and communities further north along the coast. Despite the size of Hawai'i's coastline, virtually all of the island's sugary shores are located in South Kohala. And each beach is unique – some better for lounging, others great for snorkeling. Around the resorts, find open-air shopping centers, restaurants, public beaches, golf courses, even a dine-in movie theater that serves 'ahi *poke*. Tucked throughout the landscaping are cultural sites, including natural anchialine pools and fishponds, petroglyph-dotted boulders, and traditional footpaths – all a reminder that you're not just on vacation, you're on vacation in Hawai'i. While it's possible to spend your entire trip in this resort area, we'd absolutely recommend venturing beyond.

TOP TIP

The Waikōloa Resort Area – encompassing Waikōloa Beach Resort Area, Puakō, Hāpuna Beach and several northerly resorts – spans some 8 miles along Queen Ka'ahumanu Hwy. Note that Waikōloa Beach Resort, and the Waikōloa Resort Area, are not the same as Waikōloa Village, a residential community *mauka* (up the mountain) and inland.

Resort Living

Find hidden Hawai'i among the hotels

Staying in a resort and don't want to spend your days driving? Here's an easy way to get a taste of the island within a 15-minute driving radius of most properties – and without leaving the Waikōloa Resort Area. Start off the day outdoors. Take a stroll or hit the old-school wooden calisthenics circuit on the far north end of **'Anaeho'omalu Beach Park** (A-Bay). The earlier you're there the better chances you have of catching an iconic Hawai'i sight: the local outrigger canoe club at morning practice. If you're feeling inspired to head offshore, the usually

HIGHLIGHTS
1 Hāpuna Beach State Recreation Area
2 Maunakea Beach

SIGHTS
3 Ala Kahakai National Historic Trail
4 'Anaeho'omalu Beach Park
5 Hawai'i Keiki Museum
6 Mau'umae Beach
7 Puakō Petroglyph Archeological Preserve
8 Waialea Beach

ACTIVITIES
9 Hawai'i Ocean Sports
see 11 Spa Without Walls

SLEEPING
10 Auberge Mauna Lani
11 Fairmont Orchid
12 Waikoloa Beach Marriott

EATING
see 11 Binchotan Bar & Grill
see 19 Bistro at Waikōloa Luxury Cinemas
13 Foster's Kitchen
14 Hawaii Calls Restaurant
15 Lava Lava Beach Club
16 Manta
17 Original Big Island Shave Ice Co
see 19 Pono Pastries

SHOPPING
18 Kings' Shops
19 Queens' Marketplace

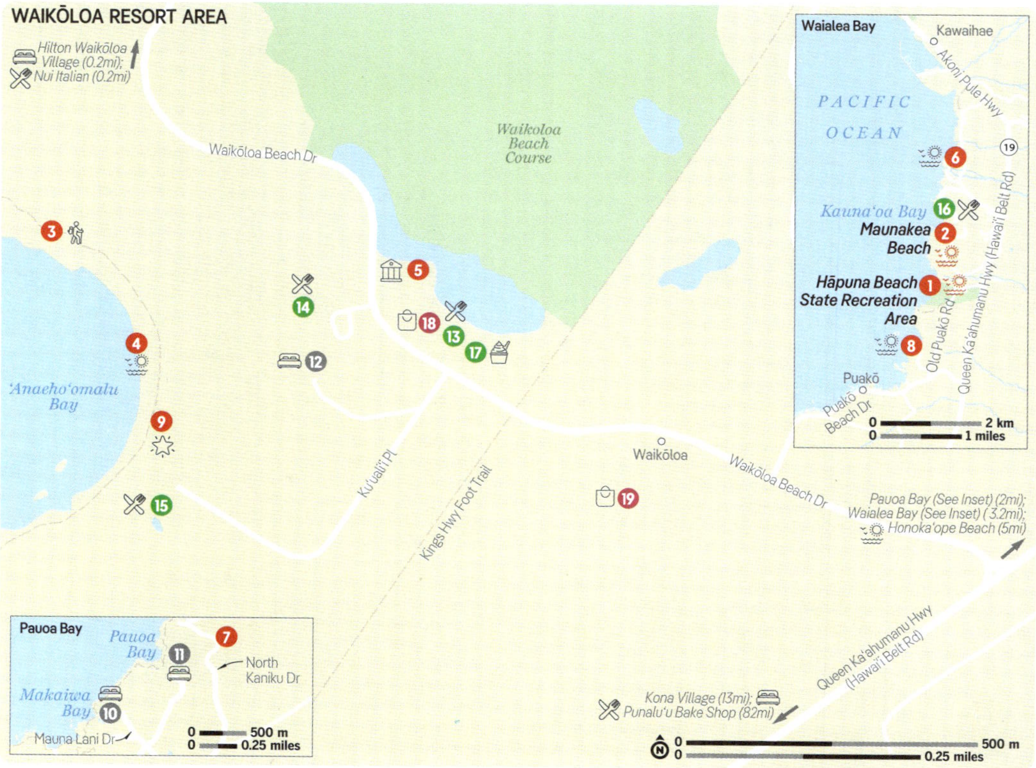

calm waters are perfect for beginner stand-up paddleboarding (SUP) and kayaking; rent gear from **Hawai'i Ocean Sports** *(hawaiioceansports.com)* fronting the Marriott.

Pampering more your thing? Get a luxurious version of a traditional Hawaiian *lomilomi* massage, starting at $275 for 60 minutes, in an outdoor thatched-roof *hale* at the **Spa Without Walls** *(fairmont.com/orchid-hawaii/spa)* at the Fairmont Orchid.

Now refreshed and recharged, put on sturdy shoes and search for ancient Hawaiian art; petroglyphs are scattered in lava-flow remnants in road medians and golf courses here. Morning guided tours departing the Kings' Shops help connect the dots, or visit **Puakō Petrogylph Archeological Preserve** on your own. Often overlooked, it's among the most concentrated and plentiful collections of the rock carvings in all Hawai'i.

Interested in cultural activities? Head to the **Queens' Marketplace** *(queensmarketplace.net)* for free *'ukulele* lessons led by Nā Hōkū Hanohano (think Hawaiian Grammys) award winner Kris Fuchigami. The Thursday night Queens' Culinary Market is worth visiting, with vendors selling an array of fresh produce, flowers, local coffee, honey and jams. Live music, too.

MOONLIGHT MUSIC

Guests staying at the **Auberge Mauna Lani** *(aubergeresorts.com/maunalani)* during weekends near the full moon are in for a treat. That's when longtime residents and local legends gather on the porch of the Eva Parker Woods Cottage, beside the restored ancient Hawaiian fishponds, for Twilight at Kalāhuipua'a – an informal 'talk story' and *kanikapila* (jam session) that can stretch late into the night with music, hula and plenty of laughter. The atmosphere is relaxed and intimate, more like spending an evening in your musical uncle's backyard than attending a formal performance.

All in the 'Ohana

Even adults will love these activities

Families looking to get away and spend more time outdoors on vacation – but within easy proximity of kid-friendly restaurants, shops and your hotel room – will find everything on their travel list in Waikōloa. Many of the hotels here cater to families, with *keiki* (child)menus and free on-site activities geared toward kids. No resort does it better than the **Hilton Waikōloa Village** *(hiltonwaikoloavillage.com)*. This 62-acre oceanfront resort boasts four pools – including the largest on the island with a 175ft waterslide and rope bridge – and a saltwater lagoon that you can explore on a pedal boat or kayak. You can also get around the resort on a canal boat or tram.

Kids will love playing on a black-sand beach, and there's one in Waikōloa. **Honoka'ope Beach** (aka 49 Black Sand Beach) is located on the coast of Honoka'ope Bay near the Mauna Lani resort. There's a small parking lot – 20 stalls, so get there before 8am – and parking cost $20 per vehicle for nonresidents. The black sand is formed from eroded volcanic material that has been broken down by waves. (Oh, and there's a restroom!) Spend an afternoon at **Kings' Shops** *(kingsshops.com)*, where the kids can interact with

EATING IN THE WAIKŌLOA RESORT AREA: FAMILY-FRIENDLY OPTIONS

Bistro at Waikōloa Luxury Cinemas: Catch a movie with 'ahi *poke* bowls, smash burgers and street tacos. *11am-8pm* **$$**

Foster's Kitchen: The menu features classic American fare, including barbecue plates, with island ingredients. *11am-9pm* **$$**

Lava Lava Beach Club: Dine barefoot on coconut shrimp, killer burgers and indulgent desserts. *11:30am-9pm Mon-Fri, 11am-9pm Sat & Sun* **$$**

Pono Pastries: Kids will love the small-batch mochi doughnuts, stuffed *malasadas* (Portuguese-style donuts) and giant cinnamon rolls. *10am-7pm* **$**

ROBERTO DANI/SHUTTERSTOCK

Petrogylph, Puakō Petrogylph Archeological Preserve

STEM exhibits at the **Hawai'i Keiki Museum** *(hawaiikeiki museum.org; adult $7-15, child free-$10)* or feast on massive shave ice from the **Original Big Island Shave Ice Co** *(obisic.squarespace.com)*. On the second and fourth Wednesdays, starting at 8pm, witness a spectacular fire knife performance at the mall – for free!

Snorkel with Mantas

A curved, white-sand beach awaits

Kauna'oa Beach, more commonly known as **Maunakea Beach**, is perhaps the region's most coveted white sandy spot. This curved, uncrowded stretch of sea is ideal for swimming, snorkeling and SUP. Come evening, you can snorkel with manta rays on a guided tour. Access is through the Mauna Kea Beach Hotel; free shoreline parking for nonguests is limited to 13 spots – to snag one, get here early or after the first wave of visitors has left in the late afternoon.

Escape the Crowds

Quieter beach but no amenities

A little over a half-mile north of Maunakea Beach, **Mau'umae Beach** is a smaller and more secluded beach. Protected from larger swells by the coastline's curves, it's a local secret and a great spot for relaxing, swimming and snorkeling. The most direct access is also via the Mauna Kea Beach Hotel – follow the old coastal road via the second right after passing through the resort gate, over two wooden bridges, and park by telephone pole No 22 on the left, where a small path leads to the shore. Parking is limited to 10 spots. You can also park at Spencer Beach Park a quarter-mile north and hike in. There are no restrooms, and dogs run freely here.

COCONUT POSTCARDS

In theory, any US post office should mail a coconut for you, but the ones in Hawai'i are far more familiar with the tradition. While you can mail almost any coconut, it's easiest to buy a painted, ready-to-ship one from a local vendor and take it to the nearest post office. Guests at the **Kona Village** (p65; *rosewoodhotels.com/en/kona-village)* can design and send a coconut postcard – a fun keepsake for travelers – at an on-property kiosk. **Punalu'u Bake Shop** (p164; *bakeshophawaii.com)* in Nā'ālehu – about a two-hour drive away – also sells hand-painted coconuts ready to mail. You can order them online, too, if you want to send a tropical surprise without making the drive.

VIEWING WILDLIFE

Hawai'i's wildlife is best viewed from a respectful distance – and state and federal laws require it. It's a felony to touch, harass, harm or kill any endangered or threatened species, including Hawaiian monk seals, with penalties of up to five years in prison and a $50,000 fine. Mandated viewing distances help protect both animals and visitors: stay at least 10ft (3m) from sea turtles on land or in the water, and 50ft (15m) or behind posted barriers for monk seals. Keep 50yd (45m) away from dolphins, and 100yd from humpback whales, a federally protected species. Observing these guidelines ensures Hawai'i's wildlife stays wild – and safe – for everyone.

Virtual Beach Playground

Hawai'i Island's biggest but with a fee

Hāpuna Beach State Recreation Park boasts the island's longest strip of white sand with convenient parking, plus public restrooms and picnic areas. But there's a fee to enter the area now: nonresidents pay $5 per person and $10 per vehicle for parking (children under three are free). It's a short, paved stroll from the parking lot to the beach. Its relaxed vibe (despite its popularity for family barbecues and birthday parties) and soft stretch of shoreline make it one of the island's best beaches. Be sure to pack an umbrella and sun protection; while picnic areas are shaded, they are set away from the shore and the beach itself is completely exposed. When the wind kicks up and whips the sand around, Hāpuna can be downright uncomfortable.

Snorklers' Paradise

Spot turtles and whales

South of Hāpuna Beach, **Waialea Beach** – known by locals as Beach 69 – has a rocky bottom but shaded, semi-private coves and soft sand. The 35-acre bay is designated as a Marine Protected Conservation District, so the diversity of marine life – including *honu* (Hawaiian green sea turtles) – is among the best along this coastline. It's not uncommon to see migrating North Pacific humpback whales offshore, too. Getting to Waialea Beach is possible via a short hike from Hāpuna Beach's southern end. The route is part of the island's **Ala Kahakai National Historic Trail**, a coastal trail network of 175 miles that spans multiple *ahupua'a* (traditional land divisions) and encompasses ancient Hawaiian cultural sites.

EATING IN WAIKŌLOA RESORT AREA: BEST RESORT DINING

Manta: Excellent fine-dining dinner specializing in local seafood with view of Kauna'oa Bay. At the newly renovated Mauna Kea Beach Hotel. 5:30-9pm $$$

Nui Italian: Within Hilton Waikōloa Village, this authentic Italian restaurant features thick-crust Roman pizza made with three-day proofed dough. *5-9pm* $$

Binchotan Bar & Grill: Order shareable plates at this northern Japanese *robatayaki* grill joint at the Fairmont Orchid. *5-9pm* $$$

Hawaii Calls Restaurant: This casual, poolside restaurant serves classic breakfast and lunch fare, and dinner features locally sourced ingredients. *7am-9pm* $$

Beyond Waikōloa Resort Area

Ancient temples, rare ecosystems, a strangely charming industrial port town and more are within a 45-minute drive of Waikōloa's resorts.

Hardened *pāhoehoe* (smooth-flowing lava) and jumbled *'a'ā* (rough, jagged lava) blanket the landscape and cup the manicured resort properties against a sparkling blue-green sea. Further north along the windswept coast, where South Kohala transitions to North Kohala, sits the boulder rock remnants of one of island's most storied temples at Pu'ukoholā Heiau National Historic Site. Just beyond, several small boat harbors give way to the small town of Kawaihae, home to a significant industrial port serving all of West Hawai'i. Inland and up the mountain from the resort region is Waikōloa Village, a residential community with panoramic ocean views and gateway to one of the island's rarer ecosystems – the dry forest.

Waikōloa Village

TIME FROM THE WAIKŌLOA RESORT AREA: **15MIN**

Explore and restore Hawai'i's dry forest ecosystem

A short drive inland from the resort area, where invasive brown fountain grass and jumbled lava rock dominate, you'll find the **Waikōloa Dry Forest Initiative** *(waikoloadryforest.org)*, just outside of the residential town of **Waikōloa Village**. Though it may not look like much, this site is one of the last remaining plots of Hawai'i's lowland dry forest ecosystem. Rare and culturally significant native plants – four endemic species of fragrant sandalwood; centuries-old *wiliwili* trees whose lightweight wood was once used to make the original surfboards; and plants such as the purple flowering *'āwikiwiki* whose vine was used in traditional medicine and woven to make fishnets – eek out an existence in an area that gets fewer than 15in of rainfall each year. In February the annual **Wiliwili Festival** here features food vendors, guided hikes and educational exhibits.

Places

GETTING AROUND

You'll need a car to get to the lesser-visited areas outside the resort area. Most rental companies operate from Kona International Airport, a 20-minute drive south, though resorts can help arrange one if you didn't grab one on arrival. Car shares (like Turo) are increasingly an option; rideshares have very limited presence here.

Many visitors are surprised by the traffic backlog along Queen Ka'ahumanu Hwy heading into Kailua-Kona from the resort area each day – plan for an extra 30 minutes if you're traveling around rush hour (7:30am to 9am and 4pm to 6pm).

BIRD TRAIL

If you want to explore another rare Hawaiian ecosystem, continue 23 miles inland – about a 35-minute drive – to the 8000ft slopes of Maunakea. Here you'll find upland dry forest filled with native māmane trees and, if you're lucky, the critically endangered *palila* honeycreeper. These yellow-headed specialists rely almost entirely on māmane seeds, and this volcano's slopes are the only place on Earth where they still survive.

For your best chance of spotting one, bring binoculars and head for the **Palila Forest Discovery Trail** in the Ka'ohe Game Management Area. A 4WD vehicle is recommended for unpaved stretches. Temperatures drop noticeably at this elevation, so pack a jacket and long pants for the trip.

GEORGE BURBA/SHUTTERSTOCK

Pu'ukoholā Heiau

Located at around 1000ft of elevation on the slopes between Maunaloa and Maunakea, and altered over time by natural and unnatural processes, the landscape is considered degraded and in need of restoration. That's where you come in. Year-round, on the mornings on the second and fourth Saturdays of each month, the 275-acre dry forest preserve opens its gates to volunteers who help build educational trails, maintain fences to keep out feral goats, clear invasive plants, collect native seeds and plant out native species to return the ecosystem to its former glory. All necessary tools are provided, but advance registration is required. If you can't make it for a designated volunteer day, consider signing up for one of its donation-based monthly Friday sunset tours, which help to fund restoration efforts. The preserve entrance is reached via Quarry Rd in Waikōloa Village. Stay to the right and follow the gravel road to the entrance gate.

Kawaihae

TIME FROM THE WAIKŌLOA RESORT AREA: **15MIN**

Visit one of Hawai'i's last great temples

Driving toward the port town of Kawaihae, where South Kohala transitions to North Kohala, it's hard to miss the massive stone structure looming large on a seaside hill. Once adorned

DRINKING IN WAIKŌLOA: COFFEE SHOPS

Island Vintage Coffee: An island-wide chain serving 100% Kona coffee alongside acai bowls and beans bagged to go. In the Kings' Shops. *6am-3pm*

Mauna Lani Coffee Co: This trendy locally owned coffee-house-style cafe serves pastries, breakfast sandwiches and lunch bites at the Shops at Mauna Lani. *6am-4pm*

HiCO Hawaiian Coffee: Kona coffee, *ube* (purple yam) and matcha lattes and a frozen coffee drink called a Froshaka. Toasts, sammies, acai bowls available, too. *6:30am-2pm*

Kohala Coffee Co: Has tons of coffee options, including nitro cold brew, all roasted in Hawai'i, and some house-made flavored energy drinks. It even has a drive-thru. *6am-6pm*

with wooden *ki'i* (god statues) and several large, thatched structures, the foundation is all that remains of **Pu'ukoholā Heiau**, a significant *luakini* heiau (human sacrifice temple) built in 1790 by King Kamehameha the Great.

Today it's a National Historic Site, and you can walk right up to its stepped base. The imposing stack of boulders – 224ft by 100ft with walls 16ft to 20ft high – were painstakingly carried by a human chain of Kamehameha's men from inside **Pololū Valley** (p194), some 20 miles away, to fulfill a prophecy: a *kahuna* (priest) told the king that if he constructed a temple to Kūkā'ilimoku (his family's war god) here, he would one day rule all the Hawaiian Islands. The prophecy came to pass nine years after the heiau's completion in 1791, and this was ultimately one of the last great Hawaiian temple structures ever completed.

Start at the low-profile lava-rock visitor center atop Pu'ukoholā (Whale Hill). The center was built to blend into the landscape and to offer excellent views of the sacred heiau; its interior is a mini museum dedicated to the site's history and importance. Don't miss the paintings by artist Herb Kawainui Kāne, a seminal figure of the Hawaiian cultural renaissance of the 1970s, depicting historical scenes of the heiau's construction and ceremonial appearance. Just beyond, a half-mile loop trail encompasses many of the grounds' highlights including the namesake heiau, an offering tower, a royal courtyard and fort site and the remnants of Hawai'i's earliest European home sites. The path also includes seaside signposts signaling the offshore location of a fully submerged temple to shark gods. It's unclear whether the temple has always been fully submerged, but black-tip reef sharks can often be found around its supposed location with their fins skimming the surface (best seen in the early morning).

An ancient seaside footpath, part of the island-rimming **Ala Kahakai National Historic Trail** (p176), makes for an excellent longer hike beyond the park – it's 3 miles to **Hāpuna Beach** (p176). The temple site and the hike are unshaded and usually hot and dry, so bring sunscreen, a hat and water.

If you're visiting between November and March, the area around the visitor center provides an excellent vantage point for spotting spouting migratory humpback whales offshore.

SHOPPING IN THE WAIKŌLOA RESORT AREA

Lava Lava Beach Club It's all island vibes at this toes-in-the-sand favorite restaurant, bungalow hotel and local hang. The merch – 70s-style surf T-shirts, sarongs, hats and coozies – is pretty great, too.

Olive Clare Boutique This family-run boutique at Queens' Marketplace is brimming with island-inspired apparel, handcrafted jewelry, and locally made home goods.

Reyn Spooner An iconic brand since 1956, this is the place to go for authentic men's and women's aloha wear. Find it at the Queens' Marketplace.

Nana's Clay Flowers The Taras started making clay flowers in Oklahoma before opening a shop at the Kings' Shops. Get clay versions of plumeria, orchids and hibiscus to take home.

EATING IN WAIKŌLOA VILLAGE & KAWAIHAE: OUR PICKS

Pueo's Osteria: Excellent hearty Italian fare in Waikōloa Village. Open late, it's one of few options for stargazers returning from Maunakea. *4:30-9pm* $$

KTA Waikōloa Village: Full-service branch of the local KTA Super Stores with deli, bakery and ATM. *6am-8pm* $

Kohala Burger & Taco: Local grass-fed burgers, tacos and milkshakes served alongside a toy and candy shop. *11am-3:30pm Mon-Wed & Fri, 11am-5:30pm Thu & Sat* $

Cipriano's Kitchen: Italian and Peruvian cuisines, with house-made pasta (no eggs, great for vegans) and a focaccia bread. *8am-3pm Mon-Fri, 8am-2pm & 4:30-7:30pm Sat* $$

DRIVING TOUR

All Kohala Loop

Want to get a feel for Kohala? This driving tour will take you there. From the resorts and beaches around Waikōloa to the plantation towns of Hāwī and Kapa'au, and the northern coast's scenic darling, Pololū Valley, plus Waimea's excellent dining with cowboy vibes there's plenty to see and wiggle room for your own exploration. Take a day to hit the highlights or spread it out to soak in this lesser-visited part of Hawai'i.

1 Waikōloa Resort Area

Begin at the resorts, Kona coffee in hand, driving north along Queen Ka'ahumanu Hwy to check out the ancient rock carvings within **Puakō Petroglyph Archeological Preserve** (p174). Further north, turn onto Puakō Beach Dr and check out the multi-million-dollar seaside mansions en route to the road's end. Take the last turnoff into the gravel lot. The water here is an astonishing blue-green and the snorkeling is excellent; enter via the rocky cove just before the start of the coral and lava rock beach.

The Drive: Take care turning left (north) onto Queen K from Puakō Beach Dr; use the center lane to help merge. Continue north, staying left at the juncture with Hwy 270 toward Kawaihae.

2 Pu'ukoholā Heiau National Historic Site

Learn about the site's significance at the **Pu'ukoholā Heiau** (p179) visitor center before walking the grounds. Continue on through Kawaihae past the port. It's easy to miss the slight right by the gas station to stay on the route; if you do, the road ends abruptly at the harbor and it's easy enough to turn around.

MARISA ESTIVILL/SHUTTERSTOCK

Pololū Valley (p194)

The Drive: It's wide-open views up the Kohala Coast now and you'll pass long stretches with little development. It's tempting to cruise here but be sure to watch for speed traps near neighborhoods. Akoni Pule Hwy brings you into Hāwī.

3 Hāwī & Kapa'au

Park on the main drag to explore downtown Hāwī (p192), once a thriving plantation town. Many of the original wooden storefronts have reemerged in more recent years as colorful cafes, art galleries and souvenir shops. Continue on to the tiny town of Kapa'au where you'll find the storied statue of King Kamehameha. (Spoiler: It spent time at the bottom of the ocean.)

The Drive: Pass through jungle gulches and over one-lane bridges along the winding road before the view opens up near the valley at road's end. Oceanside turnoffs along the route lead to tucked-away beach parks.

4 Pololū Valley Lookout

Nothing but nature as far as the eye can see. Sea cliffs plummet into Pololū, the first in a series of seven mostly inaccessible green coastal valleys. Take a postcard-worthy photo or hike the mile of switchbacks down to the worn black pebble beach and the valley floor.

The Drive: Head back to Kapa'au and take Kynnersley Rd after the statue, which becomes the scenic upland Kohala Mountain Rd (p190) after about 2 miles.

5 Waimea (Kamuela)

You'll arrive via rolling green cinder cone hills on the west side of Waimea (Kamuela; p182), the largest town in Kohala. There's an abundance of restaurants and shops here, plus farmers markets on Wednesdays and Saturdays, but the highlight is the town's proud *paniolo* (Hawaiian cowboy) heritage.

Waimea (Kamuela)

PANIOLO COUNTRY | FARMERS MARKETS | ARTS & CULTURE

GETTING AROUND

Unfortunately, Waimea doesn't have a main downtown area and the bulk of the town's shops, galleries and restaurants are scattered in strip malls and plazas across a 3-mile stretch of Māmalahoa Hwy (Hwy 19). It's a town better built for cars (or horses!) than pedestrians. Even the town's largest farmers markets, both on Saturday mornings at the same time, are held in two separate locations a mile apart.

TOP TIP

Tucked between Kohala and Maunakea volcanoes, this foothill town, at roughly 2650ft above sea level, is often windier and as much as 10°F to 15°F cooler than the coast.

Land-locked Waimea is not what most people expect when they think of Hawai'i. Its misty, rolling pasture-lands and dry grasslands (a line dividing the 'wet side' and 'dry side' runs roughly through town) conjure images of the Irish countryside and the African savannah. Yet this place is uniquely Hawai'i – its expansive ranch lands are still home to a rich *paniolo* (Hawaiian cowboy) culture, lost elsewhere in the state to time and development, and a rodeo arena hosts regular events. Local farms, which enjoy a more temperate climate, offer a different assortment of produce than your typical tropical fare at weekly farmers markets. Houses even have fireplaces (not a normal thing in Hawai'i).

Mixed in among the village's strip-mall facade is a thriving community that values art, education and fine dining. The small town is home to an abundance of art galleries, unique shopping and some of the island's best restaurants. (Note: O'ahu, Kaua'i and Maui also have places called Waimea. To avoid confusion, this area is sometimes also called Kamuela.)

Explore Paniolo Country

Horseback riding with ocean views

Connect with Waimea's cattle ranching heritage on a narrated group or private horseback-riding tour with **Na'alapa Stables** *(naalapastables.com; tours from $130)* through **Kahua Ranch** *(kahua-ranch.com)*, a historic working cattle and sheep ranch. These tours combine open-range riding in one of the most remote locales in the world, with opportunities to trot and even canter during an uphill stretch. Kahua Ranch sits at 4200ft elevation, which, on a clear day, means infinite views of the Pacific Ocean. Though the 1½- and 2½-hour tours cover only a portion of Kahua Ranch's 2100 acres, riders will immediately feel the expansiveness of the ranch. The contours of its hilly pastures, to the upland forest, and a cooling breeze and occasional drizzle create a contemplative mood.

WAIMEA (KAMUELA)

SIGHTS
1 Firehouse Gallery
2 Isaacs Art Center
3 Paniolo Heritage Center

EATING
4 Big Island Brewhaus
5 Hawaiian Style Café
6 Kamuela Farmers Market
7 Kuya Jnl
8 Merriman's
9 Moa Kitchen
10 Patisserie Nanako
11 Pukalani Midweek Market
12 Village Burger
13 Waimea Town Market

DRINKING & NIGHTLIFE
14 Hina Rae's Café
15 Surf Camp
16 Waimea Coffee Co

ENTERTAINMENT
17 Kahilu Theatre

SHOPPING
18 Uihā Hat Bar

Na'alapa Stables tours are not nose-to-tail, so riders have he flexibility to spread out and chart their own path for nost of the tour – though we recommend keeping relative- y close to the tour guide as they often point out native and ntroduced plants and wildlife along the way. For example, ou might see the endemic *'ōhi'a* tree, with its shocking red, vispy blossoms, or the *kōlea* (Pacific golden plover) – long- ange travelers that migrate to Hawai'i from Alaska in the all. Elsewhere, spot wild pig tracks, lengthy grooves running lown from the top of forested hills to open pasture, and un- ssuming black and brown Wagyu cattle grazing or gazing, nildly interested – either in you or the horses, it's hard to ell – as you cross their patch of pasture. Kahua Ranch was stablished in 1928, and some descendants of the ranch's riginal families still work the land today. If you're worried ou'll be ill-equipped, rest assured that the tour includes ev- rything you'll need to nail the equestrian look, from cowboy oots, riding cape and gloves to saddle bags for your water ottle and cell phone.

WAIMEA OR KAMUELA?

You might hear locals refer to Waimea as Kamuela – and both names are correct. To avoid confusion with the town of Waimea on Kaua'i, the US post office changed Hawaii Island's Waimea mailing address to Kamuela, the Hawaiian translation of 'Samuel.' The name was likely chosen to honor Samuel Parker, a prominent 19th-century rancher and influential figure in the region. Parker was the grandson of John Palmer Parker, founder of the historic Parker Ranch, which helped shape the town's identity and economy for generations. Today, residents use both Waimea and Kamuela interchangeably, a reminder of the area's layered history and the deep ranching legacy that continues to define this upland community.

NANI WELCH KELI'IHO'OMALU FOR LONELY PLANET

Horseback riding, Waimea (Kamuela)

Pedal Around Upcountry

Cycle through cowboy country

Cycling around Waimea with **Big Island Bike Tours** *(bigislandbiketours.com; tours from $189)* rearranges any preconceived notions of Hawai'i as a monolith. A tour along Mana Rd rumbles along the unpaved, narrow gravel road surrounded by grassy hills, grazing cattle and horses, and old, ranch-style structures that may or may not still be in use today. The mountain road traverses nearly 40 miles from Māmalahoa Hwy, up and around Maunakea before descending into Hilo.

EATING IN WAIMEA: OUR PICKS

Patisserie Nanako: This bakery specializes in Japanese-style pastries like delicate cheesecakes and pillowy breads. Go early as items sell out. *9am-3pm Tue-Sat* $

Hawaiian Style Café: Plate lunch greasy spoon with massive portions of *loco moco, haupia* (coconut cream) pancakes and crispy lechon (roast pork belly). *7am-1pm* $

Moa Kitchen: Japanese restaurant serving gyoza, ramen, oak-grilled yakitori and *nigiri*. *11:30am-2:30pm Tue-Sat, 5-9:30pm Mon-Thu, 5-10pm Fri & Sat* $$

Kuya Jnl: This takeout spot is a local fave, serving home-style Filipino food like crispy pork belly, kare kare, pancit and banana lumpia. *10:30am-8pm Mon-Sat, to 5pm Sun* $

Most tours cover just a portion of the route and include as many photo stops and water breaks as you'd like. Whether you go by standard bike or e-bike, it's a largely peaceful experience once you acclimate to some bumpy, teeth-jittering patches along the route. In addition to cows and horses, you might spot sheep and perhaps (if you're lucky) a *pueo* (Hawaiian short-eared owl).

The outfitter also operates a biking adventure (on a mountain bike or e-bike) around the 110-acre **Anna Ranch** *(annaranch.org),* located at the foothills of Kohala Mountain. Follow your guide up and around a dirt path nearly 1200ft in elevation. From this vantage point, it's possible to take in views of Maunakea, Maunaloa and Hualālai volcanoes. The ranch tour includes a detour to a hidden waterfall, currently the only way to access it legally. However, folks do find ways to pass through private land to get to the falls, and sometimes receive a citation at best, or require a rescue at worst.

Walk Through Paniolo History

A visit to Pukalani Stables

The rustic **Paniolo Heritage Center** *(paniolopreservation.org; free)* in Pukalani Stables provides an insight into all things Hawaiian cowboy culture. The stables were built in 1909 and the site of horse-breeding operations for Parker Ranch, one of the largest cattle ranches in the US. Wander among displays of original saddles, lariats, spurs and bits, many of them made in Hawai'i. One of its newer exhibits is the Hawaiian Saddle Wing, showcasing the artistry of master saddle makers and leather craftsman. There's also a room dedicated to female *pā'ū* riders. *Pā'ū* refers to the long skirt that wraps around a rider on horseback; it was originally intended as a practicality for women in the 19th century, as the *pā'ū* protected their dresses from dirt and dust while riding. Traditionally, *kukui* nuts were twisted into the flowing fabric to help secure the skirt in place while women rode astride, as opposed to side saddle. The *pā'ū* has since evolved into a colorful showpiece in festivals and parades, like the King Kamehameha Day parade in Kapa'au; the color of the skirt and flowers worn by the riders are determined by their home island. (FYI: Hawai'i Island's color is *'ula'ula,* or red.)

THE ORIGINS OF PANIOLO CULTURE

Seven cattle made their debut in Hawai'i as a gift from Captain George Vancouver to King Kamehameha in 1793. Killing the prized beasts was *kapu* (forbidden) and their tiny population boomed. By the mid-1800s, some 25,000 wild cows roamed the island, transforming the native landscape. The abolishment of the *kapu* system in 1819 paved the way for land ownership and the creation of ranches. To tame the feral cattle, vaqueros from Mexico were invited to teach Native Hawaiians to rope and wrangle and ride horses. Some think the name *paniolo* comes from a mispronunciation of what the locals called the visiting cowboys: *'Español'* (Spanish). Eventually, all cowboys in Hawai'i came to be called *paniolo.*

EATING IN WAIMEA: OUR PICKS

Village Burger: A delicious farm-to-table take on a traditional burger and shake joint. Virtually everything is sourced locally. *10am-7pm Mon-Sat, to 5pm Sun* **$$**

Big Island Brewhaus: Rustic brew pub with Tex-Mex food and over a dozen house-made beers sold in flights, pints and growlers to go. *11am-9pm* **$$**

The Fish & the Hog: This restaurant serves ribs, pulled pork, beef brisket and other *kiawe*-smoked meats with its signature barbecue sauces. *11:30am-8:30pm Thu-Mon* **$$**

Merriman's: OG location of innovative chef Peter Merriman's now statewide chain of locavore eateries. Reserve for dinner. *11:30-2pm Mon-Sat, 10:30am-1pm Sun, 5-8:30pm daily* **$$$**

WHY I LOVE FARMERS MARKETS

Catherine Toth Fox, Lonely Planet writer

Growing up in Hawai'i, I never went to farmers markets. It wasn't really a thing. We got our produce from supermarkets or vendor stalls in Chinatown – or from our own backyard. But over the past decade or so, farmers markets have sprung up across all the islands – and selling more than just fresh fruits and veggies. You can find local honey and eggs, small-batch jams, homemade desserts and artisan breads. Farmers markets are great spots to find unique gifts and souvenirs, too. Plus, you're supporting local farms, ranchers and artisans at a time when Hawai'i still imports about 90% of its food. It's a win-win!

Visit a Farmers Market

Waimea has some of the island's best

Saturdays in Waimea is meant for farmers markets – and it's not uncommon to see folks from Kailua-Kona and Hilo make the drive here. One of the largest is the **Waimea Town Market** *(waimeatownmarket.com; 7:30am Sat at Parker School)*, with over 50 vendors selling everything from Hawai'i-grown macadamia nuts to locally produced wool. The **Kamuela Farmers Market** *(kamuelafarmersmarket.com; 7:30am Sat at Pukalani Stables)* offers local produce, plants and trees, handmade wood items, fresh breads, handcrafted soaps, jams and more. The **Kūhiō Hale Farmers Market** *(kuhiohalefarmersmarket.org; 7:30am Sat at Kūhiō Hale)* is smaller and focuses on farm-to-table goods. The first Saturday of each month is known as Vintage Saturday, where vendors bring unique cultural items to sell. But if you happen to be in Waimea on Wednesday, there's a great market at Pukalani Stables. The **Pukalani Midweek Market** *(instagram.com/pukalanimidweekmarket; 8:30am)* is a lively open market with all the usual fare, plus prepared foods and live music.

Buy a Custom Cowboy Hat

Unique souvenirs from Waimea

Born in 1894, Albert Uihā Lindsey was a legendary *paniolo* foreman of Parker Ranch in Waimea, retiring in 1959 and inducted into the Paniolo Hall of Fame in 2024. His great-great-grandson, Chaz Lindsey Kamauu, opened the **Uihā Hat Bar** *(uihahatbar.com)* at the Parker Ranch Center in his honor. (Uihā is a family name, but it's also onomatopoeia for the sound of the crack of a whip.) Kamauu, who owns the *hula*-legacy-inspired clothing line Hula Tease, launched the hat bar in November 2025, shaping, branding and finishing cowboy hats, all made to order. Hats, which come in an array of colors, start at around $190 and take about 20 minutes to customize with ribbons, brooches, feathers and dried flowers, and branding from letters to Hawaiian and Western symbols.

Wander Waimea's Art Scene

Spend a day immersed in art

Perhaps it's because of Waimea's inspirational vistas, or maybe because the area's profitable ranchlands and world-class schools have long drawn monied residents, but Waimea

DRINKING IN WAIMEA: CHARMING COFFEE SHOPS

Waimea Coffee Co: Tucked away in a charming ranch-style building, this cozy cafe is popular with locals for its specialty coffees and breakfasts options. *6:30am-5:30pm*

Hina Rae's Café: Acai bowls are the main event, but waffles, grilled sandwiches and iced specialty coffees are equally great. *9am-3pm Mon-Sat*

Surf Camp: One part trendy lifestyle boutique and one part cafe serving a full menu of iced, hot and dripped island coffees. *7am-4pm Mon-Fri, 8am-3pm Sat & Sun*

Country Grounds Coffee: Drive-up shack. The usual coffee standards, fruity caffeinated refreshers and *paniolo*-themed lattes. *6am-5pm Mon-Fri, 7am-2pm Sat & Sun*

Kamuela Farmers Market

has a serious reputation as an artists town. Though it may at times feel a little like a duality – the rural *paniolo* lifestyle and the well-to-do educational and creative ethos that thrives here simultaneously – the blending of these cultural elements are a big part of what makes Waimea what it is today.

To seek out Waimea's art scene for yourself, start with the **Firehouse Gallery** *(firehouseartgallery.org)*, an exhibition, event and educational space, on your way into town. Housed in the town's historic fire station and home to the nonprofit Waimea Arts Council, one of the oldest of such organizations in the state, the gallery is staffed by volunteer docents and all art on display is made by its members.

Down the street, the **Isaacs Art Center** *(isaacsartcenter.hpa.edu)* is a hub of art appreciation. Owned and operated by one of several preparatory boarding schools in the area (the sale of art helps fund the school's scholarship program), it's a multiroom gallery of donated modern and historic art and Hawaiiana. It's the only public place on the island where you'll find such a diverse assortment of paintings, many of which have renowned provenance – the collection includes pieces by French artist Marc Chagall, Hawaiian muralist Herb Kawainui Kāne, turn-of-the-20th-century Taos Society founder Joseph Henry Sharp, classically trained Hawaiian subject painter Madge Tennent, and even Rembrandt.

If performances are more your thing, head to **Kahilu Theatre** *(kahilu.org)*, a world-class event space and the only one of its kind on the Big Island. The 490-seat theater has diverse programming – including traveling international choirs and string bands, performances by local playwrights, storytelling events and symphonies by Kamuela's own philharmonic orchestra.

FRANK LLOYD WRIGHT IN HAWAI'I

Midcentury modern fans can stay in the only Frank Lloyd Wright-designed house in Hawai'i just outside Waimea. The curvy, light-filled three-bed **Cornwell House** has a bank of floor-to-ceiling windows that help integrate the rental property into its 3-acre volcanic landscape setting and showcases the region's sweeping ocean and mountain views. It was designed in 1954 but constructed in 1995 – the plan was originally intended for a Pennsylvania family and never built. The Frank Lloyd Wright Foundation helped to facilitate construction of the architect's passive solar hemicycle design posthumously. There's just one other FLW structure in the state, another unbuilt plan begun in 1949 – at one point a home intended for Marilyn Monroe and Arthur Miller – that now serves as the clubhouse for the King Kamehameha Golf Club in Wailuku, Maui.

Beyond Waimea (Kamuela)

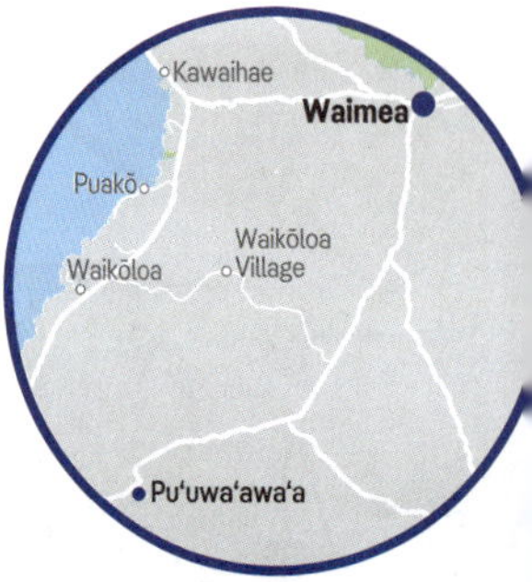

Misty pastureland and undulating ancient cinder cones with panoramic ocean views make for dreamy hikes and drives.

Waimea's surroundings are largely undeveloped. As a hub in the pastoral central uplands of Kohala, it makes a great base (or stopover) for accessing sites in all directions. When driving west to Kawaihae and east to Honoka'a through the saddle between Maunakea and Kohala, activities are limited but expansive landscapes abound. Feeling inspired to get out of your car and get in it? Pu'uwa'awa'a, the furrowed dome-shaped cinder cone on Maunaloa's slopes south of Waimea, provides an excellent vantage of the coast and surrounding volcanoes – just as long as you're willing to hike for it. Or get in your car and drive north to the former sugar town of Hāwī via the bucolic upland Kohala Mountain Rd.

GETTING AROUND

A car is essential in this part of the island. The Waikōloa Beach Resort Area is a 40-minute drive whether you route through Kawaihae and down along the coast or take the inland passage through Waikōloa Village – both are scenic drives. Note that local courtesy dictates pulling over on the shoulder to let faster traffic pass if you're tempted to take it slow for the scenery.

Pu'uwa'awa'a

TIME FROM WAIMEA: **30MIN**

See five volcanoes

About 22 miles south of Waimea, Pu'uwa'awa'a, an ancient cinder cone hill, towers nearly 1000ft above the surrounding ranchland landscape – locals sometimes call it 'the jello mold' for its bright-green color and furrowed bundt dome shape. From its summit, bird's-eye views of the Pacific and four of the island's five volcanoes – Maunakea, Maunaloa, Kohala and Hualālai – await. It's within a state-managed forest preserve 9 miles past the turnoff for Waikōloa Village from Hwy 190 (Māmalahoa Hwy/Hawai'i Belt Rd) and a half-hour drive south of Waimea. You'll be able to spot the striking feature easily from the road.

MNSTUDIO/SHUTTERSTOCK

View of Maunaloa volcano (p208)

Hike around a cinder cone

Several trails snake around the flatter foothills through endemic trees and native ground cover, but you'll want to take the longer loop path past craggy fissures around the hill's eastern flank facing Maunakea and Maunaloa to the summit. It's a gently sloping 1.5 miles up an older paved path from the gravel parking area just to reach the cinder cone's base. From there, past a gate to keep out free-roaming cattle and curly-horned moflon sheep, it's uphill in earnest. A fork near the top allows for a choice of gradient during the final ascent: stay right for a more gradual climb or veer left for a more direct route to feel the burn and hit the highest point. The dome's grassy top has a few benches to soak in the view or have a picnic before heading back down. When it's all said and done, the round-trip hike will have taken you 6.5 miles spanning some 1800ft of elevation!

Plan at least a half-day for the full trek. Before departing, fill in the register at the check-in station near the parking area. Wear sturdy shoes and bring plenty of water, rain gear and warmer layers; it can be chilly and there's often afternoon rain at this elevation. For the best chances of avoiding view-obscuring fog and clouds on the route, morning departures are best.

CHERRY BLOSSOM SEASON

The blooming of cherry blossoms signifies the arrival of spring and new beginnings, a season celebrated in Japan. But there are cherry blossom trees, or sakura, throughout Hawai'i – and in Waimea, too. In the 1950s cherry blossoms were introduced to the town and, by the 1970s, dozens were planted along Waimea's Church Row. The **Waimea Cherry Blossom Heritage Festival** is held every February to celebrate the cultural significance of these trees, which now number almost 75. The festivities include mochi pounding, sake tasting, a bon dance, traditional Japanese tea ceremonies, chef cooking demonstrations, food and more.

DRIVING TOUR

A Magical Mountain Road Trip

Kohala Mountain Rd (Hwy 250) between Waimea and Hāwī is one of the most jaw-droppingly scenic drives on the island. The 20-mile-long road traverses rolling upcountry, curving, climbing and descending between 2000ft and 3000ft of elevation. There aren't many places to stop, but the few spots that do exist are worth pulling over for a photo op. Set off early so you can add on a side trip to Pololū Valley and still have time to return for dinner in Waimea.

1 Waimea (Kamuela)

Begin your journey in Waimea (p182), the largest town in the island's northern region. Take some time to grab breakfast or a coffee; **Hawaiian Style Café** (p184; *hawaiianstylecafe.us)* and **Hina Rae's Café** (p186; *hinaraescafe.squarespace.com)* are solid options. Before heading north, peruse local art galleries (p186) or shops; Parker Sq off Kawaihae Rd is a good place to hit multiple shops in one go.

The Drive: The turnoff for Hwy 250 (Kohala Mountain Rd) is on the east side of town, just under 2 miles from Parker Sq.

2 Panoramic Views

A short distance into the drive (2.5 miles), as you ascend upland and north of Waimea, there's a scenic overlook near mile marker 8. Pull off and look around for 360-degree views that a include peek-a-boo glimpse of Waimea, sweeping pastureland with volcanoes beyond and huge swaths of

NANI WELCH KELI'IHO'OMALU FOR LONELY PLANET

Kohala Mountain Road

the Kona-Kohala Coast. On crystal-clear days (when Kīlauea isn't erupting and vog doesn't obscure the horizon), it's also possible to see Maui and the glint from its research observatory atop Haleakalā across the 'Alenuihāhā channel.

The Drive: Continue straight. If you notice that you're slowing down to enjoy the scenery, pull to the shoulder to let faster traffic pass.

3 Hāwī

From here you'll scale undulating grassy hills with the expansive Pacific beyond, before heading higher up the mountain and further inland. You'll begin to notice various ranch properties, pass through tall Norfolk pine tree tunnels and spot grazing sheep and cattle. In these higher elevation lands, it's not uncommon to pass through banks of clouds resting atop the eye-poppingly green landscape, lending an otherworldly air before making your way into the tiny sugar town of Hāwī (p192).

The Drive: Turn off the route and right onto the main town drag. The intersection is where Māhukona-Niulii Rd (to the west and toward town) transitions into Hāwī-Niulii Rd, which continues on through Kapa'au and Pololū Valley beyond.

4 Return to Waimea

After you've explored Hāwī – and time-permitting, the Pololū Valley Lookout (p194) – head back the same way you came. This road is worth seeing in both directions. Try to time the return journey back down the mountain and into Waimea to coincide with the later afternoon golden hour just before sunset (exact timing can be found at timeanddate.com) for some truly magical vistas. Back in Waimea, choose from its wide variety of dining options before calling it a day.

Hāwī

CHARMING DOWNTOWN | OUTDOOR ADVENTURES | COOL SHOPS

GETTING AROUND

Park on the roadside or in the small lot fronting the North Kohala Community Resource Center on the west side of town and then stroll east. If you can, fuel up your car before arriving in Kohala; gas prices are cheaper further south. Note that Kohala Mountain Rd (Hwy 250) is called Hāwī Rd close to town.

The main drag of Hāwī (pronounced 'hah-vee') is a colorful two-block village of cafes, restaurants, art galleries and boutique and vintage shops housed in rustic sugar plantation-style buildings. Once a hub of the Kohala Sugar Co, whose operations dominated the region for over a century from the mid-1860s, the town today is an eclectic mix of sugar workers' descendants and mainland transplants. Revitalized into a sort of artists enclave after the company's closure in 1975, Hāwī retains an independent and self-reliant streak. You won't find chain outlets or fast-food joints here. Though several small businesses along the main strip have shuttered or moved elsewhere since the COVID-19 pandemic, others are slowly starting to take their place, and Hāwī retains the unique vibe of an outpost town. Hāwī, and even tinier Kapaʻau and Halaʻula just beyond, are the last stops before the road's end at the breathtaking Pololū Valley.

Hāwī Highlights

Shops that make Hāwī worth the stop

Despite its diminutive size, Hāwī's shopping is excellent and people come from all over the island to peruse its unique wares. The all-women-run **As Hawi Turns** *(instagram.com/ashawiturns)* is a definite highlight. Inside you'll find everything from knick-knacks you didn't know you needed (miniature humans for your plant terrarium? Um, yes please!) to practical items like surf-style clothing, towels, swimsuits and slippahs. The selection changes often and you'll never know what you may find. Across the street is **Elements Jewelry & Fine Crafts** *(elementsjewelryandcrafts.com)*, a gallery shop offering mostly handmade goods – fair-trade baskets and bags from around the world and jewelry and handicrafts from island artists. Further down the main drag, **Llosh Winne Art and Design** *(lloshwinne.com)* showcases an impressive collection of exquisite hand-turned wooden bowls and vases.

TOP TIP

Hāwī is a much less crowded vantage from which to watch **Ironman World Championship** *(ironman.com)* races each October than points further south. As it's turnaround point for the biking portion of the race, and the end of the rough stretch dubbed the 'climb to Hāwī,' you'll also see the world-class athletes at a literal and emotional high point.

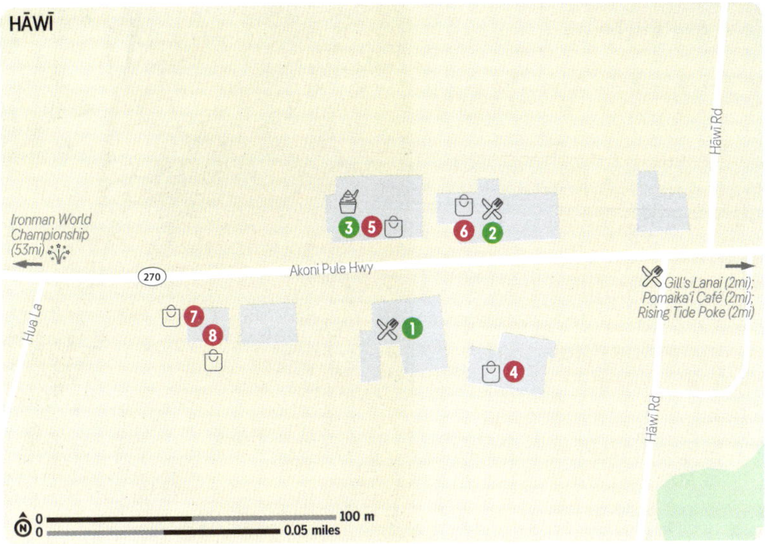

Island woods – mango, tamarind, koa and more – are shaped to highlight grain detail; some feature turquoise or lapis inlay to cover natural imperfections.

Newcomer **Sunshine Trading Co** *(instagram.com/sunshine.trading.company)* is a carefully curated boutique whose storefront looks straight out of a Wes Anderson movie. Inside you'll find home goods, cards, jewelry and upscale women's wear. **Raise Your Vibration** *(ryvhawaii.com),* whose tagline is 'good 'ol metaphysical retail store and high-vibe experience,' has essential oils, incense, singing bowls and crystals, and hosts events like sound-healing sessions and scalar wave chakra-charging sessions after hours. There are no public restrooms in Hāwī, but Raise your Vibration has a private one across the street – leave a cash donation if you'd like to use it.

For a little pick-me-up post-shopping, hit up **Kohala Coffee Mill** for your caffeine needs or **Our Founding Farmers** *(ourfoundingfarmers.com)* for locally churned farm-to-scoop ice cream. Note: Many Hāwī retailers are closed Mondays.

EATING
1 Kohala Coffee Mill
2 Mi Ranchito
3 Our Founding Farmers

SHOPPING
4 As Hawi Turns
5 Elements Jewelry & Fine Crafts
6 Llosh Winne Art and Design
7 Raise Your Vibration
8 Sunshine Trading Co

EATING IN HĀWĪ: CASUAL DINING

Rising Tide Poke: Dock-to-dish *poke.* The sides – pickled onions, kimchi cucumbers and *pipi kaula* (jerked beef) – are excellent. *10am-2pm Mon & Tue, to 5pm Wed-Fri* $

Mi Ranchito: Hāwī folks love this Mexican place, with an extensive list of homestyle fare like tacos, enchiladas and burritos. Cash only. *11:30am-4pm & 5-8pm Mon-Sat* $$

Gill's Lanai: This laid-back restaurant serves lots of locally sourced dishes, from fresh-caught fish to Big Island beef. Vegan options, too. *11am-7:30pm Tue-Sat, to 3pm Sun* $$

Pomaika'i Café: Cute spot to grab coffee, a breakfast sandwich or panini, even a Wagyu burger. Desserts like cinnamon rolls and lemon cakes are made in-house. *7am-2pm* $

TOP EXPERIENCE

Pololū Valley

At the island's northwestern tip, the road ends before the breathtaking vista of Pololū Valley. The westernmost valley in a series of seven deep valleys along the coast, forested sea cliffs plummet into lush Pololū where humongous waterfalls turn to wetlands and a stream before tumbling over water-worn pebbles into the white-capped cerulean sea. This is wild, undeveloped Hawai'i... for now.

NANI WELCH KELI'IHO'OMALU FOR LONELY PLANET

Valley Views

Pololū Valley is one of the only accessible valleys on the island's wild northern coast and a top Hawai'i Island sight. Its sea cliffs and wind-whipped waves rival Kaua'i's Nāpali Coast. Many visitors stop for the postcard-ready lookout, but those who hike the short switchback trail to the shore get immersive views without the crowds.

Human History in Pololū

Pololū Valley sheltered early Hawaiian communities for centuries, its fertile basin supporting taro, sweet potato, and later rice. It was the site of battles and the childhood refuge of Kamehameha the Great. Stones from the valley built Pu'ukoholā Heiau (p179), deepening its sacred status. Residents left in the 1940s; today only a few cattle roam the marshlands.

The Hike

The current footpath (pictured) follows an old donkey trail, descending 900ft in under a mile to sand dunes backed by creaking ironwoods. Most visitors wander the black-sand shore before returning, while the adventurous climb a steep mile to a bench overlooking Honokāne Nui. With Waipi'o closed, crowds have surged, and trail stewards now manage parking and visitor flow.

TOP TIPS

- Check with valley stewards for parking help, trail conditions and closures.
- Bring all supplies, including water; no restrooms or trash cans beyond the trailhead.
- Carry plenty of water and use shared walking sticks if the hike feels steep or unstable.

PRACTICALITIES

- hawaiitrails.ehawaii.gov/trails/#/trail/polol-trail/9

Beyond Hāwī

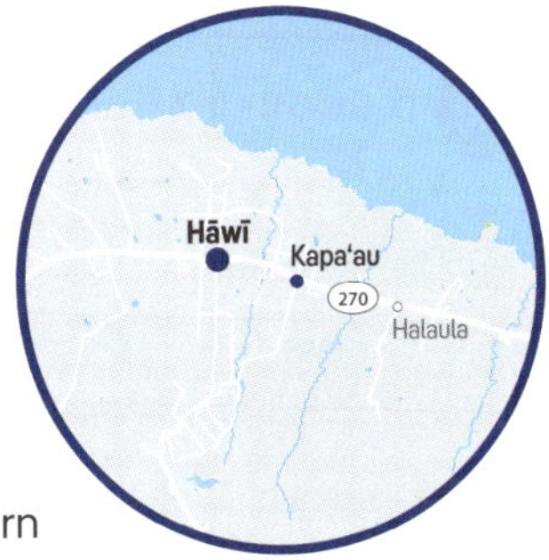

Soak in the striking natural beauty and learn about the significant cultural history of North Kohala in points surrounding Hāwī.

The upland region and down to the island's northernmost coast has a long history of settlement – this is the newest of the Hawaiian Island's geologically oldest region. Farmers, fishers and warriors have inhabited North Kohala for more than a millennium, and, as the birthplace of island-unifying King Kamehameha the Great, history was written in majestic waterfall-backed valleys here. Just one main road, Hwy 270, connects North Kohala's hub in Hāwī to the rest of the island, but many smaller backroad offshoots are ripe for exploration. Take the time to immerse yourself in this sleepy and generally underexplored region and you may find there's much more here than initially meets the eye.

GETTING AROUND

The town of Kapa'au is 2.5 miles past Hāwī heading east on Hwy 270. A Hele-On Bus rolls through in the mornings on the way to Waikōloa at 6:20am and comes back from the resorts at 5:35pm.

BILL MORSON/SHUTTERSTOCK

King Kamehameha I statue (p196), Kapa'au

DISCOVER ANCIENT HAWAI'I

Visit some of the most significant cultural and historical sites on Hawai'i Island on this half-day drive.

START	END	LENGTH
Lapahaki State Historical Park	King Kamehameha I Statue	14 miles; 5 hr

Start at 1 **Lapakahi State Historical Park** (pictured bottom far right), 10 miles west of Hāwī on Akoni Pule Hwy (Rte 270). This remote shoreline park preserves a former fishing village first inhabited about 700 years ago. A mile-long loop trail links restored and recreated heiau, shrines, a canoe house, salt pans, and a burial site.

Just north, the area around 2 **Māhukona Beach Park** holds more than a hundred ancient Hawaiian sites, including Ko'a Heiau Holomoana, a wayfinding heiau revered across the Pacific – though you wouldn't know it, as there are no signs or connecting trails. That may change soon: 642 acres of coastal land were recently protected as the Māhukona Navigational & Ecological Complex by the Hawai'i Land Trust, which now offers guided interpretive hikes.

Fifteen minutes further down the highway, turn onto Old Coast Guard Rd and follow it to the dirt path (second right) leading to 3 **Mo'okini Heiau**, said to date to the 5th century and rebuilt between the 13th and 14th centuries.

Nearby, low stone walls mark King Kamehameha's birthplace. Continue past Hāwī to reach the storied 8ft-tall bronze 4 **King Kamehameha I statue**.

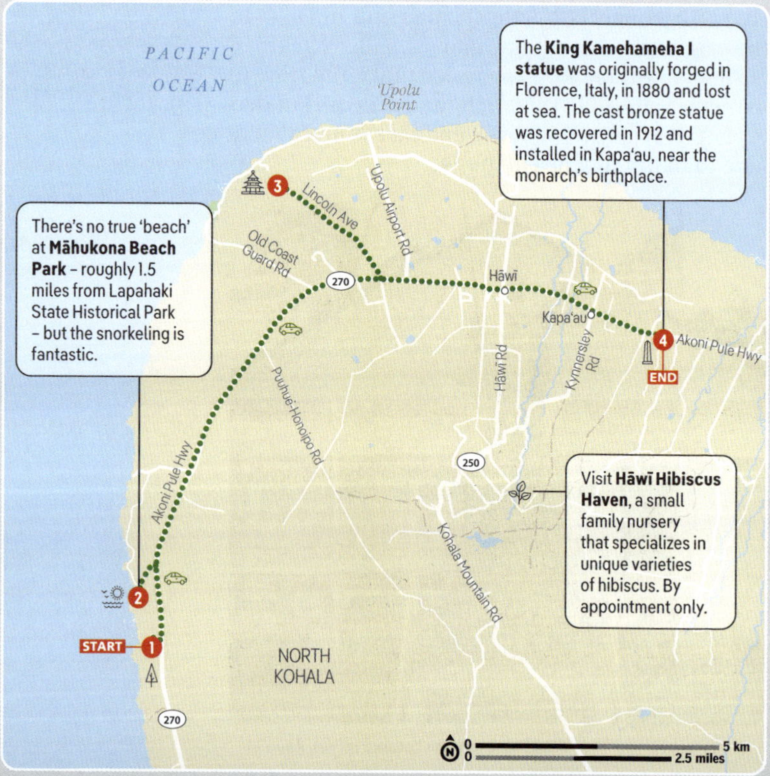

Places We Love to Stay

$ **Budget** **$$** **Midrange** **$$$** **Top end**

Waikōloa Resort Area

MAP p173

Hilton Waikōloa Village (p174) You'll love or hate the theme-park features of this mega-hotel with artificial saltwater lagoons, canal boats and trams. **$$**

Waikoloa Beach Marriott Set back from 'Anaeho'omalu Bay, this hotel is all about the water – it fronts restored fishponds and boasts three dreamy pools. **$$$**

Fairmont Orchid Elegant and almost formal (for Hawai'i), the Orchid never lets you forget that you're at an exclusive, luxury hotel. **$$$**

MEANDERING TRAIL MEDIA/SHUTTERSTOCK

Fairmont Orchid

ALEXANDRE.ROSA/SHUTTERSTOCK

Lapakahi State Historical Park

Above: Maunakea volcano (p210); Right: Saddle Road (p202)

Researched by
Jade Bremner

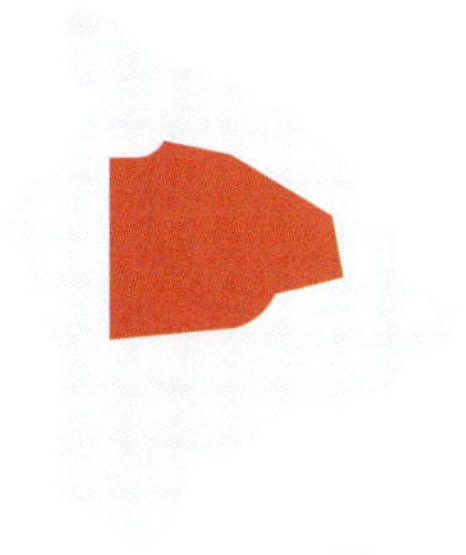

Maunakea & Saddle Road

LOFTIEST PLACE AND STARGAZING EPICENTER

This scenic road crossing the belly of the island is the gateway to Hawai'i's tallest summit.

The original hastily built Saddle Road (Rte 200) was the main cross-island route connecting the west and east. It gained notoriety as one of the most dangerous roads in Hawai'i due to its poor-quality surface, blind bends and steep grades, as well as bad weather conditions. It was completely repaved and renamed Daniel K Inouye Hwy (after a local war hero) in 2017 and is now a dreamy drive, bisecting the archipelago's two mightiest volcanoes – Maunaloa (13,681ft) and Maunakea (13,803ft) – and offering a taste of Hawai'i Island's various terrains. Rolling pastures and lush green give way to tropical rainforest and stark moon-like volcanic fields, created after historic eruptions from 150 to 4000 years ago. Hikes around the highest point of the road, Humu'ula Saddle (at 6632ft), offer a closer look at the unique and hardy flora and fauna thriving in this hostile landscape. This is also the gateway to Maunakea – a sacred place for Native Hawaiians and, technically, the tallest mountain on Earth – measuring 33,476ft from base to summit (more than half of which is underwater). With its height, lack of pollution and dry conditions, many consider it the best stargazing spot in the world. Eleven countries conduct their astronomical studies from here, at 13 observatories. A steep 4WD road winds to the summit for views above the clouds and a carpet of twinkling jewels come nightfall.

YOULI ZHAO/SHUTTERSTOCK

THE MAIN AREAS

SADDLE ROAD
East to west cross-island route. p202

MAUNALOA
The world's largest active volcano. p208

MAUNAKEA
Follow the 15-mile road to the volcano summit. p210

Find Your Way

Saddle Road connects to Rte 190 in the west, just south of Waikōloa, and travels 52 miles east to Kaumana Dr on the way into downtown Hilo, passing between Maunaloa and Maunakea.

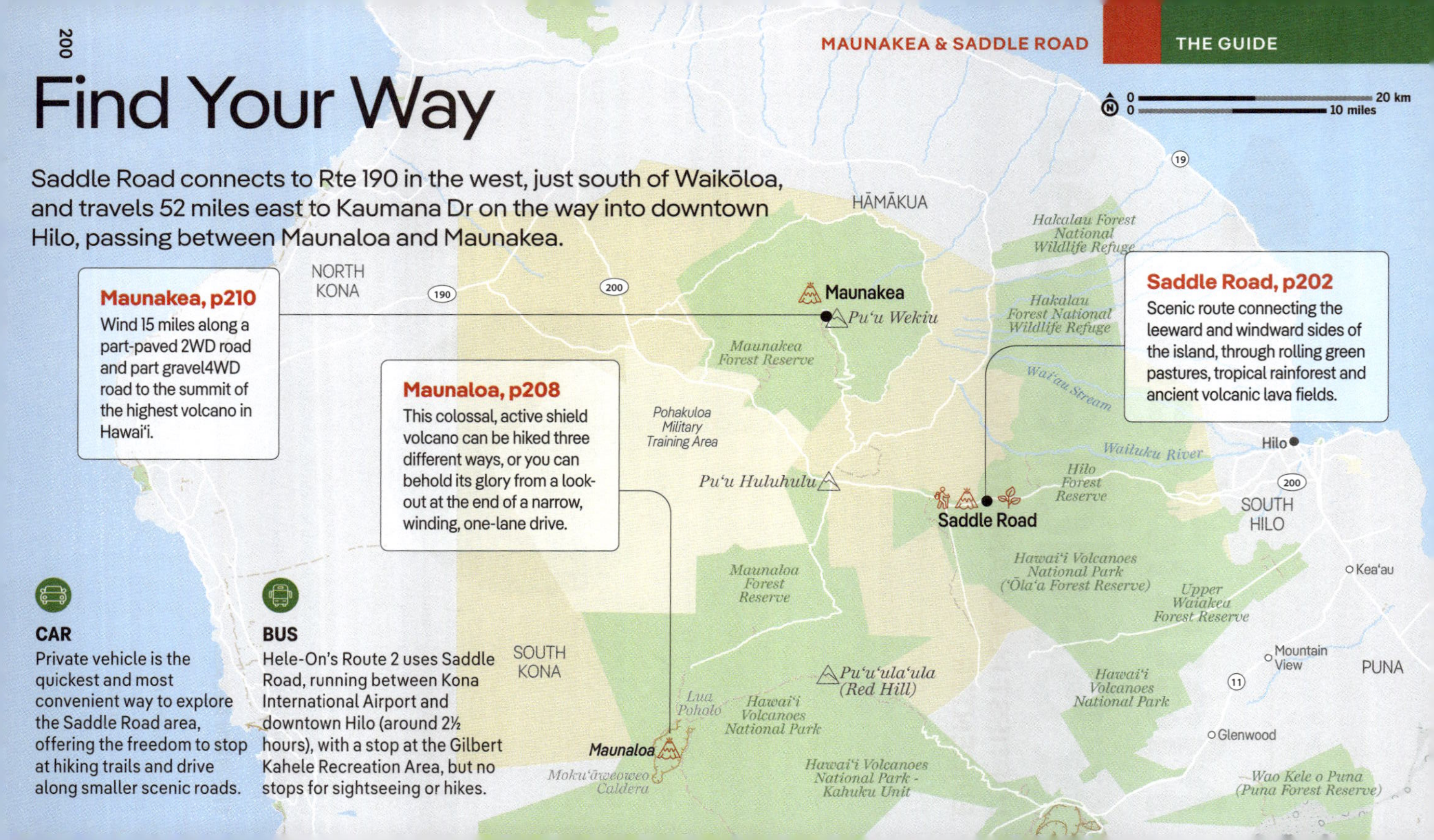

Maunakea, p210

Wind 15 miles along a part-paved 2WD road and part gravel4WD road to the summit of the highest volcano in Hawai'i.

Maunaloa, p208

This colossal, active shield volcano can be hiked three different ways, or you can behold its glory from a look-out at the end of a narrow, winding, one-lane drive.

Saddle Road, p202

Scenic route connecting the leeward and windward sides of the island, through rolling green pastures, tropical rainforest and ancient volcanic lava fields.

CAR

Private vehicle is the quickest and most convenient way to explore the Saddle Road area, offering the freedom to stop at hiking trails and drive along smaller scenic roads.

BUS

Hele-On's Route 2 uses Saddle Road, running between Kona International Airport and downtown Hilo (around 2½ hours), with a stop at the Gilbert Kahele Recreation Area, but no stops for sightseeing or hikes.

MNSTUDIO/SHUTTERSTOCK

Maunaloa volcano (p208)

Plan Your Time

It's important to take things slow at high altitudes. Don't try and pack too much in when exploring Saddle Road and Maunakea, and take plenty of breaks to appreciate the otherworldly views.

If You Only Have One Day

- Walk the 1.1-mile **Pu'u Huluhulu Trail** (p204) before driving Maunakea Access Rd to **Maunakea Visitor Information Station** (p210) for exhibits on Hawai'i's history, ecology, geology and astronomy. Settle in near the visitor center for some of the best stargazing on Earth.

If You Have Two Days

- Drive the Maunaloa Observatory Rd, climbing through beautifully desolate lava fields to the volcano's **observatory** (p209). Explore colored lava flows and the enormous **Moku'āweoweo** (p208) caldera. Bed up at the rustic high-elevation **Maunaloa Summit Cabin** (p209) for a sleep at a dizzying 13,250ft.

SEASONAL HIGHLIGHTS

SPRING
Meander the family-friendly **Kaulana Manu Nature Trail** (p202) for high-altitude flowers in bloom.

SUMMER
Stargazing opportunities are at their best, with little moisture in the air and few clouds in the sky.

AUTUMN
Last chance for hikes and stargazing on volcano slopes before the temperatures plummet.

WINTER
Maunakea is covered in snow by January and February, offering DIY skiing and snowboarding for experts.

Saddle Road

EPIC DRIVES | VOLCANO HIKING | RARE FLORA

GETTING AROUND

Hele-On Bus services cross Saddle Road from the west of the island to Hilo, but only stop once at the Gilbert Kahele Recreation Area. To scale the volcanoes on either side, or to hike the trails, a car is needed. A 4WD is required to go to the summit of Maunakea.

Connecting the east and west of Hawai'i Island, Saddle Road (officially Rte 200, the Daniel K Inouye Hwy) stretches over the belly of the island, slicing between its most gargantuan volcanoes, Maunakea (13,803ft) and Maunaloa (13,681ft), and meandering through a tapestry of rainforest, rolling grasslands and barren lava plains, with roaming feral sheep and goats. At its highest point, Humu'ula Saddle, it reaches a lofty 6632ft, and although the whole 52-mile road is well maintained, smooth and wide (it's a daily commuter route for folks on either side of the island), conditions can change quickly at these altitudes with frequent fog and low visibility. Those who embark on the drive can enjoy several kinds of terrain, almost free of human development, plus a scattering of high-altitude volcanic hikes with rare flora, birdlife, and terrific sunset views above the clouds.

TOP TIPS

Fill up on gas before you drive Saddle Road, which is a remote area with no fuel stops or stores, and very limited services. Traveling towards Kona there are fast, steep sections, which can take a toll on brakes; use a lower gear to avoid brake failure.

Rare Plant Life Walk

Volcanic fauna trail

The flat and family-friendly **Kaulana Manu Nature Trail** (0.4 miles out and back) sits at an altitude of 5583ft and meanders through a 3000-year-old kipuka (oasis) forest spared by eruptions. This is a place to go slowly – it's home to a remarkable number of plants that even the most seasoned travelers will never have encountered. Signs start pointing out significant plants before the loop; look for the endemic red-leafed fern 'ama'u *(Sadleria cyatheoides)*, used by Native Hawaiians to stain *kapa* (cloth), and the red flowering *'ōhi'a lehua (Metrosideros polymorpha)*, which has red spiky flowers

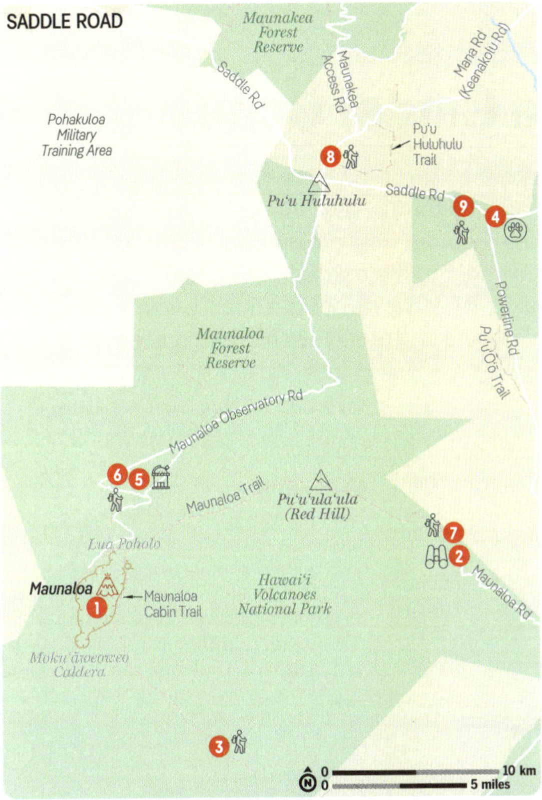

HIGHLIGHTS
1 Maunaloa

SIGHTS
2 Maunaloa Lookout

ACTIVITIES
3 ʻĀinapō Trail
4 Kaulana Manu Nature Trail
5 Maunaloa Observatory
6 Maunaloa Observatory Trail
7 Maunaloa Trail
8 Pu'u Huluhulu Trail
9 Pu'u 'Ō'ō Trail

that shoot up like sea urchin spikes. Silverswords, with their chrome-colored hairs and fleshy leaves, are only found on top of Haleakalā (on Maui) and Maunakea. Look out for the relative of this rare plant the attractive green *na'ena'e (Dubautia scabra)* grows on barren lava fields and can be spotted here with small clusters of leaves shaped like pineapple tops. Look out for the 'surfboard trees,' or koa (acacia koa) trees, the second most common tree on the islands, which can grow up to 115ft and were used by ancient Hawaiians for a multitude of things – building canoes and paddles, surfboards, spear handles, and *'ukuleles*. Around a third of the trail in, walkers will likely be surrounded by a chorus of birdsong. Dozens of rare species can be spotted and heard here. The endangered yellow *'akiapōlā'au (Hemignathus wilsoni)* makes a 'chu-wee' sound. Pause on the trail for a few minutes and listen.

WALKING TOUR

Climbing a Cinder Cone

Not to be confused with the hike of the same name in Hawai'i Volcanoes National Park, the terrific, easy, bang-for-your-buck 1.1-mile (40-minute) Pu'u Huluhulu Trail crosses an old cinder cone sitting in the saddle (adjacent to the road of the same name) between Maunakea and Maunaloa. It has views of both mighty volcanoes, plus old forest, rare plants, birdlife and stark lava fields in one easy hit.

1 Trailhead

As you drive towards Hilo from Kona on Saddle Road, Pu'u Huluhulu (meaning 'hairy hill') appears like a nipple on the landscape. A lifeboat to nature in a sea of lava, the cinder cone is rich with forest vegetation on one side and exposed to the elements on the other, with a balding surface. Park at the large gravel lot opposite Maunakea Access Rd. At the trailhead, follow five connected loops in a wobbly figure of eight.

The Walk: Start left, going up the hill onto the Pilo Trail (for an easier trail, do the route in reverse).

2 Pilo Trail

The Pilo Trail goes along an old rock wall and to the top of the mound, and on clear days there are unobstructed views of the 13,803ft dormant volcano Maunakea in all its grandeur, as well as of Summit Road crisscrossing up the mountain. Take the mini Apapane Trail onto the 'Iliahi Loop

FELIX NENDZIG

View of Maunaloa (p208) from Maunakea (p210)

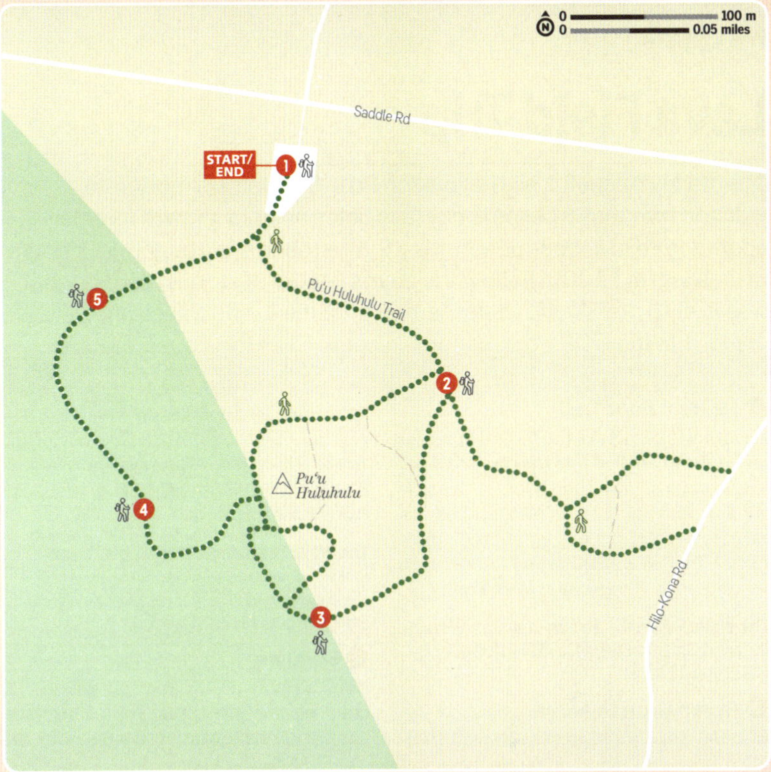

for soaring views of black lava fields beyond Maunaloa Observatory Rd at its western corner.

The Walk: Complete the loop, then rejoin the Apapane Trail to connect to the grassy forested Nail Trail and the Koa Trail.

3 Koa Trail

Take the Koa Trail clockwise for a mix of koa forest, dry mixed forest, native plants and views of Maunaloa. Although Maunakea gets all the glory, Maunaloa stands a whopping 13,681ft, only 122ft shorter than its neighbor, the highest volcano in Hawai'i. However, Maunaloa takes the gong for the largest volcano on Earth, covering half of Hawai'i Island – and it's still active (the last eruption was in November 2022). In theory, a new eruption could make it taller than Maunakea.

The Walk: Circle back down the hill through the undergrowth.

4 Old Quarry Trail

Look for endemic plants such as the *pua kala* (thorny flower), a wind-resistant pretty white poppy, and keep your eyes peeled for 33 kinds of bird, including the majestic Hawaiian hawk, only found on Hawai'i Island; the Hawaiian short-eared owl, which is active during the day; the endemic greeny-yellow-gray Hawai'i *'amakihi;* and the crowd-pleasing *'i'iwi* with its bright scarlet body and long, curved salmon bill.

The Walk: At the base of the hill, a sea of lava comes into view and the path follows a fence back to the parking lot.

5 Base of Pu'u Huluhulu

Follow the fence erected to create a safe haven, protecting the habitat from wild sheep, goats and pigs. On the way back to your car, you might see some of these hoofed mammals clambering and foraging across the expanses of the 1843 and 1934 lava flows.

WALKING TOUR

Lava Field Trip

The starkly beautiful, high-elevation Pu'u 'Ō'ō Trail is a moderate volcano hike that crosses rocky lava fields and old-growth forests, spared from lava destruction. It's a 9-mile round trip (roughly four hours of walking) at 5500ft. Follow the cairns (stacks of stones) across what was likely a prehistoric route, named after the extinct black and yellow *'ō'ō* bird. In the 1900s, this became a cattle route to Kīlauea volcano.

1 Horse & Foot Trail

The route starts near the 28-mile marker on Saddle Road. Pull into the small parking area, put on some hiking boots with ankle support for the rocky terrain (and pack a raincoat – this area has an unpredictable microclimate), and follow the wooden sign reading Pu'u O'o Horse & Foot Trail.

The Walk: Follow the well-worn initial pathway through a small section of lava field followed by green growth areas.

2 Green Growth Areas

Koa and *'ōhi'a lehua* trees and small fruit-filled trees will start to appear. Look out for the orange berries of the *pilo* shrub *(Coprosma montana)*, the red berries of the *'ākala* (Hawaiian raspberry), and the pink berries of the *pūkiawe* plant *(Leptecophylla tameiameiae)*.

The Walk: The path turns to slippery small rocks of lava mixed with smooth shelves and steps over big boulder shapes, with new growth emerging from the crevices.

3 Solitude

Once away from the road, it gets eerily quiet on this low-traffic trail. The route has very little elevation change, but the

XTREKX/ISTOCK/GETTY IMAGES

Nēnē (Hawaiian geese)

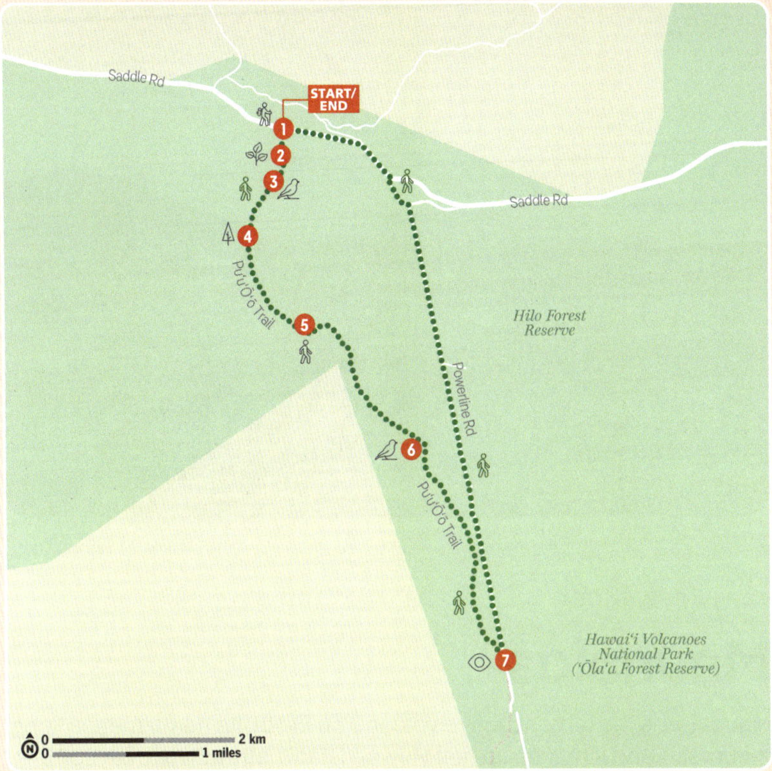

terrain requires concentration to navigate different shapes of lava.

The Walk: The path goes along smooth lava across expansive fields of stone, which would be hard to follow if it weren't for well-laid-out lichen-covered cairns.

4 Old Forests

As if from nowhere the path snakes into built-up old forests, becoming almost damp with ferns and moss-covered branches, offering a much-needed shaded canopy in the midday sun.

The Walk: The trail hits a black lava desert, created by the Maunaloa eruptions of 1855 and 1881, offering a stark contrast to the verdant habitats on this trail.

5 Moon Walking

Dark rocks and giant jagged boulders appear to stretch to the horizon. Look out for the hardy pink invasive knotweed. Several small lava tubes are visible in the rubble.

The Walk: Snake along the edge of the 38,400-acre Kīpuka ʻĀinahou Nēnē Sanctuary, established in 1974 to protect the area between the 1935 and 1852 lava flows.

6 Kīpuka ʻĀinahou Nēnē Sanctuary

Look closely for species including nēnē (Hawaiian geese), the *ʻōmaʻo* (Hawaiian thrush), and the bright-red *ʻiʻiwi* (scarlet honeycreeper), seeking refuge in an otherwise lifeless lava landscape.

The Walk: The halfway point of the trail is a 3.5-mile 4WD road to the left, which can be used as a return route.

7 Powerline Road

It's an ankle-busting road, with softball-sized lava rocks along it, but it has awesome views of Maunakea and its observatories. This route leads to Saddle Road. From here it's another mile to the Puʻu ʻŌʻō Trail parking lot, not the trailhead. Alternatively, retrace your steps.

FRANKSHIRLEY/SHUTTERSTOCK

Maunaloa Summit Trail

TOP EXPERIENCE

Maunaloa

Maunaloa is the largest active volcano on Earth. Its name means 'long mountain,' and it makes up half Hawai'i Island, stretching over 2035 sq miles. Even when the shield volcano isn't obscured by clouds, it's impossible to pick out the summit (13,681ft), as the gradual slope has built slowly over time from lava oozing down its flanks. Always check for active alerts and closures before visiting.

DON'T MISS

- Maunaloa Rd
- Maunaloa Lookout
- Moku'āweoweo
- Maunaloa Cabin
- 'Āinapō Trail
- Maunaloa Trail
- Pu'u'ula'ula (Red Hill)
- Summit Trail

Maunaloa's Eruption History

Since 1843 (when we started keeping track of volcanic activity) Maunaloa has erupted 34 times, usually starting with activity at the summit caldera before letting off pressure at its flanks along the rift zones. It had been 38 years since the last eruption when the volcano sprang back into action on November 27, 2022, with lava breaking the surface within **Moku'āweoweo**, the summit caldera. Fountains of lava soon spewed from the northwest rift zone, and flowed down within 1.7 miles of the Saddle Road. The activity lasted just 12 days, but the volcano is certain to erupt again.

PRACTICALITIES

- nps.gov/havo/learn/nature/mauna-loa.htm

Maunaloa Lookout

If you want to escape the crowds, drive the 11.5-mile Maunaloa Rd past hiking trails, majestic views and kipuka (oases). The road begins off Hwy 11 near mile marker 31, just over 2 miles west of the park's main entrance. Picnic tables and pit toilets a mile up the road are the only facilities until the top. At the end of the road lies epic Maunaloa Lookout (6662ft) and the start of the challenging and rewarding Maunaloa Trail.

Maunaloa Trail

One for your bucket list: a relentless (though nontechnical) 19.6-mile hike ascending 7000ft through surprisingly diverse lavascapes with epic views. Take at least three days, although four or five is better for a summit bid.

The first day climbs 3400ft over 7.5 miles of ancient *pāhoehoe* (smooth-flowing lava) and collapsed lava tubes to **Pu'u'ula'ula** (Red Hill), where a historic cabin gets you out of the elements. Collected rainwater is usually available, but treat it with purifying tablets before drinking. During research, it was not possible to hike beyond this point due to hazards from the 2022 eruption. The next 11.6 miles are under repair; previously the journey to the **Maunaloa Cabin** (13,250ft) was grueling but sublimely rewarding. The actual summit is on the other side of Moku'āweoweo from the cabin. The trail splits at mile 9.5, and while some hikers did the additional 5.2-mile round-trip **Summit Trail** on their way to the cabin, many elected to tackle their 16.8-mile day on the way down. Check the reopening status before embarking on the whole trail.

'Āinapō Trail

This 10.2-mile trail was part of the route used by ancient Hawaiians to leave offerings at Maunaloa's summit. Its 7600ft climb is so challenging that when geologist Dr Thomas Jaggar hiked it to observe eruptions in 1914, he immediately began lobbying for a new route – hence the Maunaloa Trail.

Access to the trailhead is via 8 miles of rough 4WD road across **Kapāpala Ranch**. You must register the day before at kapapalaranch.com/forest-reserve-access; the gate combination will be texted to you at 4:30am on the day of your hike. If your vehicle can't make it, consider splitting the hike over two days and renting **'Āinapō Cabin** *(camping.ehawaii.gov/camping; per night $60)* at Halewai, 2.7 miles up the trail.

Maunaloa Observatory Trail

This 6.4-mile, 2500ft climb starts from **Maunaloa Observatory**, accessed via Saddle Road (a two-hour drive from the park). The easiest way to stand on the top of Maunaloa is via this trail, but easiest doesn't mean 'easy.' This is a steep, exhausting, all-day adventure. Prepare for snow at any time, and take a flashlight; it'll take longer than you think. Check open status before you visit; the trail was closed at the time of research. Construction of a temporary road to access the observatory site was completed in March 2026, but access remained closed to the public at the time of writing.

HISTORIC TREKS TO THE SUMMIT

The mountain is sacred to Native Hawaiians, and throughout history holy men would make treks to the summit via the 'Āinapō Trail to set offerings at the caldera. The first European to reach the summit, Archibald Menzies, did so on his third attempt in 1794. His barometric measurements of the elevation (13,635ft) were surprisingly accurate.

TOP TIPS

- Only fit and experienced high-altitude hikers should attempt Maunaloa.
- It's essential to acclimatize first. Altitude sickness can have deadly consequences, and descent is the only remedy.
- The trail can be extremely hot and dehydrating. Heat exhaustion is a real danger.
- Sunscreen, sunglasses and a wide-brimmed hat are essential.
- When weather conditions turn windy and wet, hypothermia is possible even if temperatures stay above freezing.
- Always pack extra insulating, waterproof layers.
- For the best views of Maunaloa from the lookout, wander a short way east down the trail and you'll also see smoking Kīlauea far below.

Maunakea

HAWAIIAN SACRED SITE | EPIC STARGAZING | 4WD SUMMIT DRIVE

GETTING AROUND

The easiest way to ascend the slopes of Maunakea is by private vehicle or on an organized tour. 2WDs can only go as far as the Visitor Information Station on Maunakea Access Rd. Check weather conditions ahead of your visit; be aware that during severe weather conditions the road to the summit may be closed.

TOP TIPS

Only competent drivers in 4WDs are allowed to ascend to the summit. It's advisable to stop for at least an hour to acclimatize at the Visitor Information Station.

There is arguably no better stargazing spot on Earth: peer up and see the roof of the sky illuminated with thousands of twinkling dots, plus constellations, planets and galaxies from mighty Maunakea (White Mountain) – the loftiest point on the Hawaiian Islands, standing at 13,803ft. It is also the highest mountain on Earth – yes, bigger than Everest – if measured from base (underwater) to its summit (33,476ft). It's possible to drive from the beach to the often snowcapped (and sometimes ski-able) summit in an hour and a half, but this is not a place to rush due to the elevation. This spot offers an unforgettable steep 4WD drive in a deeply sacred Hawaiian place, or *piko* (navel). Native Hawaiians believe that Maunakea connects the land to the heavens, and it has indeed provided for thousands of years. It is here that ancient Hawaiians worked in dangerously high-altitude conditions to collect valuable basalt by hand for tools and buildings. Thanks to its altitude and dry atmosphere, there is unparalleled clarity on the summit, which has become home to 13 telescopes operated by 11 countries, and working here is the pinnacle for astrophysicists. Watching the sun set below the clouds on the top of Maunakea is a celestial experience, and as darkness falls, an otherworldly experience begins.

Get a Taste of Maunakea

History, geology and astronomy exhibitions

Non-4WD vehicles can go no further than the **Maunakea Visitor Information Station** *(free; 9am-9pm)* sitting at 9200ft; from here on in, it's 4WDs only. However, the area is a de facto base for summit explorers to acclimatize at, with dozens of tours and private vehicles waiting here before sunset

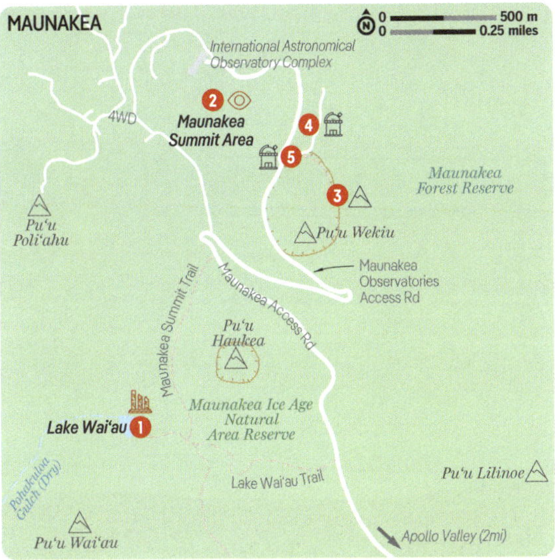

HIGHLIGHTS
1 Lake Wai'au
2 Maunakea Summit Area

SIGHTS
3 Pu'u Wekiu

ACTIVITIES
4 Gemini Northern Telescope
5 United Kingdom Infrared Telescope

viewing. Acclimatizers can entertain themselves (during the recommended hour) with informative exhibits on Maunakea's history, ecology and geology, and astronomy, plus some large bits of historic stargazing kit.

Boards have info on everything from rare wildlife on the volcano and how the Polynesians navigated the stars, to the largest primitive quarry on Earth – the Adz Quarry on the south slope of the volcano, used by ancient Hawaiians to collect valuable fine-grained basalt (known as Hawaiite). The gift shop sells water bottles, hats and gloves, books about science and Hawaiian culture, and freeze-dried astronaut food – banana, strawberry and Neapolitan-flavored ice cream. Behind the Visitor Information Station parking lot is a small walk leading to some of the most valuable plants on the volcano – the endangered Maunakea silversword (*'āhinahina*). This hardy metallic-looking subspecies grows at altitudes between 5000ft and 12,500ft and is found nowhere else on Earth. It has sword-like leaves and a spectacular, dense, shiny rosette of silver hairs that reflect sunlight and help guard against cold temperatures. These incredible plants survive virtually zero humidity and bloom only once, but live from 15 to more than 50 years. Conservationists are fighting to save the Maunakea silversword population, which declined after the introduction of feral goats, sheep, pigs and cattle to the island, plus the impacts of climate change. Tread carefully on Maunakea hikes.

ACCLIMATIZING ON MAUNAKEA

Altitude sickness is a very real risk on the summit (13,803ft) of Maunakea, especially during hard physical exertion when hiking on the volcano. It's advisable to stop at the Visitor Information Station to acclimatize for an hour before continuing to the summit.

Altitude sickness can be fatal and should be taken seriously. If you are short of breath, have a headache, stomachache or feel tired, clumsy or confused, head back down the mountain straight away. Don't go to the top of the mountain if you are unwell, if you have been scuba diving within the previous 24 hours, if you're pregnant, or if you suffer from a medical condition. Children under the age of 13 are advised not to go to the summit, due to the risk of altitude sickness.

BEST STARGAZING TOURS

Arnott's Lodge Summit Tours Terrific value and highly informative summit sunset tours with stargazing with a laser pointer. *arnottslodge.com*

Hawaii Forest & Trail Scenic sunset and starlit sky tours with hot chocolate and a Celestron optical telescope and digital deep space telescope. *hawaii-forest.com*

Mauna Kea Summit Adventures This long-running outfit offers hot dinner on the volcano, cold-weather parkas and stargazing. *maunakea.com*

Volcano Tours Knowledgeable guides, history, picnic dinner, sunset and hot chocolate with stargazing. *volcanotours.com*

Epic Tours Two-hour Maunakea stargazing tours with a pro astrophotographer and free star photos. Parkas provided. *epicbigisland.com*

LARS BENTRUP/SHUTTERSTOCK

Self-drive to the Summit

Maunakea above the clouds

The wild 15-mile ride along **Maunakea Observatories Access Rd** winds from the unique Humu'ula cinder cone (6758ft) on Saddle Road to **Maunakea Visitor Information Station** (9200ft), and then onto a gravel road up to the summit. While all cars can make the first part of the journey, up to the Visitor Information Station, from there, it's 4WD-only; there's a checkpoint where rangers make sure 4WD drivers know how to use low gears on the way down the mountain to avoid cars overheating and brakes failing due to excessive use. Brake failure has claimed lives on Maunakea. If unsure – book a summit 4WD tour.

After 4.4 miles, a gravel turnout leads to the rocky **Apollo Valley**, where astronauts have trained for missions. At mile 6.5 is the 1.4-mile (2.3 miles out and back) **Wai'au Trail**, leading west to sacred **Lake Wai'au**, one of the highest alpine lakes in the world, formed during the last ice age 10,000 years ago and fed with snowfall. The Wai'au Trail crosses

Maunakea Observatories area

the expert-only **Maunakea Summit Trail**, starting at the Visitor Information Station and climbing around 4600ft to the **summit**.

After 7.4 miles you'll reach the summit loop, where you can see several bulbous observatories up close, including the **United Kingdom Infrared Telescope**, with the second largest dedicated infrared telescope (12.5ft), and the **Gemini Northern Telescope** (26.6ft); shared by five nations and paired with the Gemini South in Chile, meaning it can cover almost the whole sky.

The true summit of the mountain is **Pu'u Wekiu**, a cinder cone opposite the UH 2.2m Telescope. Visitors are asked to respect this sacred place and to not follow the short trail to the summit, but rather to appreciate it from slightly below. There are limited parking spaces and a few porta-potties at the summit.

Note that driving at high altitudes is highly dangerous; dizziness and fatigue can cause lapses in judgment and many rental car companies do not tow cars (even 4WDs) off the mountain – check your contract before driving.

MICHELE FALZONE/GETTY IMAGES

TOP EXPERIENCE

Stargazing on Maunakea

The University of Hawai'i (UH) began observing the universe from atop Maunakea in 1968. Its summit is so high, dry, dark and pollution-free that it allows investigation of the furthest reaches of the observable universe. Today, the secret is well and truly out about this pinnacle in star-spotting. Read on for our guide to exploring the void above from Hawai'i's most sacred mountain.

DON'T MISS

- Sunset at the summit
- Ranger star talk
- Pu'u Kalepeamoa stargazing
- Telescope experience
- Space-junk spotting
- Astrological events

Sunset on Maunakea

Watching the sunset before stargazing on the volcano is one of the most popular experiences to be had on Hawai'i Island. The light disappears below the clouds, and the night sky typically appears with unparalleled clarity. Many choose to watch the day come to a close from the summit (13,803ft), via the wild 4WD Maunakea Observatories Access Rd (p212). Leave 1½ to two hours before sunset to ensure you acclimatize appropriately and have enough time to drive to the summit. Don't be disheartened if there is cloud cover at the Maunakea Visitor Information Station (9200ft) – this does not necessarily mean there will be cloud above the summit. Drivers usually pass through

PRACTICALITIES

- hilo.hawaii.edu/maunakea/visitor-information
- free
- Maunakea Visitor Information Station 9am-9pm, 365 days a year; summit closes 30min after sunset each day

the clouds, and after dark, the clouds below are often pushed away due to temperature changes as the sun sets, meaning superb stargazing opportunities at lower elevations later in the evening. Those with children under 13 years old, or without a 4WD, can watch sunset from Pu'u Kalepeamoa, or Sunset Hill, a cinder cone near the Visitor Information Station.

Nightly Ranger Star Talk

After twilight, stick around at the Visitor Information Station for the nightly one- to two-hour laser-guided night sky presentations. Topics vary depending on the time of year and what's visible in the sky above. These could range from talks on Hawaiian navigation and space discoveries to Greek constellations and astrophotography.

Self-Guided Star-Spotting

If you'd prefer a self-guided tour of the sky, you can do so from the parking lots on Maunakea, or head down the mountain to a quieter, smaller pull-out with parking, with less light pollution. Bring binoculars or a telescope and a laser for clearer star- and planet-spotting. Download a star-spotting app, such as SkyView, which works offline. Cell signal is scarce on the mountain.

Telescope Experience

Once a month, join a free private viewing experience on Maunakea, where you can see the wonders of the universe through high-spec equipment. Reservations are essential (spaces fill up quickly). Reserve spots at pay.hilo.hawaii.edu/maunakea/kuene/stargazing.php#reserve. Events are posted around two to three months in advance.

Space Junk & Satellites

The International Space Station orbits the Earth 16 times a day, and is frequently visible from Maunakea. The specific times for its passes in your location can be found via the NASA Spot the Station app *(nasa.gov/spot-the-station)*. Other satellites, like the Hubble Space Telescope, can be found using apps such as Heaven's Above *(heavens-above.com)*.

Astrological Events

Check the stargazing calendar for big astrological events during your visit. These could be everything from a total lunar eclipse to meteor showers or a Lahaina noon, when the sun passes directly overhead. A good source for these is Love Big Island *(lovebigisland.com/stargazing/astronomy-calendar)*.

Cosmic Cams

On the summit are 13 telescopes operated by 11 countries. Sadly there are no current public tours of the observatories on the summit, but many have webcams, which budding astrophysicists can log onto to see what's on view. These include the NASA Infrared Telescope Facility Cameras, the Subaru Telescope Webcams and the the NOAA cams at the Smithsonian Astrophysical Observatory's Submillimeter Array on Maunakea.

WEATHER CHECK

Expect temperatures around freezing on the summit. Warm clothes, including a big warm jacket, gloves, and a hat, are essential (skiwear is ideal). A hot drink in a flask is also recommended to lift moods during a star-spotting excursion. Check the Maunakea Observatories Forecast *(mkwc.ifa.hawaii.edu/forecast/mko)* for humidity, rain, cloud cover, and moon illumination, all of which can change stargazing possibilities.

MAUNAKEA STAR GUIDE

- **Sagittarius (Pīmoe)** The celestial trevally fish. Pīmoe is found very close to the Milky Way. Best during the summer months.
- **Orion (Ka heihei o nā keiki)** Prominent in the winter skies. Meaning 'the cat's cradle of the children' in Hawaiian.
- **Arcturus (Hōkūle'a)** Important star in Hawaiian navigation and astronomy – it passes through the zenith in Hawaiian night skies. Find it by following the arc of the Big Dipper.
- **Scorpius (Kamakaunuiamāui)** The fishhook of Maui is also known as the constellation Scorpius. It features prominently in the summer skies near the Milky Way.

TOOLKIT

The chapters in this section cover the most important topics you'll need to know about on Hawai'i Island. They're full of nuts-and-bolts information and valuable insights to help you understand and navigate Hawai'i Island and get the most out of your trip.

Wooden *ki'i* (deity images), Pu'uhonua o Hōnaunau National Historical Park (p88)

ROBERT HARDING VIDEO/SHUTTERSTOCK

Arriving

The vast majority of Hawai'i Island visitors arrive by air. Regional travelers mostly fly in from Honolulu International Airport on O'ahu and from California, including San Francisco, Los Angeles and San Diego. Flights mainly land at the Big Island's two primary airports: Kona International Airport at Keāhole or Hilo International Airport. Kona is the main entry point for tourists.

TAXI

Airport Shuttles & Taxis

Taxi fares from Hilo International Airport to downtown are less than $20, and rideshares are even cheaper. From Kona Airport to downtown, the fare is around $40 by Uber, and the Speedi Shuttle bus service around $50.

ATMs

There are ATMs at Hawai'i Island's Kona International Airport and at Hilo International Airport. These may charge for withdrawals, depending on your provider.

Fruits

Visitors to Hawai'i are not allowed to bring fresh fruit in or out of the island. This is to prevent invasive species from being transported in and out of the state. Dried fruit is allowed.

Wi-Fi

There is free wi-fi for travelers at both Kona International Airport and Hilo International Airport. Simply launch your browser and select the free wi-fi to connect.

Drive Time From the Airport

	Waikōloa	Hawai'i Volcanoes National Park	Maunakea Summit
HILO AIRPORT	1hr 10min	40min	1hr 15min
KONA AIRPORT	30min	2hr	1.5hr

RESERVE IN ADVANCE

While Hawai'i, and the Big Island in particular, is super laid-back in many ways, facilities can be in short supply. There are limited rental cars on the island; it's advisable to book one in advance for the duration of your trip if you're planning on exploring the more remote areas that are only accessible by car. Accommodations options can be limited depending on visitor numbers, and the best restaurants may also be booked up in advance. A bit of pre-planning will go a long way before arriving to Hawai'i Island.

FROM LEFT: FUSE/GETTY IMAGES, GOGLIK83/GETTY IMAGES

Getting Around

Hawai'i Island is a hugely car-dependent place, and most roads are of good quality. That said, there's a limited bus network and taxi and shuttle services for those who don't drive.

TRAVEL COSTS

Car rental **from $25 per day (plus insurance)**

Petrol **around $5.60 a gallon**

Bus fare **free for all**

Taxi fare **around $4 per mile**

Hiring a Car

This is best done at Hawai'i Island's two major airports, Hilo International and Kona International. Rates are slightly inflated compared with US mainland outlets and rental is limited, so book well in advance of a trip.

Road Conditions

Major roads on Hawai'i Island are in good condition and a normal car will be fine, unless you're planning on driving off-road or to the summit of Maunakea (a 4WD is required past the Visitor Information Station).

TIP

You can loop the entire island on the 225-mile Hawai'i Belt Rd (Hwys 19 and 11). It takes around six to eight hours to drive it in one shot.

ROAD ETIQUETTE

Driving is slow on Hawai'i Island, no one is in a rush, so expect your journey to take slightly longer, especially when factoring in sightseeing and potential dirt or gravel roads. Drives and their accompanying views are spectacular, with miles of coastline to explore, plus lava deserts and rainforests. Tailgating and honking are not the norm and people are generally polite on the road. Speed limits are obvious on the roads and enforced. Parking is abundant with a mixture of free street parking, parking lots, parking meters and private garages.

DRIVING ESSENTIALS

Drive on the right.

All passengers must wear a seatbelt.

.08

Blood-alcohol limit is 0.08%, and 0.02% for drivers under 21.

Bus

The public Hele-On Bus is semi-reliable and free to use. Around 25 routes are available around the island. Find maps on the Hele-On Bus website. Times may change due to weather conditions.

Scan for Hele-On Bus routes

Bicycle

Biking is great for journeys around towns. Avid (and fit) cyclists can do longer journeys, but the sun, wind, rain, limited hard shoulder, and elevations can be harsh. Recommended rental companies include Bike Works (Kona) and Mid-Pacific Wheels (Hilo), plus Hawai'i's HiBike bike-share program.

Taxi

Local taxis are available at the main towns of Kona and Hilo. Uber and Lyft are also available, but can be unreliable due to low car numbers. If on a time constraint, book taxi services in advance for when you need them.

Money

CURRENCY: US DOLLAR ($)

Credit Cards

Credit cards are widely accepted in shops, hotels and restaurants, and they might be required for table reservations, car rentals and for hotel bookings and deposits. Markets are unlikely to accept credit cards. Bring cash for tips for attendants, cleaners and tour guides.

Contactless Payments

More and more places use contactless payment since the COVID-19 pandemic, and most larger shops and restaurants will have this service, as will some smaller food vendors. However, don't rely on it in more rural places (some areas have little wi-fi) – take cash and a physical card, as backup.

ATMs

Cash withdrawal is available at banks, convenience stores, main airports, gas stations, and supermarkets. ATMs can be few and far between in remote areas. Fees may be applied depending on your bank.

Taxes & Refunds

A 4% state tax is tacked onto most things, including food, groceries and car rentals. There is no tax rebate for visitors.

HOW MUCH FOR A...

National Park entry
from $15

cup of coffee
around $5

museum entry
from $10

local lunch
from $15

HOW TO... Get Discounts

Various third-party companies offer coupons for discounts on activities and excursions on Hawai'i Island. Big Island Coupon, Groupon, Free Hawaii Coupon Book, GetYourGuide and Hawaii Discount all offer discounts with local businesses, including tour operators and restaurants. It's worth checking these before you book. Also, ask the concierge at your hotel if they get special rates with local tour operators.

PRICE OF PARADISE

Although Hawai'i Island is considered one of the cheaper Hawaiian Islands, along with O'ahu, in terms of costs of accommodations and goods, visitors will notice that things are a lot more costly than on the US mainland. Hefty accommodations costs are due to popularity, while the jacked-up prices on goods are down to the state's remote location in the Pacific Ocean and reliance on imports. Everything from rental cars and fuel to furniture and appliances, plus the comfort food, which visitors expect to find in grocery stores, is shipped in. Buy local brands and shop at farmers markets, food trucks and roadside vendors to save money.

LOCAL TIP

While cash is easily available, you may get a more favorable exchange rate in your home country or lower withdrawal fees on the US mainland.

Accommodations

Hotels & Resorts

Top-end resorts offer flashy stays, nearby manicured beaches, big pools and ample amenities; they're usually found in South Kohala and on the Kona Coast. Hotels and resorts can book up fast – book around three months in advance of your trip. Watch out for the added resort and parking fees.

Condos

For those looking for a more private stay, with apartment facilities – a place to cook, private entrance, washer/dryer and separate bedrooms – choose a condo. These are ideal for families or those staying on the island longer. Condos typically require multiple-night stays, but typically offer discounts for longer stays. This style of accommodation can work out a lot cheaper for larger groups.

B&Bs & Inns

Choose these for a more personalized stay, often with unique decor, characterful period properties or surrounding farmland. Sometimes the hosts live on-site and can offer local tips and recommendations. All stays come with breakfast, usually served at a set time. Accommodations are typically for solo travelers or couples. B&Bs and inns need to be booked ahead; same-day bookings are not the norm as these are local operations.

Hostels & Motels

These are no-frills affordable lodgings, with shared facilities such as a kitchen, lounge and laundry. Hostel dorm rooms are shared, but motels and some hostels provide private rooms for a higher fee. These are located in Hilo, Puna, Kailua-Kona, South Kona and Volcano. Ideal for solo travelers wanting to meet other adventurers.

Camping

There are spectacular camping spots, for those with their own gear. Campgrounds and cabins are low-cost options in scenic places. Backcountry camping is wild and remote. Permits are available at Hawai'i Volcanoes National Park's Backcountry Office. Book in advance for camping via hawaiicounty.ehawaii.gov/camping, explore .ehawaii.gov/web and hookena.org.

HOW MUCH FOR A NIGHT IN...

a campsite **from $6**

a resort **from $280**

a B&B **from $150**

ACCOMMODATIONS PRICE RANGES

$ $50–150

$$ $150–280

$$$ from $280

TOURIST TAXES & FEES

When booking accommodations, the first price is often not the actual price. When booking, read the small print, and look out for an additional resort fee, which is usually tagged onto the end of the booking – this can be as much as $50 per night. Free parking is also not a given; check if you can park your car, as it may be billed between $20 and $50 per day. In addition, the increased 'Green Fee,' implemented on January 1, 2026, adds 0.75% to accommodations bills. Short-term accommodation tax now sits at 11%. None of this typically applies to camping, which mostly includes parking and fees, but camping spots in prime locations book out fast – sometimes six months ahead of time.

Family Travel

Hawai'i Island is a magnificent destination for *'ohanas* (families), especially outdoorsy ones. With an average temperature of 80°F (26°C), there are ocean dips (in warm waters) to be had, rambles against epic rainforest and volcanic scenery, and an abundance of wildlife to meet. On rainy days, learn about local culture in the many museums.

Facilities

Condos and apartments are well suited for families, with kitchens, washers/dryers, high chairs and cots (if requested), separate bedrooms and sometimes more than one bathroom. Big resorts may offer babysitting services. Major chain stores stock standard diapers, formula and baby bottles. If your child requires special products, bring them with you to Hawai'i.

Eating

Eating on Hawai'i Island is a casual affair, and most restaurants welcome children. People eat at suitably early 6pm dinnertime. All kinds of cuisines are available, from classic American to Italian and island fare. A packed lunch is advisable for remote hikes. Fill up on snacks at in-town grocery stores.

Getting Around

Local buses are free. For further afield adventures, car rental is available. Book cars and child seats in advance; these may be limited in supply. Major attractions have changing facilities. Companies such as Babys Away rent out strollers, high chairs and toys.

Sights

Most major attractions offer concession rates. Some walking trails and beaches are not suitable for children; check ocean conditions before going swimming, bodyboarding or snorkeling at safebeachday.com/county/big-island.

STARGAZING

Inquisitive minds can explore Hawai'i Island and then venture into the universe. The sacred Maunakea is Hawai'i's highest mountain – its lofty altitude and clear skies make it one of the best stargazing spots on Earth. Tours (minimum age 13) take place from sea level up to almost 14,000ft, where, when darkness falls, the telescopes come out. There's excellent stargazing at the Visitor Information Station for all ages. 4WDs are required beyond this point due to unpaved roads. Those with younger kids can stop at the superb 'Imiloa Astronomy Center to learn about astronomy, volcanology and ancient voyaging techniques through interactive exhibits. Don't miss the planetarium show, one show included with admission.

BEST KID-FRIENDLY PICKS

Kīholo Bay
Spot sea turtles (pictured) on the northern side of this beach (p65).

Hale Cocoa
Learn all about cacao on a farm tour – with chocolate tasting! – in the tiny community of Kainaliu (p85).

Pana'ewa Rainforest Zoo & Gardens
For tropical birds, frogs, alligators, monkeys and Bengal tigers in Hilo's compact zoo (p106).

Hawai'i Volcanoes National Park
Lava deserts, craters and ranger-led activities for older kids (p140).

Hilton Waikoloa Village Lū'au
Hotel *lū'au* are cheesy, but kids love the Hawaiian cooking, music and dancing (p174).

Health & Safe Travel

INSURANCE

It's advisable to purchase insurance, especially if partaking in adventure activities such as high-altitude hikes, water sports, four-wheel driving and diving. Non-US residents should also take out travel insurance for medical care, which can be costly. Check your policy covers the activities you plan on doing and to what extent.

Vog

Short-term exposure to volcanic smog (vog) is not generally hazardous, but even limited inhalation is not advisable for pregnant women and infants. People with respiratory and heart conditions should also avoid exposure. Inhalation can cause headaches, watery eyes, a sore throat and breathing difficulties. Those who experience these should leave the area immediately.

Car Break-ins

Hawai'i Island has had a spate of break-ins in recent years. Rental cars are a particular target; hide car company branding, don't leave valuables on display in your car, and park in well-lit areas, preferably with a good amount of traffic. Use an anti-theft system if possible, such as a wheel lock or window alarm.

TAP WATER

The water from the tap is perfectly safe to drink, although it may taste a little different from the water where you live.

SWIM SAFELY

Medium hazard
Beachgoers should take caution.

High hazard
Water conditions are extremely dangerous. Do not swim.

Dangerous marine life
Shark, jellyfish, toxic algae etc might be present.

Supervised swimming area
Safe to swim and monitored by lifeguards.

Road Accidents

Road accidents are common in Hawai'i. There are roughly 10,000 serious accidents per year statewide, with Hawai'i Island registering more accidents than either Honolulu or Maui. Road conditions are generally good, but can be hazardous in rain and fog. Slow down in adverse weather, or pull over and let drivers pass.

EXTREME TEMPERATURES & COLD

In a matter of hours, you can be in tropical sunshine or in icy, freezing conditions on Hawai'i Island, which has vastly different temperatures at altitude and at sea level. Prepare for different weather conditions depending on what you are doing. Wrap up warm, in down clothing, merino wool, scarves and hats when stargazing on Maunaloa, and bring light clothing and mineral sunscreen for the beach.

Food, Drink & Nightlife

When to Eat

Breakfast (6am–10am) People rise early, but breakfast can be found until mid-morning.

Lunch (noon–2pm) Plate lunches are typical, served with scoops of rice, one scoop of macaroni salad and one meat portion.

Dinner (6pm–8pm) Fish, chicken and pork dishes are popular for dinner. Don't expect to eat late; many places are closed by 9pm.

Where to Eat

High-end restaurants Delicately presented meals

Counter and local joints Cafeteria-style places serving staple meals, usually on disposable dishes

Farmers markets Fresh produce, including local fruits and veg

Food trucks Entrepreneurial chefs serving up island *grinds*

Poke counters Fresh raw marinated fish often in grocery shops and fish markets

Cafes Sandwiches, pastries and locally roasted coffee

Lū'au Sample several Hawaiian delicacies, including *kālua pua'a* (roasted pork)

Shave ice shop Syrup-covered ice chunks

EATING PRICE RANGES

$ less than $20

$$ $20 to $50

$$$ $50 and over

MENU DECODER

Poke Cubed raw fish with rice and toppings

Loco moco Breakfast found at any basic joint, with rice, beef patty, fried egg and gravy

'Inamona Hawaiian relish made of ground *kukui* (candlenut tree) nuts and sea salt

Saimin Noodle soup topped with *kamaboko* (steamed fish cake), Spam or char siu (Chinese barbecued pork)

Shave ice Ice-based dessert covered in colored syrup (pictured)

Lomi lomi salmon Salted cubed raw fish, onions and tomatoes

Spam musubi Snack food with grilled spam and rice wrapped in a strip of seaweed

Kālua pua'a Roast pork made in an underground oven

Haupia Pudding with coconut milk, sugar, cornstarch and water

Pipi kaula Salted semi-dried beef

Manapua Hawai'i's fluffy steamed bun, filled with barbecue pork

Lava flow Rum, strawberry, pineapple and coconut-cream cocktail

Poi Steamed, pounded taro

HOW TO... Build a Poke Bowl

Poke (*poh*-kay) is usually raw, cubed pieces of 'ahi (yellowfin tuna) slathered with soy sauce and sesame oil, and tiny pieces of onion. But *poke* has evolved. *Poke* can now be any type of raw fish, or cooked shrimp, octopus, even chicken or tofu. Dressings range from citrusy ponzu to mayonnaise, kimchi and wasabi. *Poke* counters on Hawai'i Island range from fish market-style piles of cubed fish – where you order scoops by weight and take them home to make your own bowl – to *poke* counters, where you stand in line, then load up *poke* on a bed of rice or salad, before covering it with toppings such as carrot, avocado, ginger, edamame, mango, cucumber, onions, pickled veggies, sesame seeds and seaweed salad. *Poke* is nutritious, packed with omega-3 fatty acids and protein.

HOW MUCH FOR A...

shave ice
from $5

cocktail
from $10

plate lunch
around $15

pint of beer
around $10

poke bowl
around $12

HOW TO...

Eat at a Lū'au

In ancient Hawai'i, an *'aha'aina lū'au* (meaning meal gathering) was organized to celebrate landmark occasions, including weddings and big birthdays. They were usually held outdoors or in a large structure, with a feast, music and Polynesian dancing. Smaller-scale gatherings still take place in Hawai'i, and big hotels stage *lū'au* for tourists, with some 200-plus guests.

Entirely for show and not particularly authentic, hotel *lū'au* still have elements of the traditional dining experience – with communal seating, on the floor or around a low table, and an emphasis on *aloha* – being pleasant and sharing with neighbors. Commercial hotel *lū'au* usually come with tiki huts, umbrella drinks, and premixed lava flow cocktails.

At the Table

Lū'au food is typically served on *ti* leaves instead of plates, and traditionally without utensils, but commercial *lū'au* will offer knives and forks to those not keen to eat with their hands.

The main event is the *kālua* pig, which traditionally would be cooked whole in an *imu* (underground oven) on a bed of red-hot stones and covered in banana and *ti* leaves. At touristy *lū'au,* the pork is likely cooked in a kitchen, while a display *imu* illustrates how the pig would be cooked using authentic methods.

Nutritious *poi* (purple-grey steamed, pounded taro) will be on the menu. This paste has a creamy texture and sweet flavor and is served to balance out dishes like *lomi lomi* salmon – salted minced fish with diced tomato and green onion. The melt-in-the-mouth *laulau* consists of meat (pork or chicken) mixed with salted butterfish and steamed in taro and *ti* leaves. *'Ulu* (breadfruit), with a similar consistency to sweet potato, may also be served. Unadventurous eaters usually have an option of teriyaki chicken to fall back on.

COOL OFF WITH A SHAVE ICE

Not to be confused with a Snow Cone, shave ice (as it's translated from Pidgin, also called ice shave) is literally made up of shavings of ice, rather than crushed ice. It's served covered with colorful syrupy toppings. An ancient version of the dessert, named *kakigōri*, originated in Japan, dating back to the Heian period. There are records of blocks of ice being shaved and served with sweet syrup to the Japanese aristocracy during the summer months. Japanese immigrant workers who arrived in Hawai'i used their plantation tools to shave flakes off large blocks of ice to eat, coating them with sugar or fruit juice. Shave ice became a staple pick-me-up on a hot day on the island by the 1950s.

The treat can be found in shave ice shops and hole-in-the-wall joints around the islands. Usually, there's a queue for the best places, which offer dozens of fruity syrups (typically made with local cane sugar), plus adventurous ones, such as bubble gum, almond and wedding cake. To jazz up your shave ice, add a snow cap (a drizzle of condensed milk) to make it creamy. Cover it with toppings for some texture, like coconut shavings, chocolate or mochi (sweet rice cake) chunks and, for the full experience, add a filling in the middle – from anko bean paste to ice cream. Shave ice is served in a pot or bowl with a spoon. Shave ice places are casual affairs – share a communal bench or pull up a plastic chair and dig in.

Responsible Travel

Climate Change & Travel

It's impossible to ignore the impact we have when traveling; Lonely Planet urges all travelers to engage with their travel carbon footprint, which will mainly come from air travel. While there often isn't an alternative, travelers can look to minimize the number of flights they take, opt for newer aircrafts and use cleaner ground transport, such as trains. One proposed solution — purchasing carbon offsets — unfortunately does not cancel out the impact of individual flights. While most destinations will depend on air travel for the foreseeable future, for now, pursuing ground-based travel where possible is the best course of action.

The **UN carbon footprint calculator** shows how flying impacts a household's emissions.

The **ICAO's carbon emissions calculator** allows visitors to analyse the CO_2 generated by point-to-point journeys.

Eco tours

Providers registered with the Hawai'i Ecotourism Association have undergone an assessment to meet green criteria. To find the list, see the association's travel planner at sustainabletourismhawaii.org.

Reef-Safe Sunscreen

Plenty of sunscreens have harmful chemicals that damage marine life – these are banned by law in Hawai'i. Coral-safe sunscreen is readily available in local stores – don't swim in the ocean wearing anything else.

Be cautious when swimming at beaches directly after heavy rainfall or by river mouths, as road runoff and animal waste are sources of pollution. Wait 72 hours after it rains heavily on the sunny west side of the island, where possible.

Tours offer the chance to have a peek at the sustainable Hawai'i seafood industry and its practices – only hook-and-line-caught tuna is sold at auction. Visit hawaii-seafood.org/auctiontour for details.

Handling Wildlife

Many species on the islands are endangered, including Hawaiian monk seals (pictured right), nēnē geese, crested honeycreeper, and sea turtles. Swimmers must keep 50yd from spinner dolphins. While it's tempting to touch them, refrain. Wildlife can pick up harmful bacteria from humans when touched and handled.

Local Businesses

Skip chain stores, restaurants and hotels in favor of smaller independent, artisan, craft, and mom-and-pop stores. This helps feed the local economy and directly benefits local residents. Chances are they'll be using local produce too, meaning fewer food import miles.

Stay on Trail

Hawai'i Island has spectacular sights to see from its walking trails. It's tempting to leave the marked pathway to get a closer look at what's around, but hikers can unknowingly trample fragile soils and surface vegetation and disrupt the food sources for various wildlife.

Walk, Bike or Take the Bus

If traveling small distances, set off on two feet or bicycle, instead of four wheels, to help reduce car emissions, or use the free local bus services. Carpool where possible.

Rent an Electric Car

Hawai'i Island can be driven across in under two hours, meaning electric cars (which can be charged at more than 100 EV charging points in Hilo and Kona) are a solid choice if you need the freedom of your own wheels without the guilt.

Pick up Trash

Use the saying 'leave only footprints, take only memories' when exploring Hawai'i Island. This means clearing up after picnics and barbecue like you were never there, and leaving things like shells and lava where they are.

Don't Buy Water

The tap water in Hawai'i is completely safe to drink. Bring a reusable bottle to reduce plastic waste and fill up at the hotel or a water filling station – available at Hawai'i's national parks and at many recreation areas.

Join the 'agritourism' movement and visit a local farm or farm stand to get fresh produce from the source.

Consider voluntourism to help offset a trip – help on a beach cleanup or work on a farm during a stay.

Water Shortages

Hawai'i Island's drinking-water system mainly draws from rainwater. The island frequently experiences water shortages and droughts. Practice water conservation by skipping the bath, taking shorter showers and not continuously running the tap when brushing your teeth.

RESOURCES

sustainabletourismhawaii.org
For ecotour operators on Hawai'i Island.

slowfoodhawaii.com
Info on sustainable locally sourced food.

cleanrewards.org
Reference point for local beach cleanups to join.

CLOCKWISE FROM TOP LEFT: LALANDREW/SHUTTERSTOCK, LORRAINE LOGAN/SHUTTERSTOCK, BURAKTUMLER/SHUTTERSTOCK

LGBTIQ+ Travelers

The state of Hawai'i is progressive in its approach to LGBTIQ+ rights. State law protects those in the community against discrimination. While there isn't a particularly vibrant 'scene' on the Big Island, people who identify as LGBTIQ+ can travel with ease solo, as couples, or with families here.

Hawai'i Island Pride Events

While Pride celebrations on Hawai'i Island are comparatively tiny compared to those in some big cities across the world, a dedicated community runs Pride events in Kona and Hilo with all kinds of happenings, from yoga and glow stick parties to drag brunches and pool parties. **Kona Pride** *(konapride.com)* takes place in the fall (usually September), and **Hawai'i Island LGBTQ Pride** *(hawaiiislandlgbtqpride.org)* runs events during the Pride month of June in Hilo and around the island. Gay-friendly events are also posted on local forums and Facebook pages throughout the year.

ACCOMMODATIONS

Lava Lava Beach Club (p174) in Waikōloa Village is a gay-owned and -operated laid-back Hawaiian cottage, and welcomes members of the LGBTIQ+ community with open arms. The hip **Pacific 19 hotel** (p91) in Kona offers special rates for Pride attendees, plus LGBTIQ-dedicated events including a pool party and yoga sessions. **Courtyard by Marriott King Kamehameha's Kona Beach Hotel** (p91) is another option – it has previously hosted Kona Pride parties in its *lū'au* area.

Associations & Networks

Websites including gogayhawaii.com/hawaii and gayislandguide.net are sources of information for activities, accommodations and events. The Hawai'i LGBT Legacy Foundation *(hawaiilgbtlegacyfoundation.com)* is an organization across the islands that supports the community with virtual monthly drop-in Queer Mental Health Support Group sessions, advice and more.

RAINBOW WEDDINGS

Same-sex weddings are big business on Hawai'i Island. Most hotels host them, and many people choose to tie the knot here during a destination wedding, free of stigma from staff and onlookers. Enquire directly at hotels to tie the knot or contact one of the dozens of wedding planners specializing in LGBTIQ+ weddings.

LGBTIQ-FRIENDLY BUSINESSES

The LGBTIQ+ community will be made to feel welcome in various bars and restaurants, particularly My Bar and Mask-Querade Bar, both of which are in Kailua-Kona and host Pride events and meet-ups for the rainbow community. Various other businesses, including Puna Chocolate Company, Hilo Axe Lounge and the Palace Theater, to name but a few, are allies.

LGBTIQ+ Hawai'i

Pre-colonial Hawaiian society had long been stigma-free and recognized same-sex relationships, referring to them as *aikāne*. Hawaiian also includes the word *māhū*, meaning 'third gender.'

NITO/SHUTTERSTOCK

Accessible Travel

Hawai'i Island caters to travelers with disabilities to some degree. Many beaches, plus the free local bus service, are wheelchair-accessible. Dozens of hotels have accessible rooms, and there are more than a dozen accessible trails.

Airports

Both Kona and Hilo airports offer provisions for wheelchair users, including terminal to curbside assistance, accessible restrooms, and accessible parking spaces for travelers with mobility, visual and hearing needs.

Car Rentals

With advance booking, car-rental agencies can offer hand-controlled vehicles at no extra cost. Spinner knobs, swivel seats and transfer boards may also be available. Wheelchair-accessible vans can be rented from **Wheelers of Hawaii** in Kona.

Accommodations

Resorts and larger hotels have elevators and wheelchair-accessible rooms (with roll-in showers) and accessible parking. Accessible rooms should be booked in advance. B&Bs and smaller lodgings are often unable to offer the same facilities.

BEACHES

There are several accessible beaches on Hawai'i Island including Hāpuna Beach, Kua Bay, Spencer Beach, Kaloko-Honokōhau National Historical Park, Honl's Beach, White Sands Beach and Kahalu'u Beach.

TRAILS

Wheelchair users can get into nature on four trails in Hawai'i Volcanoes National Park, on the Queen Liliuokalani Garden Loop and at Pu'uhonua o Hōnaunau National Historical Park, plus the Rainbow Falls lookout and others.

ACCESSIBLE ATTRACTIONS

Wheelchair-accessible attractions include Moku'aikaua Church, Amy Greenwell Garden, Herb Kāne Art Gallery, Greenwell Store Museum, Body Glove whale-watching tours, Lavaloha chocolate farm and various hotel *lū'au*, plus some diving and helicopter tours.

RESOURCES

Disability & Communication Access Board *(health.hawaii.gov/dcab)* For info on accessible services at the airports, plus assistance animals, disability parking, and transport around Hawai'i Island.

Wheelchair Traveling *(wheelchairtraveling.com)* For Hawai'i Island and general advice on traveling with a wheelchair, visit this comprehensive website.

Accessible Travel Online Resources *(hidot.hawaii.gov/airports/ada/)* The Department of Transport lists accessibility guides for passengers arriving via Hilo and Kona airports.

Guide & Service Dogs

Guide and service animals are permitted in all accommodations, restaurants, museums and national parks. They are not subject to the general pet quarantine rules if they meet the Department of Agriculture's minimum requirements *(dab.hawaii.gov/ai/aqs/animal-quarantine-information-page)*. All animals must enter via Honolulu International Airport.

'Native Hawaiian' Versus 'Local'

Though many people outside of the islands tend to use the terms 'Hawaiian' and 'local' interchangeably, the distinction between the two is incredibly important.

The Difference Between 'Hawaiian' & 'Local'

The term 'Hawaiian' only applies to people who are Native Hawaiian – meaning indigenous to Hawaii – along with their culture, language and history. In Hawaiian, the term is Kanaka Maoli (plural: Kānaka Maoli). 'Local,' on the other hand, is used to indicate someone who is from Hawaii and not necessarily Native Hawaiian.

There is still a Hawaiian language term for locals – *kama'āina*, or 'people of the land' – although this word is now mostly used within the phrase '*kama'āina* discount,' the discount that locals can get with a Hawai'i state ID.

What's the Big Deal?

Native Hawaiian history is filled with erasure. Over the centuries since Western arrival in 1778, many parts of Native culture have been forbidden or looked down upon, including *he'e nalu* (surfing), Native Hawaiian *akua* (deities) and 'Ōlelo Hawai'i (Hawaiian language).

All of that cultural erasure doesn't even touch on the fact that American businessmen, led by Lorrin Thurston and Sanford B Dole, forcibly took the islands from Queen Lili'uokalani and the Kingdom of Hawai'i. When the United States government had the chance to return the islands to their rightful owners, it chose not to.

While US Congress did issue the Apology Resolution in 1993, it doesn't actually undo the damage that was done; the Hawaiian Islands are still under US control and Native Hawaiian culture is still struggling to recover.

When people call everyone from Hawai'i 'Hawaiian,' it continues the erasure that has plagued this Indigenous group for hundreds of years. If this practice of making 'Hawaiian' and 'local' synonymous were to become widespread, not only would Hawaiians have a stifled language and culture, they wouldn't even have a distinguishing group name. Simply put, while people from California call themselves 'Californian,' people from Hawaii will never call themselves 'Hawaiian' unless they are Native Hawaiian.

Who is 'Local'?

This terminology situation gets a little trickier when you realize that 'local' may not apply to everyone who lives in Hawai'i. For example, someone who moves to the island for six months may not be considered a local, but someone born on the islands may be, but perhaps not if they were never raised in Hawai'i and never adopted the aloha spirit. The question is, how long does it take for someone to be considered a local? Does someone have to be an active participant in the local community? Do they need to befriend locals or speak Pidgin? Ultimately, determining who is a 'local' is subjective.

MARIOSHOT/SHUTTERSTOCK

LANGUAGE

Kama'āina Hawai'i locals; literally means 'people of the land'

Kapu Forbidden; while it once meant things that were 'taboo' or against the law in ancient Hawaiian society, today it is mostly used to mean 'no trespassing,' typically when there are sacred Hawaiian spots nearby

Keiki Children

Lānai Porch, veranda or balcony

Makai Ocean (typically used for directional purposes, as in 'toward the ocean')

Mauka Mountains (typically used for directional purposes, as in 'toward the mountains')

'Ōpala Trash

Shaka A friendly hand gesture, wherein the three middle fingers are down and the pinky and the thumb remain up; can be used to mean 'thank you,' 'right on,' or 'take it easy'

Slippers/Slippahs Flip-flops

Nuts & Bolts

OPENING HOURS

Banks 8:30am–4pm Monday–Friday, some to 6pm Friday; 9am–noon or 1pm Saturday.

Bars and clubs Typically noon–midnight daily, some later.

Business hours 8:30am–4:30pm Monday–Friday.

Restaurants Breakfast 6–10am, lunch 11:30am–2pm, dinner 5–9:30pm. Hours vary by establishment, so check in advance.

Shops 9am–5pm Monday–Saturday, some open for limited hours, especially on Sunday.

Smoking

Smoking (and e-cigarettes or vaping) is illegal in all of Hawai'i Island's public spaces, including bars, restaurants and airports. Many hotel properties are smoke-free. Those aged 21 and older can buy tobacco products and e-cigarettes.

Toilets

Restrooms are available at most beach parks and all national parks.

Internet Access

Wi-fi is available at most accommodations, sometimes for a fee. There is good cell signal in towns, but it may be patchy in remote areas.

GOOD TO KNOW

Time zone
Hawai'i-Aleutian Standard Time (GMT -10)

Country code
1

Emergency number
911

Electricity

120V/60Hz

PUBLIC HOLIDAYS

There are typically 13 public holidays in Hawai'i, when banks, government buildings and schools are closed. These include the following:

New Year's Day January 1

Martin Luther King Jr Day Third Monday in January

Presidents' Day Third Monday in February

Prince Kūhiō Day March 26

Good Friday Friday before Easter Sunday (in March or April)

Memorial Day Last Monday in May

King Kamehameha Day June 11

Independence Day July 4

Statehood Day Third Friday in August

Labor Day First Monday in September

Veterans Day November 11

Thanksgiving Fourth Thursday in November

Christmas Day December 25

THE HAWAI‘I ISLAND

STORYBOOK

Our writers delve deep into different aspects of Hawai‘i Island life.

Kīlauea Iki Trail (p141), Hawai‘i Volcanoes National Park

MNSTUDIO/SHUTTERSTOCK

A HISTORY OF HAWAI'I ISLAND IN 15 PLACES

Settled by Polynesian voyagers probably around 1200 CE, Hawai'i Island – and the rest of the isolated Hawaiian Islands – initially had a rather quiet existence. But Western arrivals brought a whole new set of economic and political challenges. By Meghan Miner Murray

AS THE GEOLOGICALLY youngest, Hawai'i Island has a shorter yet no less storied past than the rest of the islands in the archipelago. It all started with voyagers from the Marquesas, who settled down in Hawai'i likely sometime between 1000 and 1200 CE. For a few hundred years, they were able to exist relatively peacefully, living off the land and sea.

Then, in the late 1700s, two major historic events happened: Captain James Cook became the first Westerner to visit the islands, and King Kamehameha I unified all of the Hawaiian Islands. The former introduced Hawai'i to global influences, economies and politics, while the latter kept the inter-island skirmishes to a minimum and created a sense of united Hawaiian identity. With the presence of Hawai'i known to the rest of the world, Hawai'i Island changed forever. Missionaries flocked to preach Christianity, dismissing ancient Hawaiian *akua* (deities). Coffee and sugar plantations popped up, bringing immigrant workers from across the globe. And ultimately, the Hawaiian monarchy was overthrown, unjustly putting Hawaiian lands in non-Native hands.

The story of Hawai'i Island is still being written, with recent events like Maunakea's TMT protests and Kīlauea's volcanic eruptions shaping the island's landscape and future.

1. Ka Lae (South Point)

THE ISLAND'S SOUTHERNMOST POINT

Most historians and anthropologists believe that the first people to settle in Hawai'i were from the Marquesas Islands and traveled the 2400 nautical miles in double-hull canoes, bringing their social structures, beliefs and culture with them. It's believed that they reached the island of Kaua'i first, but when they did finally reach Hawai'i Island, they docked at Ka Lae, beyond the cliffs at the southernmost point of the island.

For more on Ka Lae, see p160.

2. Kaloko-Honokōhau Historical National Park

ANCIENT HAWAIIAN SETTLEMENT

After settlement, Hawaiian culture and society were left to develop in isolation. In ancient Hawai'i, *ali'i* (chiefs), who were believed to be descendants of the *akua,* ruled the different *ahupua'a* (land divisions). The people built heiau (temples) to worship these same *akua*. Ancient Hawaiians also had great respect for the *'āina* (land) and picked just the produce and seafood they needed. A system of government – later called the *kapu* (taboo) system for its series of rules about what one could and couldn't do – kept their hierarchy in place. The ruins of an ancient Hawaiian settlement at

Kaloko-Honokōhau National Historical Park offer a glimpse of these aspects of life.

For more on Kaloko-Honokōhau National Historical Park, see p66.

3. Pu'ukoholā Heiau National Historic Site

A TRIBUTE TO THE WAR GOD KŪKĀ'ILIMOKU

For centuries, the Hawaiian people worked as individual communities in their designated *ahupua'a*. In 1790, King Kamehameha, then chief of Hawai'i Island, had a vision of unifying the islands under his rule. At that time, each island was a unique chiefdom, and they were often at war with one another. In order to give himself the best possible chance of overthrowing the other rulers, King Kamehameha decided to pay tribute to the gods – and specifically to the war god Kūkā'ilimoku. He and his warriors built the Pu'ukoholā Heiau, bringing the stones from Pololū Valley 20 miles away. King Kamehameha's efforts seemed to pay off, as he became the ruler of Hawai'i, Maui and Moloka'i within just five years.

For more on Pu'ukoholā Heiau National Historic Site, see p180.

Moku'aikaua Church, Kailua-Kona (p52)

LOUIELEA/SHUTTERSTOCK

4. Statue of King Kamehameha in Kapa'au

THE HOME OF A LEADER

King Kamehameha did ultimately become the supreme leader of the Kingdom of Hawai'i in 1810. Kaua'i and Ni'ihau were the final holdouts, opting to join via diplomatic treaty rather than suffer the same bloody fate as the Oahuians. The significance of unification cannot be overstated – whether positive or negative, subsequent governments had a much easier time taking control of the islands as a unit. Today, a brass statue depicting the king in royal Hawaiian regalia, near the place of his birth and fronting the old courthouse in Kapa'au, honors his legacy. The statue is itself a storied artifact – it spent two years at the bottom of the ocean near the Falkland Islands.

For more on Kapa'au and the statue, see p196.

5. Kealakekua Bay State Historical Park

CAPTAIN COOK'S START AND END

Around the time that King Kamehameha was uniting the islands, Captain James Cook arrived. His first journey took him to Kaua'i in 1778. The following year he returned – this time to Hawai'i's Kona Coast. He arrived during makahiki, a traditional Hawaiian festival dedicated to the god of fertility and agriculture, Lono. Due to his arrival time and location, the ancient Hawaiian people mistook Cook for Lono himself. This visit didn't end so well. There are a few different iterations of the story, but the gist is that Cook believed the Native Hawaiians stole one of his boats. In retaliation, he tried to kidnap the Island's king, Kalani'ōpu'u. So, the islanders killed Cook. A white obelisk, erected by the British in 1874 and fronting a popular snorkeling spot within the Marine Life Conservation District of Kealakekua Bay, marks the site of his death.

For more on Kealakekua Bay State Historical Park, see p86.

6. Moku'aikaua Church

HAWAI'I'S OLDEST CHRISTIAN CHURCH

By 1820, the first missionaries sailed to the islands. Native Hawaiians were initially cautious, and eventually, receptive. The missionaries' main goal was to convert the Native Hawaiians' beliefs to Christianity – and tangentially, to build churches in the process, like the coral stone Moku'aikaua Church (completed in 1836) in Kailua-Kona. But their influence reached far beyond that. On one hand, these missionaries meticulously documented the Native Hawaiian way of life; on the other, they deemed many aspects of Hawaiian life to be vulgar, including *he'e nalu* (surfing) and 'Ōlelo Hawai'i (the Hawaiian language), and actively worked to suppress the culture.

For more on Moku'aikaua Church, see p52.

7. Parker Ranch

THE CALIFORNIAN COWBOYS ARRIVE

In 1793, Captain George Vancouver of the British Royal Navy gave King Kamehameha a few cattle, a gift that would irrevocably affect Hawai'i's economy and ecology. Aided by a *kapu* on cattle hunting (not lifted until 1830), the original small herd proliferated into a dangerous nuisance. Wild cattle destroyed crops and houses, and even attacked people. In 1832, Kamehameha III sought help from California cowboys. Three Spanish-Mexican *vaquero* (cowboys) moved to Hawai'i and began breaking in horses and rounding up hordes of cattle. Due to local pronunciation of 'Español' (Spanish), they became known as *paniolo*. Hawaiians were quick to learn and excel in horsemanship and roping. In 1847, Parker Ranch was established; it's still the state's largest ranch.

For more on the paniolo, see p185.

8. Greenwell Farms

THE BIG ISLAND'S BIG BEAN

An 1829 attempt to grow coffee on Hawai'i Island proved to be a smart decision. By 1840, Kona coffee was widely documented, and farms – including Greenwell Farms, which opened in 1850 – started popping up all over the place. It was the bean's debut at the 1873 Vienna World's Fair that really put the island's export on the map. It's been popular ever since.

For more on Greenwell Farms, see p80.

9. Honoka'a

HISTORIC SUGAR HUB

Surprisingly, Hawai'i Island's sugar boom started after the Kona coffee industry had already established its roots. The charming town of Honoka'a served as a main hub, boasting two mills: the Honoka'a Sugar Company and the Haina Sugar Mill. Immigrants from around the world – from Japan to the Philippines to Portugal – moved to the islands to work in the industry. Though a whole host of factors were at play, the greed in the sugar industry significantly contributed to the overthrow of Queen Lili'uokalani and the Kingdom of Hawai'i in 1893.

For more on Honoka'a, see p126.

10. Laupāhoehoe Train Museum

A MODERN NATURAL DISASTER

Hawai'i Island has suffered more than its fair share of tsunamis and hurricanes, but the costliest modern tsunami by far took place on April 1, 1946. Triggered by a massive 8.6 magnitude earthquake off the coast of Alaska, this tsunami – and its 16ft waves – beat down and battered the island's east side. One hundred and seventy people, 121 people on Hawai'i Island alone, were killed.

Greenwell Farms (p80), Kealakekua

RITU MANOJ JETHANI/SHUTTERSTOCK

Among those were 24 students and teachers at a school at Laupāhoehoe Point on the Hāmākua Coast, who lost their lives when the wave hit in the early morning on a school day. The tiny Laupāhoehoe Train Museum documents the area's sugar era, including its short-lived railway and the devastating tsunami.

For more on Laupāhoehoe, see p122.

11. Hilo

HOME OF MERRIE MONARCH

After another tsunami in 1960, the island – and especially Hilo, its largest city – was feeling down and battered. Residents were looking to revitalize and energize. In 1963, some enterprising local government workers in the newly established US state (statehood occurred in 1959) banded together with a celebrated *kumu hula* (hula teacher) to create an event that would boost morale. The event was named Merrie Monarch – the nickname of King David Kalākaua – and centered around a look-alike beard contest of the King's legendary facial hair. A pivot in 1971 to focus mostly on hula helped the festival serve the dual purpose of spreading and perpetuating the Hawaiian culture, which was beginning to undergo a renaissance after decades of suppression, and drawing tourists to the still-beleaguered city. Today the weeklong festival is a world-renowned affair that gathers thousands and generates millions of dollars for the city each April.

For more on Hilo, see p96.

12. Maunakea Beach Hotel

THE FIRST RESORT-STYLE HOTEL

The Hilo Hotel, built right on the banks of Hilo Bay, claimed the title of the island's first hotel, but it burned down in 1902. While a few other small inns opened to compete with or fill the Hilo Hotel's shoes, they were typically built for the low-maintenance traveler: those looking to trek miles to see the island's volcanoes. It wasn't until 1965, when the Maunakea Beach Hotel opened on the Kohala Coast, that the first luxury-style beach resort came about. Built by a member of the monied East Coast Rockefeller family, it was so lavish it was called one of the world's greatest hotels.

For more on Maunakea Beach, see p175.

13. Kīlauea Volcano

HAWAI'I ISLAND'S GROWTH CONTINUES

Hawai'i Island is home to three active volcanoes, two of which – Maunaloa and Kīlauea – have modern eruptions. In fact, from 1983 to 2018, Kīlauea was nearly continually active. During this period of time, officially known as the Pu'u'ō'ō eruption, 48 sq miles of land were buried – including Kalapana and the old Pohoiki Beach – and an additional 500 acres created. Visitors flocked to the volcano just to see lava flowing in the distance.

For more on Kīlauea, see p140.

14. Maunakea

A SACRED NATIVE HAWAIIAN SITE

Consequences of the unjust overthrow of the Kingdom of Hawai'i are still being felt today. Maunakea, a significant place on the respected *'āina* and the location of a sacred connection between the land and the heavens, was the site of a related modern skirmish. In the late 2000s plans were hatched to add a new and even bigger telescope – the Thirty Meter Telescope (TMT) – to the collection on its summit. Native Hawaiians, who felt this news was coming after decades of mismanagement and broken promises to limit construction and overstep on their sacred places, had had enough. In July 2019, as the TMT seemed to be heading toward construction, thousands of Native Hawaiians blocked the access road – and were ultimately successful in halting its build.

For more on Maunakea, see p210.

15. Hawai'i Volcanoes National Park

THE POWER OF PELE

A visit to Hawai'i Volcanoes National Park isn't complete without beholding Halema'uma'u, the crater home of Pele, the tempestuous and violent goddess of fire. A series of eruptions within Halema'uma'u that began in 2025 and continued through the time of publication, opened several new vents in the crater and sent arcs of lava soaring taller than the height of the Empire State Building (over 1300ft). Pele's appearance (often in the form of lava eruptions) is loud and brazen, a catalyst for great destruction but also substantial creation.

For more on Hawai'i Volcanoes National Park, see p140.

MEET A HAWAI'I ISLAND LOCAL

Sure, we may be on island time – especially if the surf's up – but you can count on a Big Islander to be helpful, resourceful and adaptable in times of crisis. MEGHAN MINER MURRAY introduces her people.

A MISHMASH OF off-the-grid hippies, part-time-resident billionaires, houseless, and local families just trying to get by, Hawai'i Island residents are an amalgamation of cultures and lifestyles on a little 'big' rock in the Pacific. There's something that drew us (or our ancestors) to one of the most remote inhabited places on the planet; no one really ends up here by accident.

To stay here, though, we have to work for it. Among the challenges: the steep cost of imported goods, affordable housing, the distance from modern conveniences, and the proximity to raw nature (including, but not limited to, one of the world's most active volcanoes).

At 4000 sq miles, Hawai'i Island is larger than all the other islands combined and has just 13% of its population, yet it is one of the state's most affordable places to live. In fact, we were the only island to experience positive population growth between 2020 and 2024.

Hawai'i Island is governed as a single county, but residents tend to identify most closely with their district: Hāmākua, Hilo, Puna, Ka'ū, Kona or Kohala. Hilo is the administrative seat, with many government offices. It has the island's only outpost of our state university and the largest concentration of residents at roughly 22%. It's also a cheaper place to live than along the Kona/Kohala Coast, where Kailua-Kona (the second-largest population center) and the bulk of the island's beaches, resorts and tourism infrastructure lie. Waimea (Kamuela), the island's third-largest 'city', has a unique American Western-meets-Hawai'i vibe thanks to its sprawling upland ranches and deep *paniolo* (Hawaiian cowboy) history.

Outside of those three large towns, most Big Islanders would consider themselves members of a small, rural community. (You'll likely encounter bumper stickers that say: 'Keep the Country Country!' and 'Big Little Island'). Over 60% of the state's agriculture activity happens on Hawai'i Island. From Kona and Ka'ū coffee, to Big Island beef and macadamia nuts, Hāmākua mushrooms and Waimea strawberries and greens – 'local' is a premium brand and an industry worth more than some $290 million dollars annually.

Many People, Many Ways

Hawai'i Island is the single most racially diverse county in the United States according to the last US census and, in recent years, the only county in the state to experience positive population growth.

Many residents have adopted routines that follow the sun. Despite diverse geography and climates island-wide, our seasons are much less varied than on the temperate mainland, and we enjoy continuously pleasant outdoor weather (and growing seasons). We are early risers and early sleepers, too. It helps that it's daylight from roughly 6am to 6pm year-round, with about an hour wiggle room in either direction. You'll find plenty of coffee shops open at 6am, but don't expect much of a late-night scene beyond a smattering of bars in Hilo and Kona.

Despite our differences, and because of our shared place, we are still one Big Island community, and we band together in times of need. There's space to breathe here, and we like it that way.

I LIVE IN SOUTH KONA

I arrived in Hawai'i in 2014 with my fiancé on a one-way ticket; I'd never visited. I was convinced that tropical beaches and a 'later brah' attitude were the answer to early career burnout and the long, cold winters of Michigan. More than a decade on, I've grown roots; we've developed a diverse friend group, and my parents and a cousin live here as well. We have two poi dogs, a small plot of land where I grow bananas, guavas and *liliko'i* (passion fruit), and, in 2024, my husband and I welcomed our very own *kama'āina* baby.

My story isn't unlike many, particularly in and around beachy Kona, where the community is awash in transients trying to find their peace, purpose and place. Those who persevere revere Hawaiian culture and sense of place, and maintain a high tolerance for minor inconveniences and regular natural disasters. We all have different stories, ways of doing things, of understanding the world around us, but we unite in that we steward this special place together.

Lava falling into the ocean from Kīlauea volcano (p140)
EDUARDO CABANAS/SHUTTERSTOCK

LIVING IN THE LAND OF FROZEN FIRE

Hawai'i Island continues to shape-shift, thanks to its four active volcanoes, which both destroy and create. Many residents live on active volcanoes, and in the potential path of lava flow.
By Jade Bremner

HAWAI'I ISLAND, YOUNGEST of Hawai'i's islands at around half a million years old (Kaua'i is the oldest at 5.1 million), is still alive and growing. This is thanks to magma spewing from the Earth, caused by shifts in the Pacific Plate. And you don't have to be peering into a crater to see evidence of Hawai'i Island's volcanic activity – it lies all around, with miles of jagged boulder-strewn lava fields, rocky coastlines and jet-black sandy beaches, all punctuated by verdant green rainforest.

The island has four of Hawai'i's six active volcanoes (Kīlauea, Maunaloa, Maunakea and Hualālai), plus two dormant volcanoes (Māhukona and Kohala Volcano). Mighty Maunaloa is the world's largest active volcano, and moody Kīlauea is the island's most active – with a 2018 eruption destroying hundreds of Hawai'i Island homes but also forming new land. 'About 875 acres of new land was added to the coastline,' explains Matthew Patrick, a geologist at the USGS Hawaiian Volcano Observatory. 'Many of the eruptions reach the shore; this addition of new land will certainly continue in the future,' says Patrick.

It's also possible that active Maunaloa could overtake Maunakea as the world's tallest mountain. 'Maunaloa is larger in volume than Maunakea but just a hair shorter,' says Patrick. 'Maunaloa is still in the prime of its life, so it will continue to erupt, while Maunakea is past its prime and won't be erupting nearly as much in the future. Maunaloa may exceed Maunakea at some point, but this will almost certainly take some time, more than just one eruption.' Maunaloa last erupted in November 2022 (at the time of writing), with lava spilling into Halema'uma'u crater. Visitors can get up close to the ever-changing calderas of Maunaloa and Kīlauea inside Hawai'i Volcanoes National Park and responsibly watch active eruptions and red-hot fiery lava (Kīlauea erupts multiple times a year).

Spiritual Significance

Hawai'i Island is the place to fully understand the power of Pele, or Pelehonuamea, the goddess of fire and volcanoes, who Hawaiians believe is the creator of the Hawaiian Islands and is currently residing in the active Kīlauea volcano. According to religion, she is embodied in eruptions and is volatile, both destroying towns and forests and creating new land. Many Indigenous people consider Pele a family member, who deserves the utmost respect – many say they can feel her presence on the summit of Kīlauea. When visiting, it is important

FROM LEFT: DRAGONWEN/SHUTTERSTOCK, ROBERT HARDING VIDEO/SHUTTERSTOCK

Steam vents, Kīlauea volcano (p146)

to do so respectfully. It's believed that those who take lava or rocks away from the islands will feel the wrath of Pele.

Maunakea also holds great spiritual significance in Hawaiian culture. The highest mountain in the world (from its base on the ocean floor to its peak) is believed to connect the land to the heavens. When traveling to the peak, visitors are advised to avoid standing on the true summit, the sacred Pu'u Wekiu cinder cone.

Price of Paradise

Hawai'i Island is split into nine lava hazard zones – Zone 1 being the riskiest. People do live in all zones, but as you would expect, housing is cheapest in Zone 1 – the rift zone of Kīlauea and Maunaloa. In 2018, the gated residential community of Leilani Estates had 24 volcanic fissures open up, dispensing molten lava, which ate up hundreds of properties.

Long-term Hawai'i Island resident and Arnott's Lodge guide Andras Toth was there during the eruption. 'I was cooking dinner, and my neighbor was running down our driveway. "OK, guys, run! There's lava in the block behind our street," said my neighbor. He was in US Special Forces, so he doesn't scare easily. He was kind of gray in color.' Toth was one of more than 700 Puna residents whose homes were engulfed by lava in the months-long Kīlauea eruption.

His house, all its contents, plus his 3000-sq-ft plot of land were destroyed. He and his wife, Eszter Kreisz, had time to grab one bag and their pets before leaving. 'Kīlauea had not had any major volcanic activity in 60 years,' says Toth, who was attracted to this paradise location due to its price. 'We looked around, and we thought, "Wow. This is a luxury community. It's super lush, with beautiful people." It was a really, really nice neighborhood – especially for someone coming from New York City... to my wife's credit, she got the maximum insurance possible on our home.'

Living in an affordable area allowed Toth and Kreisz to build their own home, a unique geodesic dome, which they enjoyed for just over a year before the eruption. The couple has since built another geodesic dome in a different Hawai'i Island neighborhood with their insurance payout. Many unlucky residents are still battling insurance companies about settlements.

Going with the Flow

Sara Garcia has lived in Zone 2, close to Pahala, for 11 years, but is not fearful. 'You sort of don't feel the sense of danger. I think people can get used to anything,' she says. But some live here out of necessity, as it has cheaper land, with lower property taxes.

'These higher-risk areas have kind of become a last refuge for the people being marginalized and pushed out [of other areas] for financial reasons,' says Hawai'i Island homeowner David Collier. 'They would rather have that risk than have to leave the islands.' Collier explains that although there are inextricable socioeconomics tied up with living on a volcano, a silver lining is that residents are almost insulated from the development seen on other Hawaiian Islands. 'Because of the volcanoes, residents are protected from those forces... In a lot of ways, it's like going back to a different era of Hawai'i. It's so removed from the Waikiki culture. There's also a real appeal for people who want to get back to a more natural, often agricultural lifestyle.'

HAWAI'I ISLAND HAS MILES OF JAGGED BOULDER-STREWN LAVA FIELDS, ROCKY COASTLINES AND JET-BLACK SANDY BEACHES, ALL PUNCTUATED BY VERDANT GREEN RAINFOREST.

Lava fields, Hawai'i Volcanoes National Park (p141)

Garcia describes the resilient, almost frontier mentality of those living in high-risk lava areas, where many properties are not connected to mains water or electricity. 'There's a hippie vibe in some areas, with people who want to live freer, be off the grid, have a community and live in nature,' she says, maintaining that her neighborhood is the perfect place to be. 'I have never regretted moving here, not for a moment. Anywhere you live, you're in danger of something. In Washington, we were in danger of wildfires and occasional hurricanes; in Texas, I was in danger of tornadoes, and so on.'

Stresses of Volcano Life

Despite the benefits of living in a volcanic community, there are obvious physical and psychological stresses. Garcia could see Kīlauea erupting from her house in 2018, and while there was no immediate threat to her life, she had a big problem with vog (volcanic smog). 'There was so much vog and sulfur in the air that the air quality was in the red. We taped plastic over all of our windows, stuffed towels under the doors, and then just ran air purifiers all day long,' she says.

After an eruption warning, Kreisz admits that worry creeps into daily life. 'We were told we'd have to leave our home [ahead of the 2018 Kīlauea eruption] at a moment's notice,' she says. 'Every little shake or noise kept me awake. I was so exhausted, and I was completely out of it by the time the lava reached us.' The build-up, the escaping, the roller-coaster weeks of worrying if her property would survive – it all had an effect. 'I do have PTSD,' she says. Even though she is settled in a new Zone 3 house, 'there is always a risk.'

Living on the slopes of Maunaloa, Collier also felt anxious during the December 12 eruption in 2022. 'It wasn't necessarily rational, the flow was 15 miles away or so, but we had just had our baby and I could see the lava from my yard. I knew it was still a long way off, but I couldn't sleep, because historically the flows have come down into where my house is.' By incredible fortune, the flow dramatically slowed down after four or five days and Collier's property remained unharmed.

Luckily, Hawai'i's lava flows are typically very slow-moving. 'Life is rarely imperiled,' says Collier. 'I see a lot of people who have lost their homes, but they are thankful, not that they lost their homes, but that they had them to begin with. We can view Pele through the lens of destruction, but everything that Hawai'i has to offer is a product of volcanic processes.'

PROTECTING HAWAI'I ISLAND'S WILDLIFE

Invasive species, overtourism and climate change threaten Hawai'i Island's creatures and ecosystems. By Ashley Harrell

STEWARDSHIP OF NATURAL resources is a traditional Hawaiian value, reflected in *aloha 'āina* – respect for the land. But Hawai'i has also been called the extinction capital of the world, with nearly 500 species listed as threatened or endangered, and Hawai'i Island's diverse ecological zones are under tremendous pressure. Here's why – and how you can help.

Invasive Species

After the Big Island emerged from the sea as a barren lava mountain hundreds of thousands of years ago, plants and animals started to arrive in three ways that all start with the letter 'w': waves, wind and wings. The creatures that survived the journey evolved into new forms and new species, with many losing the defenses that were once crucial to their survival. This is one reason the endemics of Hawai'i fare so poorly against the onslaught of environmental changes brought about by humans.

Each new predator, insect, or disease that arrives here finds an ecosystem not accustomed to novel threats – and the results have been disastrous. For example, feral pigs uproot native plants, disturb soil and increase erosion, while strawberry guava grows dense thickets that outcompete endemic vegetation and alter forest ecosystems. Meanwhile, several hundred species of endemic plants and animals have disappeared entirely, and hundreds more likely went extinct before being documented. Many more species remain at extreme risk of extinction. Here are a couple of the most pressing issues, along with some guidance for how to avoid becoming part of the problem.

Rapid Ōhi'a Death

While hiking, you may encounter signage and shoe-cleaning stations that call your attention to Rapid Ōhi'a Death (ROD). This fungal disease grows inside of *ōhi'a* trees, which are the backbone of most of the island's native forests. They protect watersheds, provide habitat and food for native birds and plants, and keep coral reefs healthy by preventing erosion. When the fungus enters the tree, it cuts off the flow of water, and infected trees begin to die within a few days to a few weeks. Thousands of ROD-infected trees have been found in all areas on Hawai'i Island, and there is no remedy or cure.

DIDI_SETIYADI/SHUTTERSTOCK

Coconut Rhinoceros Beetle

To avoid spreading the fungus, don't cut branches or scruff up roots, which can allow the fungus to enter the tree. At the shoe-cleaning stations installed at trailheads by the Department of Land & Natural Resources, brush the soil off your shoes and spray them with rubbing alcohol when it's provided.

Coconut Rhinoceros Beetles

A tiny beetle is becoming a big threat on the island of Hawaiʻi. The invasive coconut rhinoceros beetle has been spreading across the island since it was first detected in 2023, killing coconut palms and endangered native *loulu* palms. The beetles lay their larvae in mulch, compost and nursery materials, which makes them easy to accidentally transport. Despite the urgency of the problem, state regulations have yet to catch up, and forests across Hawaiʻi are at risk.

To avoid contributing to the problem, don't transport plants, mulch, soil or green waste between areas or islands, even unintentionally. Stick to reputable nurseries if buying plants, clean mud from shoes and gear before hiking in different regions, and follow any posted biosecurity rules. Supporting local conservation groups and learning about invasive species before visiting also helps.

Overtourism

Tourism is the largest industry on the island of Hawaiʻi, with nearly 2 million visitors spending more than $3 billion a year. As the number of tourists rises, the strain on Hawaiʻi Island's creatures and ecosystems ramps up. Building tourist infrastructure such as large-scale developments and golf courses is synonymous with deforestation and habitat loss for thousands of species; moreover, additional humans around means more burning of fossil fuels, more water shortages, and excesses of waste and other kinds of pollution. In addition, today's tourists have become increasingly problematic in their travel style. With GPS and cell phones, people are more prone to venture off the beaten track for that cool selfie like the one they saw on Instagram.

In an attempt to manage tourism more responsibly, the Hawaiʻi Tourism Authority, in partnership with local residents and community organizations, has developed a Destination Management Action Plan. Protecting culturally and ecologically significant places is top of the agenda, along with spearheading education and community-based programs. On Hawai'i Island, these efforts are part of a broader shift toward regenerative tourism, which seeks not just to minimize harm but to actively restore ecosystems, support Native Hawaiian culture, and ensure visitors leave a positive impact on the land and communities they visit. In recent years, a few new policies protecting ocean life have also gone into effect, offering a ray of hope.

Spinner Dolphins

Hawaiian spinner dolphins are some of the most fascinating and playful cetaceans around, and for many who visited the Big Island over the last few decades, seeing them was a highlight of the trip. In 2021, though, the National Ocean & Atmospheric Administration banned swimming with dolphins (p65), and some 70 tour operators were forced to stop offering encounters. This might seem strange, considering that dolphins often approach boats and swimmers, and even seem enthusiastic about the interactions. In fact, this is exactly the problem.

Dolphins are social creatures, and when they spend time around humans, that's time they don't spend on their normal behaviors, such as resting. Over time, as more humans show up to interact with dolphins, those diversions reduce the amount of energy the dolphins have for activities like foraging. It leads to a decline in overall health, leaving dolphins less capable of fighting diseases, protecting themselves and reproducing.

Although the tours have been outlawed, some people still aren't following the regulations, while others have attempted to get rid of them. In 2023, 33 swimmers were cited and fined for harassing a pod off Hōnaunau Bay, inciting outrage. And over the last several years, two women who ran a dolphin therapy businesses attempted to overturn the regulation in court (they failed in late 2025). Do your part by staying 50yd away, and do not harass, feed, pursue, approach, surround, swim with or attempt to touch dolphins. Limit your time observing them to 30 minutes, then get on with your life so they can too.

Spinner dolphins

MARTY WAKAT/SHUTTERSTOCK

Green Sand Beach

Papakōlea (p156), the famously green beach on Hawai'i Island's southernmost point, is a place of wonder and awe. Its volcanic, olivine sand has drawn countless visitors in recent years, and for those willing to make the exposed, dusty hike, it's really a beautiful thing. The problem has come with the travelers who instead climb into the backs of trucks driven by locals, who off-road through the dunes to the beach for a fee. Many travelers don't realize that the rides are illegal and harm the coastal ecosystems. The deep ruts and dirt paths created by the vehicles have caused damage to delicate dune plants like *ōhi'a*, a native shrub boasting vibrant orange and red blossoms. Furthermore, the loose dirt stirred up by vehicular traffic eventually reaches the ocean, posing a threat to coral reefs by obstructing essential sunlight. In addition, the area holds sacred significance to Native Hawaiians, as *iwi kūpuna* (ancient bones) are interred here.

Do your part to honor the culture and environment of Hawai'i by passing up the truck ride and hiking to the beach instead.

HAWAI'I'S WATERS TEEM WITH TROPICAL FISH, BUT OVERTOURISM HAS PUT THE ISLAND'S FRAGILE CORAL REEFS UNDER PRESSURE.

Tropical fish

JULIE MEYER/SHUTTERSTOCK

Coral Reefs

Hawai'i's waters teem with over 500 species of tropical fish, but overtourism has put the island's fragile coral reefs under pressure. Rising visitor numbers increase the risk of damage, while warming waters and ocean acidification due to climate change add another layer of stress, making coral more susceptible to bleaching and slow to recover.

Travelers can help protect reefs by keeping a safe distance from coral to avoid touching or stepping on it, and wearing high-UPF clothing instead of harmful chemical sunscreens, which are banned in Hawai'i. In addition, visitors can choose reef-friendly tours and donate to community restoration projects in places like Kahuwai and Kealakekua bays, where coral colonies are being regrown. For a more hands-on experience, you can also volunteer with organizations such as Reef Check Hawai'i, helping to monitor, restore and safeguard coral ecosystems for future generations.

Climate Change

Long-term shifts in global temperatures and weather patterns are taking a toll on Hawai'i Island. As the planet warms, largely due to the burning of fossil fuels, clouds over the island are thinning, which means less rain. At the end of 2025 there were widespread rainfall deficits across the island, compounding drought conditions and stress on natural systems. Prolonged dry periods weaken native vegetation that can't adapt to such conditions, while fire-prone invasive grasses – which thrive in dry environments – continue to create elevated wildfire risk across leeward and lowland areas.

Meanwhile, rising seas and intense storms are eroding the coast and compounding wastewater issues. In 2025, research from Arizona State University found that sewage-contaminated groundwater discharge – much of it linked to tens of thousands of cesspools and outdated septic systems – is entering coastal waters and threatening fragile coral reefs. Additionally, a 2025 University of Hawai'i at Hilo study used dye tracer tests to show that wastewater from cesspools and treatment systems reaches shoreline waters quickly, highlighting serious water-quality concerns.

Climate change has major impacts on residents, especially Native Hawaiians who rely on fish populations, and farmers facing drought and unpredictable weather. Travelers can help by flying on fuel-efficient aircraft, supporting ecofriendly local businesses, packing light, walking or biking when possible, and avoiding products wrapped in paper or plastic.

Hikiau Heiau (p87), Kealakekua Bay
CASCADIAN/ISTOCK/GETTY IMAGES

COLONIZATION & RESISTANCE: A HISTORY OF HAWAIʻI

Many tourists arrive unaware of how Native Hawaiians still carry the island's colonial history in their hearts. Kona Au-Love writes about how that history impacts her community today.

WHEN I WAS five years old my father told me that we would be moving from Arizona to Hawaiʻi, fulfilling his dream of raising his children surrounded by our Hawaiian culture. I spent the next few months envisioning my family on a small mound of sand in the middle of the ocean with a single palm tree on it. Having grown up in the desert, I wasn't sure what to expect. Everything I knew about islands at that point was informed by the cartoons I watched, so when my dad mentioned Hawaiʻi I thought of the things I associated with islands – sand, the ocean, and some kind of palm or coconut tree.

As an adult, I've found that these are common associations people make with Hawaiʻi. When I travel, both in the United States and abroad, and I tell people I am from Hawaiʻi, people usually respond by asking about the beaches, the surf, or the lush valleys and vegetation (of course there are sometimes other questions, like where exactly is Hawaiʻi? Or, do you dance hula, or paddle a canoe to work? But these are becoming less frequent). For most people, Hawaiʻi is more or less what I imagined it to be before moving here: islands in the middle of the ocean, a place where one can find rest and experience paradise while still accessing modern luxuries. This image is fed by movies and media that show the world exactly that: white-sand beaches, clear blue waters, and sun and surf galore. And while I cannot deny the beauty of these islands (in fact I often boast of the excellence of this place like a proud parent), Hawaiʻi is so much more than a slice of paradise. For Kānaka Maoli (Native Hawaiians, also Kānaka ʻŌiwi), this is our home, our ancestor and relative, and a place whose history should be known by those who wish to visit our amazing shores. The events that I will discuss below occurred in the past, but the legacies of European colonialism and American settler colonialism continue to impact the lives and wellbeing of Kānaka Maoli, making it as prevalent an issue today as it was over a century ago.

The Impact of Early Western Contact

Traveling to and from Hawaiʻi is not a new tradition. For centuries, Kānaka Maoli had a vibrant sailing tradition that connected them to islands and communities throughout Oceania. Kanaka Maoli *moʻolelo* (histories and stories), *mele* (songs) and *oli* (chants) teach us that Kānaka Maoli had rich relationships with other places. Our voyaging practices went dormant after the 1300s, but began picking up once again when English Captain James Cook

KAMEHAMEHA . I

arrived in 1778. While Western accounts claim that Kānaka Maoli thought of Cook as a god, our own *mo'olelo* demonstrate that our ancestors initially understood him to be an exalted chief, one who in our world-view had the lineage of a god and was to be treated with a high level of respect and decorum. Kānaka Maoli were dissuaded from such notions after spending more time with him and his crew, and he was ultimately killed after attempting to kidnap one of our *mō'ī* (sovereigns).

Following Cook's mapping of Hawai'i, other vessels began arriving on our shores, often resupplying while on imperial voyaging explorations. These vessels brought opportunities for Kānaka Maoli to once again explore the world, but they also brought diseases and practices that ravaged our population. While exact numbers are debated, anywhere from 300,000 to 1 million people inhabited this *pae'āina* (archipelago) at the time of Cook's first voyage. Four decades later, this number was reduced to approximately 135,000. Epidemics brought about by foreign viruses caused mass death across our communities, a situation exasperated by the introduction of alcohol, prostitution, and a drastic change in the native diet.

An Illegal Coup & Native Resistance

During this time Hawai'i was also experiencing an array of political upheaval, with several *ali'i* (chiefs) and *mō'ī* competing to consolidate power across the archipelago. Kamehameha I from Hawai'i Island eventually won, taking control of the islands and making himself the first king of all eight islands. The Kamehameha line eventually created a government that was grounded in Kanaka Maoli principles, and combined our own structures with those introduced by European and American advisors, known as the Kingdom of Hawai'i.

In 1843, following an attempted coup by English Captain George Paulet, Hawai'i became one of the first non-European nations to be officially recognized as a sovereign nation by the world's 'Great Powers' at the time. In July of 1843, Admiral Richard Thomas from Great Britain was sent to Hawai'i on behalf of Queen Victoria to disavow Captain Paulet's attempts to assert British sovereignty over the Hawaiian Islands. This date, later known as Lā Ho'iho'i Ea (the day sovereignty was returned), is still a celebrated holiday in Hawai'i today. Later that year, on November 28, the United Kingdom and France signed the Anglo-Franco Proclamation, officially recognizing the sovereignty of the Kingdom of Hawai'i. November 28 continues to be celebrated in Hawai'i as independence day, Lā Kū'oko'a.

The United States of America never formally signed any proclamations recognizing the sovereignty of the Hawaiian kingdom; however, they did establish a number of treaties with our kingdom, by default forcing them to acknowledge us as a sovereign nation. The first reciprocity treaty between the US and the Hawaiian kingdom was signed in 1875, and allowed for the sale and export of duty-free sugar from Hawai'i. When the first reciprocity treaty was set to expire, the US tried to get the *mō'ī* at the time, King David Kalākaua, to sign another treaty that would continue to allow for duty-free sugar sales, in addition to the US having access to Pu'uloa (later named Pearl Harbor). Pu'uloa's natural depth made it an ideal harbor for navy vessels, and the US was keen to access these lands. King Kalākaua refused to sign the treaty, thus marking the start of increasingly hostile relations between the US and the Hawaiian kingdom.

In 1887, what is now known as the Bayonet Constitution was signed into law by King Kalākaua. As the name implies, the king was held at gunpoint, and told to sign the constitution or risk the execution of him and his wife. This constitution disenfranchised labor immigrants and Hawaiians without property, income, or literacy, reduced the power of the monarchy, and transferred the majority of legal authority to the legislature and cabinet (two bodies that drastically changed once Hawaiians were prohibited from voting). Once this new constitution was enacted, the Hawaiian kingdom signed a second reciprocity treaty with the United States that ceded Pu'uloa to the US.

King Kamehameha I statue, Kapa'au (p196)

ALEXANDRE ROSA/SHUTTERSTOCK

In 1892, following his death, King Kalākaua's sister, Queen Lili'uokalani, became the new *mō'ī* of the Hawaiian kingdom. After the queen began promulgating a new constitution that would return voting rights to Kānaka Maoli, the 'Committee of Safety' arrested the queen and gave her the ultimatum of ceding sovereignty to the provisional government or having US Marines flood the shores and take the country by force. To avoid bloodshed, the queen temporarily ceded sovereignty to the US, and then petitioned the US government to conduct an inquiry into the coup of her nation. Commissioner James Blount affirmed that an illegal coup led to the creation of a provisional government and the overthrow of Queen Lili'uokalani. President Cleveland ordered the provisional government to stand down, but they refused. Between 1894 and 1896, the Republic of Hawai'i instituted numerous laws prohibiting Kānaka Maoli from speaking our language and continuing our cultural practices. In November of 1896, William McKinley was elected president of the US, and by June of the following year signed a treaty of annexation with the Republic of Hawai'i and submitted it to Congress for ratification.

Following the Bayonet Constitution and in the wake of the Committee of Safety's coup, Kānaka Maoli organized protests and rallied against US interference with our sovereignty. In 1897, Kānaka Maoli gathered approximately 38,000 signatures by those who vehemently opposed annexation; this petition was used by Kanaka Maoli delegates to successfully convince Congress not to ratify the treaty. To this day, a treaty of annexation does not exist between Hawai'i and the United States. On July 6, 1898, the US Congress passed the Newlands Resolution, making Hawai'i a territory of the United States without any input from Kānaka Maoli. In addition to affecting our sovereignty, this resolution placed roughly 1.8 million acres of Kanaka Maoli Crown Lands into the hands of the US government, where they remain today.

Canoe

BIGWEST1/ISTOCK/GETTY IMAGES

Kānaka Maoli Today

Following WWII, imperial nations such as the United States were supposed to hold referendums to allow territories to decide for themselves if they want to remain territories, become fully incorporated into other nations, or retain their sovereignty. When the US held the vote in Hawai'i, residents were given only two options: remain a territory, or join the union and become an official state. The majority of residents at the time, most of whom were not Kānaka Maoli, voted for statehood, and in 1959 the *Admissions Act* created the State of Hawai'i.

A century after the arrest and overthrow of Queen Lili'uokalani, the United States passed what has come to be known as the *Apology Act,* wherein the US acknowledges the overthrow of the Hawaiian kingdom as a historically significant event that resulted in the 'suppression of the inherent sovereignty of the Native Hawaiian people.' The Act is carefully worded, and is clear that this acknowledgement cannot be used for any legal recourse, leaving many Kānaka Maoli to view it as an empty apology.

This colonial legacy lives on in Hawai'i, and manifests today in high rates of poverty, houselessness and incarceration among Kānaka Maoli, as well as high costs of living that consistently price Kānaka Maoli out of our homelands. Despite these challenges, however, Kānaka Maoli continue to perpetuate our culture and language, and fight for our access to and control over our *'āina*. In recent years, there has been a push in the tourism industry here to educate tourists on this history and its ongoing effects, resulting in campaigns encouraging visitors to be mindful of where they are, and to engage with local organizations. There are amazing organizations across the islands that are teaching our language and cultural practices, while also doing important land restoration work, and many of these groups encourage visitors to volunteer with them.

HAWAI'I IS OUR HOME, OUR ANCESTOR AND RELATIVE, AND A PLACE WHOSE HISTORY SHOULD BE KNOWN BY THOSE WHO WISH TO VISIT OUR AMAZING SHORES.

Lili'uokalani Gardens (p111), Hilo

RITU MANOJ JETHANI/SHUTTERSTOCK

It's been a couple decades since I first pictured Hawai'i as that lump of sand in the middle of the ocean with a palm tree on it, and to this day when people ask me about Hawai'i the sand is still the first thing I think of, except now instead of an abstract pile of sand, I picture my favorite beach. I see the curve of its small bay, the glistening blue of its waters, and the crop of ironwood trees in the distance. I see my home, with all of its beauty and its cracks, a place that can welcome newcomers, but that requires mindfulness, and an attention to our past and culture.

INDEX

Map Pages **000**

Map Pages **000**

W

Z

NOTES

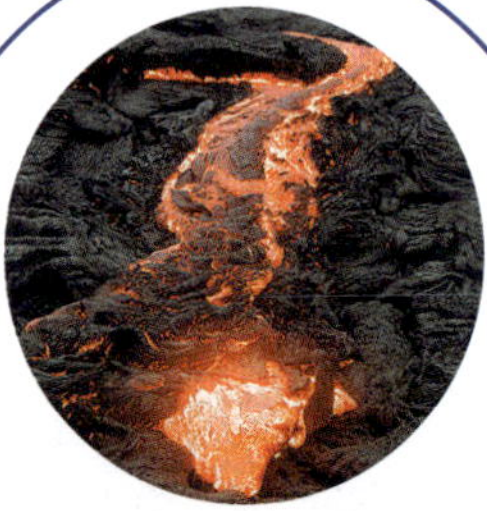

Hike above the clouds at Hawai'i Volcanoes National Park (p140) to see Kīlauea's steaming crater and fountains of lava.

Peer through the clear waters of Kealakekua Bay (p86) to see colorful tropical fish, green sea turtles and coral forests.

FROM LEFT: ANNA WOLTERS/SHUTTERSTOCK, RUGLIG/SHUTTERSTOCK

Mapping data sources:
© Lonely Planet
© OpenStreetMap http://openstreetmap.org/copyright

THIS BOOK

The 7th edition of Lonely Planet's *Hawai'i Island (The Big Island)* guidebook was written and researched by Jade Bremner, Catherine Toth Fox, Ashley Harrell and Regis St Louis. The previous edition was written by Jade Bremner, Ashley Harrell and Meghan Miner Murray. This guidebook was produced by the following:

Destination Editor Melissa Yeager

Production Editor Amy Lysen

Image Researcher Clara Monitto

Cartographer Alison Lyall

Coordinating Editor Andrea Dobbin

Assisting Editor Laura Crawford

Cover Researcher Matthew Dekneef

Thanks Ronan Abayawickrema, Sarah Etinas, Jenna Myers, Kat Rowan, Saralinda Turner

MIX
Paper | Supporting responsible forestry
FSC™ C021741
www.fsc.org

Paper in this book is certified against the Forest Stewardship Council™ standards. FSC™ promotes environmentally responsible, socially beneficial and economically viable management of the world's forests.

Published by Lonely Planet Global Limited
CRN 554153
7th edition – Nov 2026
ISBN 978 1 83869 797 6

10 9 8 7 6 5 4 3 2 1
Printed in China